I S D N
Clearly Explained
Second Edition

AP PROFESSIONAL
1300 Boylston Street, Chestnut Hill, MA 02167
World Wide Web site at http:\ \www.apnet.com\approfessional

An imprint of ACADEMIC PRESS
A division of HARCOURT BRACE & COMPANY

United Kingdom Edition published by
ACADEMIC PRESS LIMITED
24-28 Oval Road, London NW1 7DX

Library of Congress Cataloging-in-Publication Data

ISDN clearly explained / Ed Tittel . . . [et al.]. -- 2nd ed.
          p.   cm.
          Rev. ed. of: ISDN networking essentials / Ed Tittel, Steve James.
          Includes index.
          ISBN 0-12-691412-5 (alk. paper)
          1. Integrated services digital networks.   I. Tittel, Ed.
II. Tittel, Ed. ISDN networking essentials.
TK5103.75.I82   1997
004.6'6--dc21
                                                                      97-18892
                                                                      CIP

Printed in the United States of America
97 98 99 00 IP 9 8 7 6 5 4 3 2 1

Contents

to write another one? The answer's in the concept behind the series and in how it informs this book.

The *Clearly Explained* series aims to fill the gap between theory and practice for networking. It offers solid, practical networking information, without jargon or unnecessary detail. It explains all its topics in clear, concise language and plainly defines terms that may be unfamiliar.

The series is divided into the topics that are most likely to be of use to networking professionals or serious users, from setting up a network, to finding problems with it, to more specialized topics such as mobile computing, ISDN, and electronic messaging. Each book takes a gentle, lighthearted approach to the material that focuses on the basic principles you absolutely must know to master a topic or technology, with plenty of tips and proven techniques gleaned from the authors' wealth of practical experience in putting theory into practice.

ISDN Clearly Explained

Where ISDN is concerned, what makes our book different from some of the others is that we assume little or no foreknowledge of computer telephony, digital signaling, or broadband ISDN (B-ISDN) and lead you into each topic as best we can. In fact, we've tried to lay out the materials so there's something for everyone, whether beginner, novice, or seasoned cybernaut.

What makes our book different from some of the other ISDN tomes is that we don't attempt to provide an encyclopedic reference to all conceivable ISDN protocols, services, and abilities: Our book is designed as much to provide a set of techniques for you to do your own investigation and installation as it is to provide a road map to what's involved in using and working with ISDN. Finally, our book is designed to provide useful tools and techniques to help you learn for yourself and to supply you with the essential information you'll need to be able to navigate and cope with the many viewpoints, implementations, and discussions you're likely to find surrounding ISDN.

Tell Us What You Think

The authors want to hear from you about these books. Please write to us, care of the publisher, or contact us through the electronic mail addresses below:

Ed Tittel	etittel@zilker.net
Steve James	snjames@wetlands.com
David M. Piscitello	dave@corecom.com
Lisa A. Phifer	lisa@corecom.com

We'd like to hear more about what you liked and didn't like about these books and your ideas for other topics or more details that you need for your networking life.

In closing, we'd like to say thanks for buying this book. We hope you find it worth the money you've paid for it and the time it takes to read!

Introduction

Welcome to *ISDN Clearly Explained*! This book is aimed squarely at the following audiences:

- people who are curious about how ISDN works and what it can do for them at a personal or small business level
- people in small or home offices with PCs who want to establish a working ISDN connection, probably to improve the performance of their Internet link
- network administrators or power users on small networks (15 nodes or less) who want to link their users to the Internet or another information provider on a network basis

have to obtain the necessary ingredients to establish a working ISDN connection.

Here's the short list of what's necessary to bring ISDN into your home or office:

- You'll have to determine that ISDN service can be delivered to your home or office. The best way to find out if it's available in your area is to call your local phone company. Ask to speak to their business service department (even if you're thinking about a home installation), and then inquire about the availability of ISDN service. If the response isn't satisfactory (e.g., nobody knows if it's available or not), call the phone company's headquarters location and ask them instead. ISDN is new enough that only a select cadre within the phone company should be considered "ISDN friendly" if not "ISDN knowledgeable."
- Assuming that ISDN service is available (right now, the odds are about even; actually, they're greater if you're in a metropolitan area and much less if you're in a rural setting), you'll need to schedule an ISDN installation. Before you do that, be sure to ask how much this will cost you and whether any special promotional deals or considerations are available. If you make the commitment, ask for a date for installation (in many areas a four- to six-week wait is not unusual).
- Once you know your installation date, you can schedule the remaining activities around it. You'll want to arrange to have cables installed from your phone company's demarcation point ("demarc") on your premises to wherever you want to attach your ISDN equipment. You can install this wiring yourself, but we recommend hiring a qualified cable installer to do the job. Look in the Yellow Pages under "Telephone Installers" or "Computer Wiring and Installation" to find prospective candidates for the job. Ask for two or three bids, and take

Basically, you're looking at spending between $500 and $2100 to establish your ISDN connection and between $90 to $230 a month (or more) for recurring charges. Equipment costs aside, this compares favorably with the cost of a business line in most parts of the United States, but is considerably more expensive than residential phone service.

Can You Do It Yourself?

By this point, you've probably gotten the idea that (a) ISDN is kind of expensive and (b) it's not the simplest connection technology in the world to install and get working. Both of these points are true and should lead you to another question, namely, "Can I do this myself?" If you're smart, you might even have phrased the question as "Do I want to do this myself?"

Although your budget will have a strong bearing on the answer, we're inclined to suggest that you should consider hiring a consultant to help with the installation, no matter what your financial circumstances might be. Of course, you can still decide to go it alone, but it's worth considering that you may have to devote significant amounts of time and effort to get ISDN up and running.

We need to warn you plainly that doing it yourself might mean spending a "mere" 20–30 hours on the task, including researching the hardware selection, arranging for installations, and going through the installation on your PC. But it could also mean spending 40, 60, or even 80 hours or more on the phone with your ISDN provider, your Internet service provider, the network termination type 1 (NT1) vendor, the ISDN interface vendor, and your communications software vendor as you try to puzzle out why your chosen combination of components isn't working.

Therefore, if your time has value, you also need to consider the potential "opportunity costs" of being an ISDN do-it-yourselfer. Our advice is that if 30 hours of your time is worth more to you than the costs of hiring a consultant for your installation, you should locate and hire a consultant without giving the matter too much further thought. If you can't afford the costs, or don't want to spend the money, be prepared to spend some significant time and effort in getting your ISDN installation up and running!

About This Book

ISDN Clearly Explained has been formulated with four primary goals in mind:

1. To help you understand enough of the workings, costs, and capabilities of ISDN to decide whether you want to use it or not.
2. To provide you with sufficient information about available ISDN hardware and software offerings to equip you to make informed purchase decisions.
3. To supply you with sufficient background and terminology to be able to survive the rigors of the installation process.
4. To acquaint you with the best sources for up-to-the-minute ISDN information so that you can temper what's included in this book with the latest and greatest technical and product information.

To that end, this book has been structured into three parts, with appendices, to provide the information you'll need to reach each of these four goals:

1. Part I of the book introduces the fundamentals of ISDN technology and terminology and explains what it is and how it works.
2. Part II of the book introduces current ISDN hardware and software options, with rating and pricing information to help you select the items appropriate for your needs and your budget (Appendix A lists ISDN service providers to help you locate one in your area, and Appendix B includes a comprehensive listing of ISDN vendors).
3. Part III of the book covers the installation and troubleshooting of a typical PC ISDN setup in order to acquaint you with the pro-

cess and to equip you to deal with the kinds of problems or questions you might encounter along the way.

4. The remaining appendices provide bibliographic and online resources to help you stay current on ISDN technology and products, including pointers to the very best resources on ISDN, whether in print or in electronic form.

We suggest that you read this book from start to finish if you're relatively inexperienced with ISDN. If you're already somewhat knowledgeable, you can probably skip Part I and delve into the areas of Parts II and III that interest you. We also suggest that all of our readers sample the various appendices, if only to determine what kind of information they contain and to see if their contents might provide some useful pointers to vendors, consultants, or other sources of ISDN enlightenment.

Whatever your approach to this book, we hope you find it useful. Please feel free to correspond via e-mail with any of the authors. We welcome your feedback, whether critical or otherwise.

Part I

ISDN Technical Overview

The Integrated Services Digital Network has been the topic of fear, hype, and speculation for years now. But it's only since early to mid-1994 that there's been any realistic hope of having that technology delivered to your home or office in a usable way.

For years, this led technohumorists to decode the ISDN acronym as "I Still Don't kNow" or "It's Still a Dream, No?" But today, the only problem in obtaining ISDN is a lack of universal coverage. Virtually all of the former "baby Bells," the Regional Bell Operating Companies (RBOCs), are offering ISDN to their customers, at least in pilot implementations, and other carriers, like MCI and Sprint, are entering this business as well. Although universal ISDN coverage is as much as a decade away in the United States, ISDN is no longer a pipe dream.

1

In this, the first part of the book, we introduce the underlying terms and technologies that constitute and explain ISDN. Starting in Chapter 1, we discuss the basics of digital and analog communications and explain what makes ISDN so interesting and special for computer-to-computer and human-to-human communication. In Chapter 2, we lift ISDN's hood a bit to examine the transmission structures, interfaces, and protocols that make ISDN possible. Then, in Chapter 3, we discuss the various kinds of private and public networks that can accommodate ISDN traffic and what their relationships are. Finally, in Chapter 4, we take an in-depth look at the specifications for ISDN, including protocols, bearer services, signaling regimes, and more.

Our goal in Part I is to equip you to understand the terms and concepts behind ISDN so that you can better understand the technology and its capabilities. Along the way, you'll find yourself learning more about the operation of the telephone system, both long and short haul, than you ever dreamed possible. We hope you enjoy the trip!

1

Digital Communications and ISDN

Nothing ever just happens. Circumstances, coincidences, and events converge; cultures combine, individuals act and react; or natural forces combine and recombine in patterns that have never existed before or in different patterns that have been replicated since the beginning of time. The natural world supports the occasional revolutionary change, but all change is essentially evolutionary when taking the long view.

Since the origins of humanity there has been technology. The history of human civilization goes hand in hand with the history of technology. There is a logical and natural set of circumstances and perceived needs that has led us from the stone ax, the lever, and the wheel to electric guitars, in-the-door ice dispensers, and digital communications. What we call state-of-the-art technology has its roots back in the "dream time" of human history.

What do these ruminations have to do with the Integrated Services Digital Network (ISDN)? Our point is that ISDN, while it appears to be a revolutionary way of handling communications, is the natural result of evolutionary processes that began back when digital communications meant holding up two fingers and pointing at a herd of mastodon.

Since the beginnings of human history, computing systems and communications systems have been evolving from the simple to the complex. Although the importance of nonverbal digital communications in Stone Age hunting strategy should not be minimized, it is a subject somewhat outside the scope of this book. The intent of this chapter is to show that the Integrated Services Digital Network is the result of and a synthesis of evolutionary processes in communications and information processing technology.

Communications Basics

ISDN really represents the inevitable convergence of two related technologies: communications and modern distributed computing. Each field grew up more or less independently of the other. As the development of each one progressed, the benefits of their conjunction became more obvious and more of a necessity.

Communications technology, most particularly telephone communications, has developed out of a perceived need to provide the benefits of face-to-face communications over long distances. The developers of the telephone set out to develop a technology, *telephony,* that would allow the sound of a human voice to be carried over long distances and recreated at a receiving station. In a little over 100 years, telephone technology has been refined to create the modern worldwide network that we take more or less for granted today.

Computer technology results from the perceived need to process and store volumes of information generated in normal human interactions. The need to solve problems, and to store and distribute information, has been common to humanity from the days of painting on cave walls up to present-day enterprise computing. The modern solution to this need has been the development and refinement of more flexible and more powerful computer technology. In a short 40 years, computer technology has evolved rapidly from the batch-processing, vacuum-tube mainframes chugging out jobs to modern enterprise local area networks (LANs) and wide area networks (WANs), supporting state-of-the-art distributed systems.

Analog Communications

Telephone communication is based on human speech. The original goal of the telephone's developers was to provide a means of transporting the human voice faithfully (or at least audibly) over long distances. In its beginning phases, digital telephony wasn't even a pipe dream. Early practitioners of the telephonic arts used the human voice, which they were determined to transmit and recreate, as the basis for development of their systems.

Human voices generate sounds that travel through the air in continuous waves. These waves are known as *analog* signals. Analog voice signals cause vibrations on a membrane in the human ear, which converts the waves into recognizable sound. Not surprisingly, a conventional telephone receiver acts much like the human ear: Speaking into the phone transmits vibrations onto a membrane that generates electric impulses that are transmitted as a continuous wave over the phone lines. On the other end of a connection, telephone receivers interpret these electrical impulses and recreate corresponding sound waves as close to the original as the limits of the equipment will allow.

Since these electric pulses are analogous to the sound waves that generate them, telephony is said to be based on analog transmission, in the same way that human speech is based on analog transmission.

Computer Design

While the telephone network was reaching worldwide, the development of modern computing began. All communications inside computing machines, between computers and their peripheral devices, and between interconnected computers are handled digitally.

Whereas the telephone system was originally based on analog transmission and evolved from that point, there has never been a precedent for analog transmission in a computing environment. Computers have always been based on digital information and instructions. Thus, communications inside the computer and among devices attached to computers have always been digital.

Construction of the Telephone Network

The original phone system was made up of a single transmitter connected to a single receiver over a single wire. Early commercial telephone implementations offered phone service only to sites directly connected by discrete wires. As the popularity of phone service grew exponentially, the basic components that now make up the international telephone network began to be developed and brought on line.

The first addition to the phone system was the addition of *central offices* (COs), which provided a common switching point for all the phone lines in a given geographic area. All telephone system end users were connected to the CO by their *subscriber loops.* A call would come through the central office over a subscriber loop and a connection to the receiving subscriber would be made. At first these connections were made manually by operators by physically connecting wires on patch panels to establish the connections between subscribers.

In the next phase of elaboration, COs were linked by trunk lines. Multiple COs could also be linked by *tandem offices.* A tandem office contains a *tandem switch* that can switch transmissions over trunk lines and handle the routing of calls between COs. Tandem switches lower the cost of phone transmission by providing links between COs that do not require a dedicated direct trunk line.

Since 1984 the United States has been divided into 161 *local access and transport areas* (LATAs), made up of local loops, COs, and tandem switches. Long-distance calls are handled by inter-LATA carriers. COs or tandem offices switch calls to the inter-LATA carriers, and calls are transmitted and switched between LATAs in the same way as they are transmitted and switched between COs. This may sound complex (and in many ways it is), but it also means that almost any call in the United States can get between caller and callee by going through fewer than six involved parties: two local loops, two LATAs, and one or two inter-LATA carriers. Logically, this bespeaks a complex and pervasive communications grid.

Digital Communications

Computers have always used digital signaling methods to control local devices and for communications over local buses. The development of the local area network led to a slightly more complex form of digital communication, namely communication between and among computers. LANs permitted powerful new applications for computer technology. In fact, many industry pundits argue that the development of LAN technology was an important first step toward a new widespread use of computers, the linking of LANs into wide area networks.

Widespread adoption of WANs has led to large-scale use of the telephone network to complete the links between widely separated computers. Computer network nodes on a WAN may be connected not only by local cables but also by telephone links.

Normally, this requires that digital computer signals be converted to analog signals for transmission over the phone systems and then reconverted on the receiving end by *mo*dulating and *dem*odulating equipment (modems). Even though this conversion causes considerable time delays and increases network overhead, the benefits of wide area networking make it practical and necessary. Widespread use of telephone lines for data transfer created a new use for phone switching and transmission equipment and has been a key factor in the push for a fully digital telephone system.

Evolution of the
Integrated Digital Network System

The development of digital computer technology fomented a revolution in the way organizations created, stored, and transferred information. Many key innovations originally developed for computer technology were quickly adapted for use on the telephone network.

Analog to Digital (and Back Again)

Telephone networks depend on the coordination of many separate and distinct parts for their operation. Development of these parts has traditionally been concentrated in two major divisions: transmission and switching. Developments in computer technology have traditionally been adapted for use in the telephone network to lower cost and improve the quality and reliability of service.

The first major use of computer, or digital, technology in the phone network was in transmission. Although most local subscriber loops in the United States are still analog, the more sophisticated transmission functions of telephony have been converted to digital. The first digital lines used in the United States were *digital first carrier systems* (T1), made up of two wire pairs, one for transmission and one for reception. T1 lines were introduced into the phone network to provide a high-volume link between COs and between COs and tandem offices. Analog signals are converted to a digital bitstream and transmitted over the T1 line, where they are reconverted to analog on the other end.

Analog Signal Transmission

Analog signals are continuous signals consisting of waves traveling in cycles. Human voice, video, and music are all examples of analog signals. The frequency of an analog signal is measured in hertz (Hz), or cycles per second. The *passband* of an analog channel is defined as the range of frequencies that can be carried simultaneously.

The *bandwidth* is the width of the passband required for transmission. Different channels may use different passbands within the frequency range of transmission.

The passband of an analog telephone link is defined as approximately 300 to 3400 Hz. The human voice produces sounds between 50 and 1500 Hz. Obviously, the passband of the physical phone link isn't adequate to carry the full range of human voice, but research has shown that the majority of human voice frequencies fall between 300 and 3400 Hz. Telephone links are optimized to carry these frequencies, which contain enough of the range of human sound to recreate clearly recognizable speech.

The bandwidth of voice communications is limited on a telephone network so that multiple phone conversations can take place over the same physical channel, or link.

Digital Signal Transmission

For digital transmission over T1 lines, and to take advantage of digital switching, analog voice must be converted into a digital bitstream. The continuously varying values of an analog signal are sampled 8000 times per second and converted to digital values using a coding algorithm called µ-law (pronounced "mu-law") encoding. A continuous set of 8 bits carries this digital value. After the value is obtained it is mapped to one of 254 different numerical volume, or amplitude, numbers.

Commonly, an analog signal is generated, converted to a digital stream, transmitted, and then deconverted at the receiving end into analog signals. Ironically, the use of computer modems adds another set of conversions to each end of the stream, where digital data is converted to analog for initial transmission over the local loop and, on reception from the local loop, converted back from analog into digital.

Multiplexing

Using a common link for many simultaneous connections is called *multiplexing*. Multiplexing in the telephone network allows multiple conversations or connections to occur over the same physical connection.

Analog and digital signals are multiplexed in different ways. The analog telephone network uses *frequency division multiplexing* (FDM) to carry multiple conversations. FDM apportions the total available bandwidth into channels or bands that belong to an assigned user for the duration of the connection. For voice transmission, each conversation is assigned a different passband with a bandwidth of 3100 Hz.

Digital signals are multiplexed over a link using *time division multiplexing* (TDM). TDM gives each separate channel the entire frequency range for a very tiny increment of time, before switching to the next transmitter waiting in line. That's why TDM is sometimes called a "time-slicing" approach; nobody gets the whole bandwidth all of the time, but everybody gets a slice for their portion of each unit of time.

Switching

The first switching devices on the telephone network were electromechanical switches called *step-by-step* switches. As their name implies, step-by-step switches react to each digit dialed by the user and make physical connections in the switch to route the call. The next step in switch development was to provide *common control* of the switching function within the switch. Common control switching is based on a series of electromechanical relays, with instructions for handling the switching functions statically defined by the internal wiring inside the switch.

Stored program switches were made possible by the development of the transistor. These switches allowed easier reprogramming of connections and call control within the phone network. The first stored program switches were installed in the early 1970s. Essentially they were digital switches, so their inclusion in the telephone network, combined with the implementation of T1 lines, marks the beginning of digital telephony and the beginning of the evolution of ISDN.

The inclusion of digital switches and high-volume digital transmission lines required a high volume of analog-to-digital and digital-to-analog conversions within the network. Although these conversions were practical and necessary, considering the evolution of the phone network, they also added considerable overhead and cost to transmission of phone calls without adding any value to the connections. Engineers in the phone network immediately began to convert more of their transmissions and switching functions from analog to digital, in order to cope with this overhead and its associated costs by reducing the number of conversions required.

LANs and WANs

Meanwhile, the development and implementation of computer technology continued at an incredible pace. New ways to construct and use computers were envisioned, developed, deployed, improved, and replaced by more efficient methods in a ceaseless quest for the best and fastest technologies.

One of the most significant changes in computing followed the move from batch-oriented mainframe processing to distributed computing. Following this change in physical organization, innovations pushed computing toward decentralized processing and storage. Most of this push resulted from the deployment of local area networks composed of powerful desktop computers spread willy-nilly around many enterprises.

At the same time, these newly deployed LANs were linked by telephone circuits to form wide area networks that vastly increased the desktop computer user's access to application processing, storage capacity, and sources of information.

The widespread implementation of LANs and WANs placed a new burden on telephone transmissions. Primarily designed and built to provide analog voice transmission, the telephone network was increasingly called on to provide the transmission of digital data.

As we mentioned earlier, digital computer signals are converted to analog signals (modulated) on the sending end of a transmission,

and deconverted back to digital signals at the other end (demodu-
lated). Modems are designed to handle this task to enable computer
communications over the telephone networks. But because the infrastructure of the telephone network was increasingly shifting
from analog to digital, it was invariably the case that computers had
to go through an extra layer of modulation and demodulation, simply to use what was primarily a digital medium in the first place!

The Move to an Integrated Digital Network

As more and more phone circuits are used for digital computer data
transmission, new developments and evolution in digital hardware
and software continue to bring down the transmission and switching costs and overhead necessary for the operation of the telephone
network. From the beginning, it has been obvious for reasons of
economy, expedience, and accuracy that conversion and deconver-
sion of analog and digital signals over the telephone network
should be eliminated.

As early as 1959, when the first experimental digital telephone technology was being tested and debugged, it was proposed that the
global telephone network should move from its analog beginnings
and be converted into an integrated digital network (IDN), in
which switching and transmission facilities could be combined for
efficiency.

Users and implementers of wide area networks have always recognized the value of and sought the implementation of end-to-end
digital connections for transfer of computer information. Telephone
network technicians sought the cost savings, increased load capacity, and tighter control that can be provided by eliminating analog-
to-digital conversions inside the system.

ISDN

The word "integrated" in IDN implies the integration of switching
and transmission. IDN has meaning in the context of the interna-

tional telephone network and embodies the goal of the total digitalization of telephone technology.

The concept of ISDN is somewhat broader. In ISDN, "integrated" means that data transmission of many types—voice, video, sound, and data—may be seamlessly included in the digital switching and transmission capabilities of the IDN.

ISDN Standards

Standards are defined as "a prescribed set of rules, conditions, or requirements concerning definition of terms; classification of components; specification of materials, performance, or operation; delineation of procedures; or measurement of quantity and quality in describing materials, products, systems, services, or practices."

Several standards organizations have involved themselves in defining the standards for the proposed ISDN. The preeminent body in this group is the International Telegraph and Telephone Consultative Committee (CCITT).

The CCITT definition of ISDN is as follows: "An ISDN is a network, in general evolving from a telephony IDN, that provides end-to-end digital connectivity to support a wide range of services, including voice and non-voice services, to which users have access by a limited set of standard multi-purpose user-network interfaces."

In 1984 the CCITT defined the following *principles* for ISDN.

1. ISDN should support a range of voice and nonvoice applications. Service integration for an ISDN should take place using a limited set of connection types and user-network interface arrangements.
2. ISDNs support a variety of applications, including switched and nonswitched connections. Switched connections should include both circuit-switched and packet-switched connections.

3. New services introduced into ISDN should be arranged to be compatible with 64 Kbps switched digital connections.

4. ISDNs will contain intelligence for the purpose of providing service features, maintenance, and network management functions. This intelligence may not be sufficient for some new services and may have to be supplemented by either additional intelligence within the network, or possibly compatible intelligence in the user terminals.

5. A layered protocol structure should be used for the specification of the access to an ISDN. Access from a user to ISDN resources may vary depending on the service required and upon the status of implementation of national ISDNs.

6. It is recognized that ISDNs may be implemented in a variety of configurations according to specific national situations.

Furthermore, the CCITT recommends the following evolutionary pattern for the move to ISDN.

1. ISDNs will be based on concepts developed for telephone ISDNs and may evolve by incorporating additional functions and network features including those of any other dedicated networks such as circuit switching and packet switching for data so as to provide for existing and new services.

2. Arrangements must be developed for the interworking of services on ISDNs and services on other networks as transition from pre-ISDN to ISDN networks proceeds.

3. An evolving ISDN may also include at later stages switched connections at bit rates higher and lower than 64 Kbps.

A Visualization of ISDN

The natural evolution of ISDN communication reached critical mass in the 1970s, when digital switches and transmission lines were introduced and started to become ubiquitous in the world telephone network. Evolution and rapid improvement in computer technology expanded the computer's role in communications while the

IDN became a reality. Implementation of standards for the envisioned ISDN makes the union of the two technologies complete.

Summary

The first worldwide network to establish interconnecting links was the telephone network. The telephone was developed to provide over long distances capabilities for communications that were analogous to human speech.

As more and more users got into the phone network, various additions and improvements were made to allow for the increase in demand and keep the cost of services as low as possible. Original telephone operations were improved and linked up with the new technologies to create networks of telephone links that covered the entire world. Many components of the original analog system were replaced by digital equipment as it became available, making it possible for overhead and costs to be lowered.

Computers have always been based on communications using a stream of binary bits. In other words, computers have always used digital communications. At the end of the 1980s, computers started to become more powerful, more flexible in their uses, and more affordable. Traditional mainframe batch processing has been mostly phased out and replaced by distributed, or enterprise, systems made up of multiple desktop computers linked together in local area networks (LANs), which are in turn linked, often over telephone lines, to form wide area networks (WANs).

Developments in the computer field made possible the creation of digital switches and transmission lines to make telephone communications simpler and cheaper. Introduction of the first digital trunk lines in the 1960s and the first digital switches in the 1970s marked the beginning of the transformation from analog to digital telephony. The goal of this transformation was the creation of an international integrated digital network (IDN) that could provide end-to-end digital connectivity.

The overhead and time required to transform digital stream computer signals to analog signals for transmission over the telephone network cause sluggish, sometimes unacceptable performance on computer networks. The need to transmit a variety of data types, including voice, video, music, print, and numeric data, continues to drive a requirement for more flexible communications through the phone network. The demand for faster and more accurate transmission of computer information over telephone systems has pushed the move to a completely digital phone network, the Integrated Services Digital Network (ISDN).

By definition, ISDN calls for the transmission of video, data, and voice over the telephone network. But seamless digital connectivity is only one benefit of ISDN. A variety of services are available on the ISDN, and they can be accessed at will by their potential users.

Seeing the need for development of ISDN, standards bodies around the world, led by the CCITT, have set key standards for ISDN implementations. Standards deal with the description, concept, and architecture of ISDN and provide for the ultimate evolution from analog telephony and digital distributed computing to one network standard, ISDN.

Proposed implementations of ISDN define standard devices and interfaces, called reference points, between the devices on the ISDN. Four major types of ISDN channels are defined in the standards, as are the basic rate interface (BRI) and primary rate interface (PRI) access interfaces. In the chapters that follow, you'll learn all about these types of channels, and the access interfaces that provision them.

2

ISDN Structures and Functions

In Chapter 1 we introduced most of the concepts that make up ISDN without going into much detail on how all those pieces fit together. In this chapter we'll take a closer look at how information is passed over an ISDN and how users can access the functionality of the ISDN.

Transmission Structures

Prospective ISDN users will contract with an ISDN access provider for a digital pipeline to allow them to access the ISDN. The size of this pipeline will be predetermined, and users can consume any or all of the available bandwidth as needed. To meet these needs, ISDN access providers supply *access interfaces* of two basic types. These interfaces will be composed of combinations of *logical channels*. We'll elaborate on these concepts and this terminology in the sections that follow.

ISDN Channels

In a traditional telephone network the user is connected to the network central office (CO) by a local, or subscriber, loop. A local loop consists of one analog channel that is used for signaling to the network—dialing a call for instance—and for information transfer, which may be transfer of a conversation, sound, video, or binary data.

In an ISDN, the local loop carries only digital data, although it may be of any type available in today's environment. The ISDN local loop connects the ISDN equivalent of the CO, the *local exchange* (LE), to the ISDN user's equipment. The ISDN local loop is composed of separate logical channels that may be combined to provide the user's interface to the ISDN.

These logical channels are divided into three basic types. Each of these channels exists in a time slot over the local loop pipeline through the process of time division multiplexing (TDM), which we introduced in the preceding chapter. Furthermore, ISDN channels are categorized by their use, whether for signaling or data transfer, and also by the standard transmission rate for a particular channel type.

The various types of ISDN channels are listed in Table 2.1.

Table 2.1   ISDN channel types.

Channel Type	Definition
D channel	(Device channel) used for transfer of signaling information between the user and the network and for packet transmission.
B channel	(Bearer channel) used for data transmission over the local loop.

Table 2.1   Continued

Channel Type	Definition
H channel	(Higher rate channel) used for services that need higher transmission rates than a single B channel.
B-ISDN	(Broadband ISDN) channels will enable applications requiring speeds higher than those defined for H channels. B-ISDN standards allow transmission rates as high as 622.08 Mbps.

D-Channel Transmissions

The D channel is used primarily to carry signals between the ISDN user and the ISDN network itself. Different ISDN user devices, such as telephones, fax machines, and computers, have different ways of connecting with the ISDN, but they all share a common protocol for signaling and receiving signals from the network and they all use the D channel for this communication.

Signaling data does not consume the entire bandwidth provided for the D channel at any given time. Thus, a secondary use for this channel is possible whenever bandwidth is available. Although such use is not terribly common, this extra bandwidth can be used for packet-switched transmissions like Internet protocol (IP) or X.25.

The D channel may have a rate of 16 or 64 Kbps, depending on the type of access interface provided to the user.

B Channel

An ISDN B channel, sometimes called a *bearer channel*, is used to carry the information needed for ISDN services. Essentially this means the B channel is used to carry user information, such as digitized voice, video, audio, and binary data, and can be multiplexed to carry any combination of these data types limited only by the bandwidth of the channel.

The B channel is the fundamental user data channel described in the standards for ISDN. The B channel was defined at a rate of 64

Kbps, which was the bandwidth required for effective transmission of a digital voice conversation at the time these standards were set. B channels are used to make circuit-switched, packet-switched, or semipermanent connections (the ISDN equivalent of a leased line).

H channel

Some user applications require more bandwidth than a B channel can provide. Standard configurations of bandwidth, known as H channels, provide such higher bit rates. Applications such as video teleconferencing, high-speed data transmission, and the multiplexing of large numbers of lower bit rate transmissions all require more than 64 Kbps. H-channel configurations are offered to provide this bandwidth.

An H0 channel is a logical grouping, or its equivalent, of six B channels operating at a bit rate of 384 Kbps. An H1 channel is made up of all available H0 channels on a single-user interface employing a T1 line (this consists of 23 B channels, operating at a bit rate of 1472 Kbps, plus a 64 Kbps D channel). An H1 channel is equivalent to four H0 channels and provides 1.536 Mbps altogether.

Broadband ISDN (B-ISDN)

D, B, and H channels were defined in the first standards for ISDN and provide a considerable improvement in carrier transmission rates. But, things being what they are, even this increase in bandwidth isn't enough. ISDN users want to use the ISDN for video teleconferencing, high-definition television, and other bandwidth-intensive applications that just won't perform acceptably over the original ISDN. These original ISDN standards define what is now known as narrowband ISDN (N-ISDN).

Standards for broadband ISDN (B-ISDN) call for bit rates in the 600 Mbps range. B-ISDN is described in the standards as service oriented, allowing the transmission of multimedia information integrating data of many types. B-ISDN services are loosely grouped into *communications services*, analogous to traditional phone services, and *conversational services*, which provide ISDN users two-way end-to-end information transfer capability for applications like video teleconferencing or high-speed data transfer. B-ISDN transport involves sophisticated *cell-relay* technology, called asynchronous transfer mode (ATM).

Access Interfaces

Access interfaces provide the connections between ISDN users and the ISDN, and they are made up of logical groupings of channels provided by the network or service provider. ISDN is designed to allow multiple information flows over one physical connection, so ISDN access interfaces allow users to switch among available services on demand.

ISDN standards define two different access interfaces, the *basic rate interface* and the *primary rate interface.* These interfaces define the bit rates used for transmission and are differentiated by the numbers of B, D, and H channels they support.

Basic Rate Interface (BRI)

The basic rate interface is made up of two B channels and one D channel. The designation for the BRI is 2B + D. The BRI D channel always operates at 16 Kbps. Taking these channels together, the BRI has a total bit rate of 144 Kbps; including additional overhead bits brings the actual bit rate up to 192 Kbps.

The BRI provides basic phone service to users and allows simultaneous access to voice communications and a variety of data applications. BRI is intended for small office and home use.

Primary Rate Interface (PRI)

PRIs are provided to users with large capacity requirements, such as offices with digital private branch exchanges (PBXs) or local area networks (LANs). The PRI in the United States is configured to conform to the T1 transmission rate of 1.544 Mbps. The channel structure for the primary rate interface is 23B + D. The D channel in the PRI has a rate of 64 Kbps.

Perhaps needless to say, the PRI is designed for larger companies with multiple ISDN devices in operation. Really big companies using ISDN might even use multiple PRIs, but today only service providers typically consume PRIs in multiples.

User-Network Interfaces

ISDN pipelines from the ISDN access provider and the user site have been described as basic or primary rate interfaces. These interfaces are broken down into channels used for signaling the network for services and channels for carrying the services provided. That's what the ISDN access provider provides to the user site. What about the ISDN user site itself?

ISDN standards describe the user-network interface of an ISDN as a combination of *functional groupings,* which describe the different devices on the user premises that use the ISDN, and *reference points,* which are logical points of interaction between the functional groups.

Devices on a user's premises may be physical devices such as ISDN phones or virtual devices that perform an ISDN interface function transparently. These devices are grouped by the role they play in the interface between the customer site and the ISDN access provider.

The ISDN standards define the following devices, or functional groupings.

1. Network termination type 1 (NT1)
2. Network termination type 2 (NT2)
3. Terminal equipment type 1 (TE1)
4. Terminal equipment type 2 (TE2)
5. Terminal adapter (TA)

Each of these types of devices performs a set of required functions. We'll describe those in detail in this section. But an understanding of the *reference points* is critical to understanding a diagram of the user-network interface. These reference points are the conceptual points that divide the functional groups.

In other words, reference points describe the interactions between functional groupings, generally keeping associated functions grouped together. The interactions at the reference point are prescribed by protocols, the rules of the road for the transfer of information around an ISDN user site and onto the ISDN. ISDN standards describe various reference points called R, S, T, and U. We'll expand those initials into explanations in this chapter and show how these functional groupings and reference points can effectively define an ISDN user site.

Functional Devices

ISDN functional devices fall into the following categories:

- *Network termination type 1* (NT1). Represents the physical termination of the ISDN user's interface. NT1 may be provided by the ISDN access provider and handles OSI level 1 functions such as the physical connection between the ISDN and user devices, line maintenance, and performance monitoring. The NT1 supports multiple channels in the BRI and PRI and handles the multiplexing of bitstreams using time division multiplexing. An NT1 is the ISDN equivalent of the modular plug in the old analog phone system, where multiple ISDN user devices can be connected to the ISDN network.
- *Network termination type 2* (NT2). A device that, depending on its level of intelligence, may provide OSI level 1, 2, and/or 3 capabilities. NT2s are used for concentration of user ISDN devices or for switching between those devices. Examples of NT2s are digital PBXs, LAN gateways, and any packet-switching devices. NT2s may not

be necessary at small sites where ISDN devices can be directly attached to the NT1.

- *ISDN terminal equipment* (TE1). The TE1 is any ISDN end user device that uses ISDN protocols and supports ISDN services. ISDN telephone, ISDN fax, and ISDN workstations are examples of TE1 equipment.
- *Non-ISDN terminal equipment* (TE2). End user devices that are not ISDN compatible, such as standard analog telephones.
- *Terminal adapter* (TA). Allows non-ISDN devices (TE2s) to communicate with the ISDN.

Reference Points

Many device-to-device connections are defined in ISDN standards. Each connection type, or interface, requires a defined protocol. Each of these interfaces is described as a *reference point.*

The four most important reference points defined by ISDN standards are the R, S, T, and U reference points. These are defined in the following list:

- R reference: describes the interface between non-ISDN terminals (TE2s) and terminal adapters (TAs).
- S reference: describes the interface between an ISDN terminal (TE1) or terminal adapter (TA) and a network terminating device (NT1 or NT2).
- T reference: describes the interface between a local switching device (NT2) and the local loop termination (NT1).
- U reference: exists between the NT1 and the ISDN local exchange (LE) and defines the standard for communications between the two. CCITT standards define the NT1 device as part of the local network and do not deal with standards on the local subscriber loop. American National Standards Institute (ANSI) standards in the United States define transmission standards over the local loop.

ISDN protocols, which we look at in the next section, are the rules that define how legal communications can occur at defined reference points.

ISDN Protocols

In the world of computer technology, and networking in particular, protocols are used to describe succinctly the relations between entities in a communications environment. Protocols are the rules that prescribe how interactions take place. Earlier, we described the different reference points in the ISDN architecture. Each of these reference points, which operates as an interface, has associated protocols that describe what takes place at that interface.

Planes

As defined by the CCITT, the ISDN architecture is made up of four planes:

1. *Control* plane (C plane)
2. *User* plane (U plane)
3. *Transport* plane (T plane)
4. *Management* plane (M plane)

C-plane protocols deal with control communications between users and the network, such as requests for bearer services and establishing and terminating calls. U-plane protocols deal with the transfer of information between user applications. Transport plane protocols handle the physical connections required, and management plane protocols keep an eye on protocol interactions inside and between the planes.

The U and C planes delineate the paths used in ISDN for signaling to the network (C plane) and transfer of user information (U plane). U-plane protocols, dealing with the B channel, are basically transparent to the ISDN. The bulk of ISDN protocols deal with the interface between the user site and the network over the D channel.

OSI and ISDN

ISDN protocols for the D channel map more or less agreeably to the first three layers of the OSI model.

1. Layer 1 (physical layer): Describes the physical connections between ISDN devices and the network termination device (NT1). Calls for a synchronous, serial, full-duplex connection. The connection may be point to point over the BRI and PRI or point to multipoint over the BRI.
2. Layer 2 (data link layer): Handles error control over the physical link. Creates the connection between the user site and the ISDN. The ISDN protocol at this layer is Link Access Procedures on the D channel (LAPD).
3. Layer 3 (network layer): These protocols deal with signaling between users and the ISDN for establishing, maintaining, and disconnecting calls, and calls for supplementary services. Layer 3 protocols deal with user/network signaling over the interface between the user site and the ISDN. Signaling system 7 (SS7) protocols handle signaling within the ISDN.

ISDN Connections

ISDN standards require the availability of three types of service for end-to-end connections:

- circuit switched on the B channel
- packet switched on the B channel
- circuit switched on the D channel

The B channel, which delivers *bearer services,* can be used for circuit switching, semipermanent circuits, and packet switching. The D channel is used primarily for messages between the user and the network related to connection setup and calls for services.

Circuit-Switched Connections

An ISDN voice connection is established over one of the B channels. Control information necessary to establish the connection is sent over the D channel. The BRI will allow two voice connections simultaneously over ISDN, as it has two B channels to carry bearer services. Even if the two B channels are being used, the D channel is still available to carry signaling information for additional calls. The D channel manages calls or can be used to invoke supplementary services such as call hold and call waiting, up to 15 levels deep in most ISDN environments.

Packet Switching

For packet switching, a circuit-switched connection is set up on the B channel between an end user and a packet-switched node using the D-channel LAPD control protocol. The B channel may be multiplexed using the time division multiplexing scheme to provide a number of virtual channels. Packet-switching capability may be provided by the ISDN itself or by a separate packet-switching network attached to the ISDN. Packet switching may take place over the B channel or over the D channel.

Addressing

The world telephone network depends on a numbering system of addresses for the individual devices (telephone, answering machine, etc.) attached to the phone network. The telephone number you dial to reach someone is the unique address of that person's telephone device. Each subscriber in the phone network must have a unique number to route calls and to let access and service providers know whom to bill and how much.

In an ISDN, a number and an address are slightly different things. An *ISDN number* is the network number of an ISDN user site. An *ISDN address* is made up of an ISDN number with some additional address bits that identify a specific device at the user site.

According to this scheme, the ISDN subscriber is assigned an ISDN number that identifies the subscriber site. A digital PBX at this site has this ISDN number as its address. ISDN addresses allow direct connections between devices at ISDN sites.

ISDN addresses are made up of a combination of the following:

- Country code: A one- to three-digit number that specifies the country or geographic area of the call (country codes are already defined in the existing standards for telephony).
- National destination code: The designation of an area within the country, used to access destination networks inside the designated country. Comparable to the area codes in use in the national telephone numbering plan.
- ISDN subscriber number: The designation of an individual ISDN subscriber site.
- ISDN subaddress: The designation of a specific user site device on the ISDN.

Basically, each T reference point is assigned an ISDN number, and each S reference point is assigned an ISDN address.

Interworking

With all the standards in place and with ISDNs operating all over the world, the brave new world of ISDN still hasn't really jelled into one. Instead we find different nations and continents using slightly different flavors of ISDN. And that's just ISDNs. There are various non-ISDN public networks in operation that predate the implementation of ISDNs.

For the goals of the ISDN to be realized, there has to be a method for communicating among different ISDNs and between ISDNs and existing network components. *Interworking,* the interaction of different types of networks, is critical to the evolution of a worldwide ISDN. Interworking requires that a set of internetwork translation functions be implemented either in the ISDN or in the network accessed by the ISDN.

Interworking of network addresses between ISDNs and other types of networks depends on the ISDN to route the call to the called party's network and on the called network to complete the routing of the call to the call party. This approach is called *single-stage* addressing. A *two-stage* addressing scheme is also allowed by ISDN standards but is not recommended. Two-stage addressing calls for use of an interworking unit to handle address number transformation.

To provide a compatible connection between an ISDN and another type of network, certain predefined functions must take place. A short list of these functions follows:

- provide interworking of network numbering plans
- match physical layer components
- maintain error and flow control over the interconnection
- collect billing data
- provide multiplexing and frame construction conversion

For these functions to be defined, additional reference points and their associated protocols have been outlined in the ISDN standards:

- K: Interface with existing non-ISDN network. Internetworking is performed by the ISDN.
- L: Same as K, but responsibility for internetworking falls to the non-ISDN network.
- M: Interface with specialized non-ISDN network requiring adaptation functions performed in the non-ISDN network.

- N: Interface between two ISDNs. Protocols determine requirements for compatibility of service.
- P: Specialized connection within the ISDN providing access to separate components.

At present, these reference points are more targets for future implementation than actual working entities. But they do point to potential methods for integrating heretofore incompatible ISDNs and pre-ISDN telephone systems.

Summary

Users who hook up to an ISDN must contract with an access provider for a digital pipeline. The size of the pipeline will be determined by mutual agreement between the customer and the provider based on the user's requirements and budget.

This pipeline is defined as a set of access interfaces. ISDN standards define two access interfaces between customers and ISDN access providers, the basic rate interface (BRI) and the primary rate interface (PRI). The BRI and PRI are defined by the channels that are carried over the interface. A BRI, the basic small-company interface, contains two 64 Kbps B channels to carry bearer information and services and one 16 Kbps D channel used for communication between the customer and the ISDN. The PRI is made up of 24 channels (23 B channels and 1 D channel), each with a bit rate of 64 Kbps. Certain customers may require a connection made up of multiple PRIs.

The user side of the user-network interface is described by a schematic made up of functional groupings, or collections of devices with similar functions, and reference points, which are the defined points of protocol-defined interactions between functional groupings.

ISDN adheres to a protocol architecture based on the concept of planes, which can be mapped generally to the OSI network architecture model. Most ISDN protocols deal with user-to-network and network-to-user signaling over the D channel. Protocols dealing with the D channel can be mapped to the first three layers of the OSI network model.

ISDN addressing has been implemented to provide routing of calls. The current ISDN scheme is evolving on the model of the telephone network. ISDN numbers refer to customer sites and ISDN addresses refer to ISDN devices used on the customer sites. As the ISDN evolves, the issue of ISDN interfaces with preexisting public networks must be dealt with. ISDN interworking with these networks will require some type of address resolution between the separate schemes.

ISDN interworking has been defined by protocols, many of which are still under development. The operation of these protocols is defined by additional reference points, which correspond to the points of interaction between the ISDN and other network types.

3

ISDN Communications Service Links

The basic concept behind ISDN is end-to-end digital connectivity, that is, a completely digital signal channel all the way from sender to receiver and vice versa. This idea is relatively simple to understand, but the implementation has been a long time coming. ISDN standards are based for the most part on existing carrier technology; therefore, to fully understand ISDN's implications, you must understand ISDN evolution in terms of communications services that are already in place. In this chapter, we're going to examine various types of existing communications and their relationships to ISDN.

You've already seen how disparate elements in ISDN have evolved from existing telephone and computer technology. You've also learned that ISDN is a long-planned standard for the union of those two technologies. Here's where we'll try to explain how this convergence will actually occur.

Any significant technological development is pushed along by factors in the marketplace. The need to lower the costs involved in telephone transmission and switching eventually led to digital carriers and integrated digital switching. Improved performance and falling prices for computers and peripherals have fueled the dramatic spread of desktop and distributed computing. The same general market factors are also driving related technologies to create a similar union in ISDN.

Markets respond to many factors, and the interplay of these factors keeps them in flux. Few markets are changing as fast in size and scope as the telecommunications and computer technology markets. In these fields, change has become a constant, and technology consumers are wary. One day's cutting-edge technologies may become obsolete within a period of months. Technologies that represent a perfect solution for one company's needs may have little to offer to others. It takes time, and proven technology, to meet market demands.

ISDN technology must prove itself with existing technology as well as integrate new ideas. ISDN has been designed to emulate or incorporate existing technologies but also to be flexible enough to incubate developing ones. Here, we'll take a look at the market and at some of the different ways in which ISDN relates to communications and processing technologies already in common use.

T1 Networks

T1 lines are full-duplex digital circuits designed specifically to carry digital signals. T1 digital carrier lines began to be integrated into the telephone network in the early 1960s. T1 lines were originally installed as trunk lines internal to the telecommunications network, and they were intended to provide increased transmission capability and lower the cost of the telecommunications infrastructure. Digital transmission allows more channels to be multiplexed over a single trunk line than is possible over an analog trunk. As advances were made in digital technology, the high cost of T1 began to erode, and T1 lines were extended to customer sites for dedicated, or leased, line service.

When it was first introduced, the cost of T1 service was very high. Advances in digital technology have brought about rapid improvements in the capabilities of T1, both for telephone carriers and for end users. T1 lines are often used by companies to set up private wide area networks. On a T1 WAN, the telephone network carrier's central office acts as a hub to switch T1 links that tie together remote stations. Data and voice traffic can be multiplexed for transmission over the links.

T1 Anatomy

The T1 line is made up of twenty-four 64 Kbps channels multiplexed to carry voice and data. The T1 architecture is based on the digital signal hierarchy used in North America to describe telecommunications links. During the setup of the analog POTS (plain old telephone service) it was discovered that the optimal bandwidth for human voice transmission (that's why they invented telephones) was 56 Kbps. With a few overhead bits for transmission control, the optimal channel required was 64 Kbps. Digital transmission cuts down on the overhead required during transmission and allows use of the entire 64 Kbps. The 64 Kbps is the basic unit of the digital signal hierarchy, the DS-0.

- DS-0: 64 Kbps
- DS-1: 1.544 Mbps

A T1 line can be represented as a bundle of 24 DS-0 circuits combined to give an aggregate bandwidth of 1.544 Mbps, corresponding to the DS-1.

T1 Hardware Requirements

T1 links, at the physical layer, may be of diverse types. A T1 connection could be made over coaxial cable, fiber-optic cable, infrared, microwave, satellite, or, most commonly, over an enhanced metallic local loop.

To enhance the local loop, the telephone company places units at appropriate intervals along the customer loop to regenerate the digital signal. Thus, the installation of a T1 link does not usually require the installation of upgraded cabling but does require additional hardware to upgrade the loop.

For connecting a T1 line to customer site hardware, the following equipment is required:

- Channel service unit (CSU): This device represents the actual interface between the T1 link and the customer site. The CSU maintains line quality, monitors the actual connections across the user-network interface, and acts as the physical termination point for the T1 line.
- Data service unit (DSU): The DSU is responsible for the actual conversion of LAN and voice signals into the digital signals used by the T1. The DSU is connected on one side to the CSU and on the other to *customer premises equipment* (CPE), such as LAN bridges and routers, and multiplexing devices.
    A CSU and a DSU are commonly combined into a single device with connections for the T1 on the CSU side and LAN connections on the DSU side. This device is the physical manifestation of the user-network interface between a customer site and the local telephone carrier.
- Multiplexers: Devices responsible for the channeling of circuits in the T1. A multiplexer allows a mix of voice and data over the same link.
- Bridges and routers: These well-known LAN devices usually connect LAN traffic to the DSU.

T1 Costs

Most telephone carriers today offer T1 services to their customers, with T1 circuits typically leased on a month-to-month basis. An initial setup charge is standard, and the actual month-to-month charge for T1 links is determined by the distance of the link. Charges are usually based on a per-mile rate, plus a monthly service charge. T1 lines are used primarily for links within one telephone local access and transport area (LATA). If the T1 link spans multiple LATAs, the charges are based on the services of the linked LATAs and may include charges from an interexchange carrier (IEX) as well.

Prices for T1 local service average about $2800 per month nationwide. Long-distance T1 usage drives rates up rather sharply. The cost of a coast-to-coast T1 link may be as high as $25,000 per month.

T1 and ISDN

The ISDN primary rate interface (PRI) was deliberately described in CCITT standards to conform to the T1 architecture. ISDN, of course, provides much more flexibility than T1 service. And ISDN tariffs are substantially lower than those for T1 service.

T1 multiplexing allows the sharing of single channels for voice and data, as does ISDN. ISDN, however, allows the user to configure combinations of 64 Kbps channels for higher bandwidth requirements.

Private Branch Exchanges (PBXs)

Private branch exchanges, in the communications world, are the user site equivalent of the central office. A PBX is a telephone exchange at an office or business that provides circuit switching between the various extensions and devices and provides an interface between the public communications network and the local site. PBXs can be used to connect devices for data transmission, to connect voice calls, and to provide access to public network services such as Frame Relay and X.25 packet service.

PBX Connections

Devices

As you might imagine, almost any communications or data processing device can be connected to a PBX. Incoming voice transmission may be switched by the PBX to analog phone sets or digital telephones. PCs and workstations may be separately connected to the PBX, or they may use the same wire pair as the analog or digital phone set. PBXs have long been used to link mainframe devices in Systems Network Architecture (SNA)-based mainframe network environments.

Control

A PBX may be manually operated, as is done at most small businesses, or it may be completely automated. Management and control functions are built into the PBX so that an attendant or operator can provide maintenance and error checking functions as well as switching capability.

PBX Networks

A PBX may operate by itself in a corporate environment, but it is most probably linked to other PBXs to provide a distributed wide area private switching system. PBXs on a small exchange may be linked to higher level PBXs that link multiple exchanges. Through a hierarchical arrangement of multiple PBXs operating at different levels, a private distributed PBX network may be established. Multiple PBXs are usually connected over leased or dedicated lines. The combination of leased lines and multiple PBXs provides organizations with the equivalent of a private telephone carrier network.

Centrex

Most public telephone carriers offer what is known as Centrex service. With this type of service, user devices such as telephones, fax machines, mainframes, and PCs are all directly linked over customer access loops to the public phone network central office (CO). Users could use a private PBX network or a Centrex system and get equal functionality. The major difference between the two systems, as it appears to the end user, would be the access number (called an escape digit) required to leave the PBX network and access the public carrier lines. A PBX network requires the escape digit for outside access. The user of a Centrex system, using carrier-provided switching, has transparent access to the public carrier network.

PBX and ISDN

PBXs are used in an ISDN environment in much the same way that they are used in the analog telecommunications environment.

ISDN PBX

An ISDN PBX may perform the same function as an analog PBX, but the functions are described differently. User devices attach to the ISDN PBX over a two-wire-pair connection at the S interface. This connection supplies each device with a basic rate interface (BRI) connection or some segment of a BRI. The ISDN PBX is connected to the exchange carrier switching office (CO) over the U interface. An ISDN PRI provides the communications channel between the user site and the CO. The PBX provides network termination (NT1) and customer premises switching (NT2) functionality.

Centrex and ISDN

In an ISDN Centrex system, BRI connections are made from the user's equipment directly to the local CO. A user device would be connected over the S interface to an NT1 at the user site and directly over the U reference point (local loop) to the Centrex carrier. The channel between user and CO would be a BRI throughout, and the Centrex network would supply the digital switch necessary for connectivity.

Local Area Networks (LANs)

Considerable work has been done to design and deploy devices to provide interconnections between LANs and ISDN. ISDN is by its nature a wide area network (WAN) service. Standards encourage the linking of LANs to ISDN to provide wide area network service.

ISDN can, if desired, provide LAN services to a user site if parameters for local network performance allow.

LANs and PBXs

Traditionally, an organization has computers interconnected over a
local area network. Telephones are connected to a local PBX. The
two networks, voice and data, are not connected. The PBX is connected to user devices (phones) at the user site and connected to the
local exchange (LE) carrier over the local subscriber loop. Computers are connected by cabling specified physical links into LANs.
LANs can be connected by bridges and routers, devices that can direct traffic from one LAN into another.

In this type of configuration, the LAN and the PBX do not normally
interact. However, a gateway computer can be configured to make
remote links in a WAN through the PBX. However, given recent developments in computer telephony, as well as Novell's Telephony
Services application programming interface (TSAPI) and Microsoft's Telephony API (TAPI), the gap between LANs and PBXs
has narrowed dramatically and should continue to do so over the
next two or three years. At some point, the distinction between a
network server and a PBX will become far more academic than it is
today.

ISDN LANs

An ISDN LAN operates in much the same way as a Centrex PBX. In
fact, Centrex data services are offered by most exchange carriers.
ISDN services can be supplied to networked PCs connected to
ISDN over the BRI or PRI. Individual PCs in such a configuration
are linked to the ISDN provider, either directly or through a PBX in
the manner just discussed in the preceding section on PBXs.

Performance is a major issue in this type of configuration. Ethernet
LANs offer transfers at 10 Mbps, and 100 Mbps LANs are not uncommon. An ISDN LAN operating over B or D channels could not
exceed the B channel's 64 Kbps "speed limit."

Nevertheless, this configuration could be useful to organizations just migrating to LAN technology and is a good first step toward total integration of ISDN services.

Centrex LANs

Centrex data service, offered by most local exchange carriers, is a popular transmission mechanism that integrates voice networks and data networks. A Centrex LAN functions in much the same way as a Centrex PBX. Computers and devices are linked directly to the CO, which acts as the local bus for the LAN. Voice devices (telephones) also directly linked to the CO. Typically, one telephone and one computer share a single local loop.

Centrex LANs depend on a device called an *integrated voice/data multiplexer* (IVDM). On the user side, the IVDM changes voice and data traffic into an integrated digital stream. On the network carrier side, another IVDM decodes the digital transmission into voice and data transmission, which is switched accordingly to either a voice or data switch for delivery to the destination on the LAN.

LAN Interconnection

An ISDN is by definition a wide area network. The most LAN-related use for ISDN is to provide a link between remote users and LANs or to provide a link between remote LANs.

Integrated Voice/Data LAN (IVDLAN)

The IEEE 802.9 committee has presented standards for the integration of voice and data traffic on LANs that have broad implications for ISDN. IVDLAN standards define a connection between user devices (IVDTE) and an ISDN. The 802.9 standards call for IVDTEs linked to an access unit (AU), which is in turn linked to the ISDN.

Services provided by the AU travel over channels that correspond to ISDN channels.

- B channel: a 64 Kbps channel identical to the ISDN B channel
- C channel: a circuit-switched channel providing multiple 64 Kbps circuits similar to ISDN H channels
- D channel: a user network signaling channel exactly analogous to the ISDN D channel
- P channel: packet channel; provides 802 LAN functionality

TCP/IP (Internet Protocols)

The Transmission Control Protocol and Internet Protocol (TCP/IP) constitute what is arguably the most widely used protocol suite in existence today. Without going into too much detail, it should be understood that TCP/IP protocols deal with network interactions above the data link layer of the OSI model. This means that TCP/IP can run over any data link and physical link protocols. The manner in which TCP/IP is transferred over ISDN is outlined in a series of documents called *requests for comment (RFCs)*. RFCs are issued by the Internet Engineering Task Force (IETF), the governing body of the worldwide internetwork called the Internet.

The Internet is a set of LANs and host computers connected by links such as T1 and T3, satellite, radio, POTS and ISDN. The one thing all these diverse end stations have in common is that they are all using the TCP/IP suite, the standard set of protocols for the Internet.

Internet Protocol

The fundamental protocol of the TCP/IP suite is IP. IP is a connectionless datagram protocol that is used for communication between network nodes and internetwork gateways and for communication between gateways. IP is packet oriented and provides for TCP/IP addressing, delivery, and packet formation. IP is a layer 3 protocol and is supported by the ISDN in much the same way the X.25 packet service, asynchronous transfer mode (ATM), and Frame Relay are supported.

Requests for Comment

Provisions have been made for the use of many data transfer methods in the ISDN. RFC 1294 deals with Frame Relay. RFC 1356 deals with the X.25 public packet-switching network. ATM is also described as it relates to TCP/IP transfer.

TCP/IP protocols are described in documents known as requests for comment. RFC 1356 describes IP packet transmission on the ISDN. Protocol standards have been adopted by the CCITT and the International Standards Organization (ISO) for interworking between the ISDN and IP networks.

Network Layer Protocol Identifier

An 8-byte identifier, the *network layer protocol identifier* (NLPID), in an ISDN packet identifies the type of higher layer protocols in use. IP has an identifier of 11001100 (0xCC). In an ISDN data packet, the NLPID is the first octet of the call user data field of the packet.

Summary

There is a salient fact about ISDN that has been implied but not yet stated. ISDN represents a wholesale shift in the way public telephone networks are organized, implemented, and operated. Years of evolution in the communications industry have finally provided the building blocks for a nationwide ISDN.

Many of the steps along the way to the adoption of ISDN have offered ISDN-like services, and many more blocks must be put in place to complete a comprehensive ISDN. ISDN represents a fundamental shift in the technology used in the public communications networks. This shift has been taking place more or less gradually.

The implementation of digital switching in the local exchange CO was an important step, as was the widespread deployment of T1 digital transmission lines.

ISDN will provide a substitute for many technologies and services now in use. ISDN BRI and PRI are priced in such a way that many dedicated T1 links may no longer be necessary. Customers may receive T1 bandwidth over local loops already in place.

ISDN operations can emulate LAN technology or may be used to provide increased LAN services. Connections between LANs and WANs will be much more flexible, and probably cheaper to use, over the ISDN. ISDN can provide more efficient transfer and increased access to services for users of the worldwide TCP/IP network, the Internet.

Progress toward a nationwide ISDN has been slow and deliberate—too slow for many, too fast for some. One reason for this slow pace is the magnitude of technological and strategic change that must be considered. ISDN marks a convergence of a multitude of related technologies and creates a multitude of considerations. Almost every step taken in the development and implementation of digital and communications technology brings us closer to ISDN.

4

ISDN Technical Specifications

ISDN Protocol Architecture

ISDN has its own architecture. The ISDN model is segmented into *planes* that describe the structure and function of ISDN. In this chapter we examine the four planes that constitute this model for ISDN.

We can also map the ISDN model to the Open Systems Interconnection (OSI) model. The planes of the ISDN model cross over the bottom three layers of the OSI model. ISDN is unconcerned with user layers 4–7 of the OSI stack, because ISDN deals solely with network access and not with end-to-end connections between nodes. Generally, applications on the host machines communicating over the network are expected to provide their own end-to-end services (or to draw on protocols, such as TCP/IP, that can provide such services).

45

ISDN Planes

ISDN standards call for a number of *channels* that, taken together, constitute the ISDN pipeline. The ISDN interface bandwidth is split into combinations of D and B channels, which carry signaling information and bearer services, respectively. Different sets of protocols are used to describe these different types of channels. The protocol sets make up the *planes* that are the fundamental units of the ISDN architecture (Figure 4.1). You'll remember that there are four planes in the ISDN model, the *control* plane (C plane), the *transport* plane (T plane), the *user* plane (U plane), and the *management* plane (M plane).

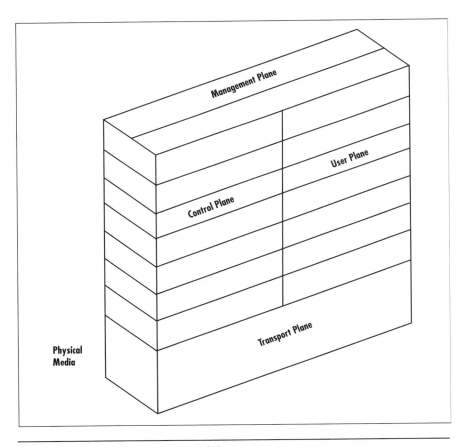

Figure 4.1   ISDN architecture model.

The D and B channels represent the paths for signaling and user information through the ISDN pipeline. These channels have distinct purposes, uses, and protocols that define them. Because B channels carry information or bearer services for users, the B channel is described in the ISDN user plane. Physical standards are defined by the CCITT for ISDN. The transport plane protocols describe the nature of physical connectivity. Protocols of the management plane have been described as the traffic control protocols. The management plane makes sure that ISDN traffic is directed to, and handled by, the correct plane.

OSI and ISDN

ISDN is used for user-to-user communications and for user-to-network communications. A working knowledge of the planes of ISDN and their relationship is helpful in describing these functions. For describing intercommunication between user networks already in place, however, we must compare the planes of the ISDN architecture with the OSI model.

Although ISDN planes contain the functionality of the layers of the OSI model, there are certain aspects of ISDN that cannot be fully explained in terms of the OSI model. The most important of these aspects deal with the relations between ISDN protocols, the setting up of multimedia calls over ISDN, and the setting up of conference, or multipoint, calls over ISDN.

A look at Figure 4.2 shows another important aspect of ISDN when compared with the OSI model. ISDN is concerned strictly with network operation and as such is described completely at the bottom three layers of the OSI stack. Layers 4–7 of the OSI stack deal with connection management and end-to-end connectivity. ISDN expects higher level functions to be provided by the hosts involved in the communication.

We can also see that different protocol sets are necessary to define the B channel and the D channel above the physical layer. Both the D and B channels use the same interface at the physical layer, so the same standards and protocols apply. Above the physical layer,

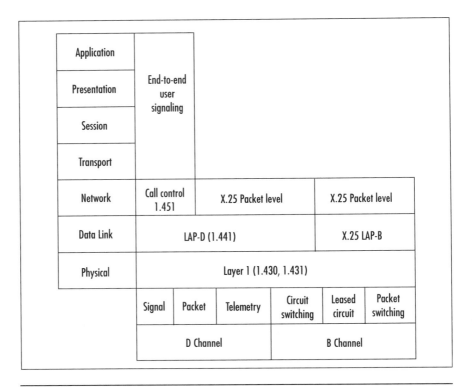

Figure 4.2   OSI and ISDN.

however, different protocols apply to these separate channel types. In fact, most CCITT protocols for ISDN deal with user signaling over the D channel.

Physical Layer Protocols

Layer 1 of the OSI model is concerned with the physical characteristics of a network connection. The ISDN physical layer, corresponding to OSI's layer 1, has the following functions:

- encoding of digital data
- duplex transmission over the B channel

- duplex transmission over the D channel
- multiplexing of basic rate interface (BRI) or primary rate interface (PRI) connections
- activation and deactivation of the virtual circuit
- provision of power from NT1 to terminal
- terminal identification
- faulty terminal isolation
- D-channel contention/access

Remember that ISDN *devices* are connected at *reference points*. ISDN *protocols* describe the nature of the connection and the interaction that occur at these reference points. Figure 4.3 shows the different ISDN devices and associated reference points.

The Basic Rate Interface (BRI)

CCITT Recommendation I.430 defines the physical layer specifications for the BRI. The BRI, as defined in the standards, supports point-to-point and point-to-multipoint connections. The CCITT has defined physical layer protocols for the S reference point, representing the connection between terminal equipment (TEs), terminal adapters (TAs) and a digital routing device (NT2), and for the T reference point between an NT2 and network terminating equipment (NT1).

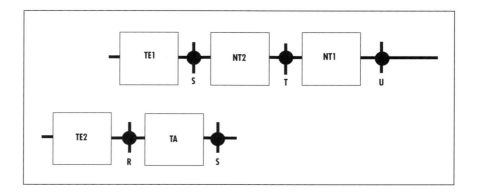

Figure 4.3   ISDN devices and reference points.

Configuration

The point-to-point configuration supported by the BRI allows a distance of 1 kilometer between the NT device and the connected TE. Multipoint connections are defined as being either short passive bus or extended passive bus. In the short passive bus configuration, the NT and up to eight TEs can be connected over a single bus. TEs cannot be more than 200 meters from the NT device. The extended passive bus calls for a grouping of multiple TEs separated from one another by no more than 50 meters. The TE grouping can be up to 1 kilometer from the NT device.

B channels can be used by only one device at a time. User-network signaling ensures that only one TE is assigned to one B channel at any particular time. Multipoint configurations allowed by the BRI must share the D channel simultaneously so that messages can be exchanged between the users and the network.

Connections

Standards for the BRI specify full-duplex transmission between the local network and the ISDN provider. The physical connection between the NT and the TE is made over at least two wire pairs. One pair is used for each direction of transmission.

Power

In the traditional telephone system, often called the plain old telephone system (POTS), power for telephone devices is supplied by the local phone service provider. In an ISDN, the customer is responsible for powering devices at the customer site. The local loop, the connection between the customer site and the access provider, is defined by the CCITT as a digital transmission facility. This means that no AC power can be carried over the local loop. CCITT standards describe power sources for ISDN devices:

- Power source 1: The NT gets power from the network or from a local AC power source or batteries supply power to the attached TEs. In Europe this is sometimes the case;

in North America, power is not and will not be supplied by the network provider.

- Power source 2: Power is derived locally at the NT device, either from batteries or from a local AC source. There is a capability to connect all ISDN equipment to a central power source or battery backup source. Devices may be connected to the NT and derive power from the NT, or they may be separately connected to a central power supply unit.
- An ISDN terminal may plug directly into an AC or DC power supply.

Digital Signal Transmission

Digital signal transmission is based on the transmission of 1 and 0 values. The most common way to transmit these values is to use different voltage levels on the line to represent one or other of the binary digits. An encoding method is implemented that designates a digit and its corresponding voltage. The encoding method for the BRI is called *pseudoternary coding*. Pseudoternary coding dictates that a 0 is always represented by either a positive or negative voltage, and a 1 is always represented by no voltage. The binary 0 pulses must alternate in voltage from positive to negative. Certain bits in the BRI frame are used to balance the voltage on the line, ensuring that there is no net DC component on the line.

Frames

The BRI is a synchronous time division multiplexed structure. This means that transmission across the physical medium takes place within sections of bits called *frames*. Each BRI frame (Figure 4.4) contains 48 bits. For a BRI in the configuration 2B + D, the total bit rate is 192 Kbps, allowing transmission of 4000 frames per second. Each frame carries 16 bits for each B channel and 4 bits for the D channel. The bits are interleaved in a particular order in each frame as described in the following:

Channel:	B1	D	B2	D	B1	D	B2	D
No. of bits:	8	1	8	1	8	1	8	1

The BRI can be configured as 1B + D, or possibly as only a single D channel. If one of these optional configurations is used, then the unused bits in the frame for that channel are filled with 1s so that no signal is transmitted.

The other 12 bits in the frame deal with handling and timing of the frame:

- E bits: Frames traveling from the NT to the TE carry E bits, which repeat the bits last transmitted on the D channel. E bits manage contention for the NT by the attached TEs. Because only one device may use a B channel at any one time, there is no problem with contention on the B channel. But all devices must share the D channel for signaling. TEs monitor E bits to know if they can keep transmitting. If a transmitting TE receives an E bit with a value different from that of its last D bit, it knows it no longer controls the channel and has to stop transmitting.
- L bits: DC balance bits enforce the requirement for an even number of 1 bits in the frame, thereby making sure that there is no net DC current. The L bit will be 0 if preceded by an odd number of 0s and 1 if preceded by an odd number of 1s.
- F bit: A 0 bit used for the beginning of a frame. Each F bit is followed by an L bit to balance the voltage on the line. The F bit L bit configuration acts to signal the beginning of the frame to the receiver.
- A bit: Activation bit. Used to activate or deactivate a TE device.
- FA bit: Auxiliary framing bit. Always set to zero unless used in multiframing.
- N bit: Reserved for future use in multiframing. Always set to 1.
- S bit: Reserved.

Contention

As mentioned earlier, E bits help to manage contention between TEs for the S or T interface. B channels are always assigned to one

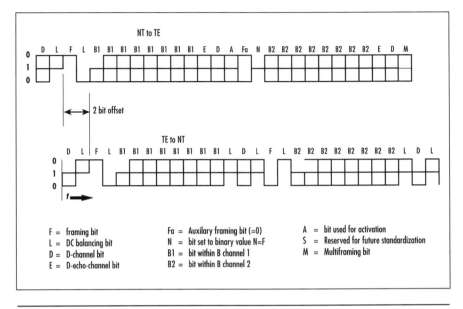

Figure 4.4   A BRI frame.

TE or another, so there is no need for contention resolution. Contention resolution on the D channel of the BRI is handled as follows:

1. A TE with nothing to transmit sends out a series of binary 1s. In the BRI encoding scheme this means no signal on the line.
2. The NT echoes back the signal as an E bit with a value of 1.
3. A TE wishing to transmit monitors E bits. If it hears enough E bits with a value of 1 it assumes no transmission on the line and transmits.
4. If a TE detects E bits with different values than it is transmitting, it assumes another TE is transmitting and breaks off contention for the D channel.

The U Interface

CCITT standards do not address the U interface, the connection between the NT1 and the local exchange (LE) carrier. These standards have been described in the United States by the American National Standards Institute (ANSI) standard T1.601. These standards call for serial, synchronous, full-duplex point-to-point connections at the U reference point. ANSI standards allow the use of existing twisted pair local loop wiring in the BRI.

The Primary Rate Interface (PRI)

The PRI physical layer is defined in CCITT Recommendation I.431. These standards call for full-duplex, serial, and synchronous transmission using two wire pairs. Unlike the BRI, the PRI standard supports only point-to-point connections. The PRI is usually defined at the T reference point. At the T reference point, a digital private branch exchange (PBX) or local area network (LAN) concentration device controls multiple ISDN terminals and provides them multiplexed access to the ISDN. The PRI is based on the DS1 transmission structure used in North America for T1 transmission services.

The PRI multiplexes twenty-four 64 Kbps channels in a normal configuration of 23B + D, where the D channel is a 64 Kbps channel. Some configurations are made up of 24 B channels, with D-channel services provided over an additional PRI.

Framing

PRI frames are made up of one F bit plus 1 byte of information from each of the 24 channels of the PRI. This makes up for a total frame length of 193 bits per frame. A transmission rate of 8000 frames per second adds up to a total bit rate of 1.544 Mbps.

Framing bits are organized into *multiframes* that provide information about synchronization and error checking. The 24 framing bits provide information about synchronization, frame checking, and maintenance.

Six of the bits in a multiframe form a repeating pattern. If a receiver loses synchronization of frames in a transmission, it just needs to identify this pattern in five consecutive multiframes. This 6-bit pattern is called the *frame alignment sequence* (FAS).

Another 6-bit sequence is the remainder from the cyclic redundancy check and is used to determine errors at a bit level in the previous multiframe. This 6-bit sequence is the *frame check sequence*.

Twelve of the multiframe's framing bits are used to form a side channel used for network management and for messaging. This 4 Kbps channel is called the maintenance channel.

Timing

Density requirements for the PRI specify that no more than fifteen 0 bits occur consecutively on a link and that at least 1 bit out of every 8 bits is set to a 1. The coding method recommended to provide the proper number of 1 bits is called bipolar 8 zero substitution (B8ZS).

When using B8ZS, if an all 0 set of 8 bytes occurs, it is replaced by the bit pattern 00011011. B8ZS encoding represents a binary 0 by no line signal and a binary 1 represents a positive or a negative pulse. Binary 1 pulses must alternate in polarity. B8ZS encoding ensures that the wire maintains neutral polarity.

H Channels

The PRI may also be configured to allow H0 or H1 channels as well as B channels. The PRI can support three H0 channels with a D channel, or four H0 channels with no D channel. An H0 channel is the equivalent of six B channels and can be made up of any six B channels available on the PRI. The H11 channel uses all 24 channels on the PRI.

The U Interface

For the PRI, there is no discernible difference between the T reference point and the U reference point. Standards across the U interface call for two wire pairs, a traditional T1 link, and standards across the S and T reference points carry the same requirement. Both carriers provide full-duplex transmission over two wire pairs.

The D-Channel Data Link Protocol

The data link layer of the OSI model is where reliable communications between physically connected machines take place. Protocols at the data link layer deal with the setup, maintenance, and disconnection of this type of communication. In an ISDN, all of this activity takes place over the D channel. For this reason, ISDN data link protocols deal almost exclusively with the D channel.

ISDN's data link protocol is the *link access protocol D* (LAPD). LAPD is defined in CCITT standards I.440 and I.441. LAPD is a bit-oriented protocol based on the *high-level data link control protocol* (HDLC) defined in OSI standards. Like all bit-level protocols, LAPD transmits as a stream of bits defined in a structure known as a frame. At the receiving end of a transmission, information in the frame is interpreted bit by bit as it comes off the transport medium.

LAPD's purpose is to prepare and transmit information between ISDN layer 3 entities. LAPD uses the D channel to define logical connections between users (TEs) and the network across the S reference point and between users and the network across the T reference point (Figure 4.5).

LAPD Services

LAPD is designed to provide two types of service. LAPD must be able to handle multiple terminals on the user-network side of the S or T reference point, and it must be able to support communications between multiple layer 3 protocols operating on the ISDN. Two types of service are provided:

- unacknowledged information transfer service
- acknowledged information transfer service

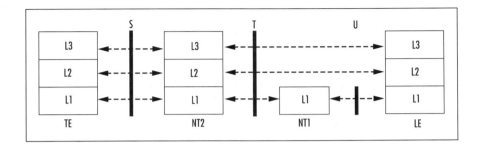

Figure 4.5   LAPD connections (TE or TA to NT2 or LE across S or T...NT2 to LE across T).

Unacknowledged Transfer

Transfers frames with no acknowledgment. Connectionless datagram service does not guarantee delivery and provides no monitoring, flow control, or error control. Supports either a point-to-point or a broadcast transmission. With almost no overhead, unacknowledged transfer is quick and dirty.

Acknowledged Transfer

Creates a logical connection between LAPD layers. Like all acknowledged transfer protocols, LAPD transmission involves a setup or connection establishment phase, a data transfer phase, and a connection termination phase. In the setup phase, two ISDN entities agree to exchange information. A connection request from one entity is acknowledged affirmatively and a logical connection between the entities is established. During the data transfer phase the data is monitored for sequencing, error control, and flow control.

These types of operation may occur simultaneously on the D channel. Multiple acknowledged transmissions can be set up at the same time that acknowledged operation supports multiple logical LAPD connections.

Link Access Using the D Channel

LAPD Frame Structure

Like any data link, bit-oriented protocol, LAPD transmits information in frames (Figure 4.6). LAPD frames have the following fields:

- Flag: Indicates the beginning and the end of a frame. Always a set of 8 bits in the pattern 01111110.
- Address: Important to function of D channel. LAPD addressing allows multiplexing of the physical connection between ISDN devices and the network.
- Control: Specifies the type of frame transmitted.
- Information: Carries control signaling and packet information.
- Frame check sequence: Used to detect errors in transmission with cyclical redundancy checking.

Flag

Flags indicate the beginning and the end of an LAPD frame. The flag at the end of a frame can also be the indicator of the beginning of the next frame. The LAPD flag is 01111110.

One common problem with bit-level flags is that this sequence could occur naturally as a combination of consecutive bit values in other fields of the frame. To avoid this problem, LAPD uses a process known as *bit stuffing,* or zero-bit insertion and removal. Using this process, LAPD counts the 1 bits it transmits. If five 1 bits occur in a row, then LAPD inserts a 0 bit, ensuring that the flag sequence occurs only where it is needed.

Flag	Address	Control	Information	Frame Check Sequence	Flag
8 bits	16 bits	8-16 bits	Variable up to 2080 bits	16 bits	8 bits

Figure 4.6   An LAPD frame (fields and lengths).

Address

The structure of the LAPD address field gives LAPD its ability to multiplex several logical connections over the physical layer. An LAPD address is formally called a Data Link Connection Identifier (DLCI).

LAPD handles two types of multiplexing. LAPD allows multiple devices at the customer site simultaneous access to the physical link, and it deals with both control signaling and packet data transfer. To handle these types of traffic, LAPD uses a two-part address consisting of a *terminal endpoint identifier* (TEI), which identifies devices, and a *service access point identifier* (SAPI), which identifies a layer 3 process operating on a device. The TEI and the SAPI, taken together, make up the DLCI.

TEIs are usually assigned dynamically as a TE device comes on line. In some cases they can be assigned manually by the network administrator, but care must be taken to ensure that no two TEs on a customer network have the same TEI.

SAPIs are used to identify a level 3 process in operation on an ISDN device. Four SAPI values are defined in CCITT standards.

- call control: manages setup and disconnects on the B channel
- 16: X.25 packet mode transmission on the D channel
- 63: management information
- frame bearer service transmission on the D channel

Control

The control field indicates the type of LAPD frame being transmitted. LAPD uses three types of frames:

- information transfer frames (I frames)
- supervisory frames (S frames)
- unnumbered frames (U frames)

I frames carry user information. S frames are used to provide flow control and error control data to LAPD; they control the transmission of I frames on the link. U frames are used to support the unacknowledged transfer capability of LAPD. Logical links are established, maintained, and terminated using U frames.

Information

Information fields are found only in I frames. Information field bits may be in any order in the field, but they must, in the aggregate, make up a certain number of full bytes, or octets. The length of the information field may vary significantly depending on the system in use, but may not be more than the 260 octet maximum.

Frame Check Sequence (FCS)

These bits provide some error checking functionality. CCITT standards for cyclic redundancy checking define the operation of the FCS. With any given block of data r bits in length, there is an associated FCS number of f bits. $r + f$ should, when divided by a predetermined number, have no remainder. If a remainder occurs, then an error condition is detected.

LAPD Operation

As mentioned earlier, LAPD can operate on the D channel in acknowledged or unacknowledged mode. LAPD, like most bit-level transport methods, is based on transmission of command and response messages.

Acknowledged LAPD Operation

Acknowledged mode requires the transfer of I frames, U frames, and S frames between a TE and the network. Acknowledged mode transfer has three stages:

* connection establishment
* data transfer
* disconnect

Connections

A logical connection in ISDN may be requested by an ISDN device or by the network by the transmission. Usually this request is in response to a request by an ISDN level 3 process. Peers exchange LAPD connection information and the connection request is either accepted or rejected.

Transfer

If a connection is requested and confirmed, information transfer begins. Information is carried across the physical link in I frames. Error checking and flow control information is also exchanged during this stage using S frames.

Disconnect

Either LAPD entity involved in a logical connection may terminate the connection by sending a U frame containing the disconnect signal. The receiver sends back a U frame with bits set to accept the disconnect. Both LAPD instances inform the layer 3 entities associated with the connection that it is terminated.

Unacknowledged LAPD Operation

LAPD also supports unacknowledged operation over the D channel. Unacknowledged operation has no provisions for flow control or error correction. LAPD user information is transmitted in frames called *user information* (UI) frames. An LAPD user passes information to LAPD in a UI frame, which is received and passed up to the layer 3 entity. Although no acknowledgment is sent, errors are detected and frames in an error condition are discarded.

Additional LAPD Management

LAPD is also responsible for the assignment of TEIs to ISDN devices. Assignment takes place either on start-up of the device or when a request is made for an LAPD connection. LAPD also can negotiate the use of nondefault parameters for the transmission. Parameters are defined as standard defaults, but under some conditions LAPD peers can negotiate the use of optional defined parameters.

LAPD Multiplexing

The ISDN BRI supports point-to-multipoint connections. Because multiple ISDN devices may be connected, LAPD must provide services to multiplex any number of logical connections over the D channel. In addition, there may be multiple traffic types traveling between devices. LAPD is responsible for addressing the proper device and the correct process on that device.

TE devices are assigned an identifier, already mentioned, called the *terminal endpoint identifier.* Automatic TEI assignment allows users to install and remove equipment from the user network side of the interface without having to update database tables manually throughout the network.

Service access points are the interfaces between level 3 processes operating on a TE and LAPD. Each of these access points is assigned a unique identifier, the *service access point identifier.*

ISDN standards dictate that network to user interface transmission or user interface to network transmissions be established between peer services at the local exchange (LE) and the *terminal endpoint* (TE). LAPD uses the SAPI to locate and connect the correct layer 3 process, or service requested, and uses the TEI to differentiate between terminals that may supply that process. The combination of the two identifiers gives LAPD a logical identifier that allows the multiplexing of the D channel to allow these connections. The combination of the SAPI and the TEI is the *data link connection identifier* (DLCI). Unique DLCIs identify the logical communications channels between the user interface and the LE.

LAPD Channel Priority

The multiplexing features that enable point-to-multipoint connections in ISDN can lead to contention problems. Multiple devices are connected over a single physical interface (BRI or PRI). The physical connection is further multiplexed, as multiple devices may have multiple layer 3 services. The DLCI ensures that the multiple processes may be connected over the user interface in a manner we've already discussed.

This multiplexing demands some type of control mechanism to assign priority in transmission between the multiple channels over the single link. ISDN implements a contention resolution scheme called perfect scheduling with prioritization and fairness that is one of the functions of LAPD.

Pseudoternary Coding

We've already covered how LAPD handles device contention on the ISDN interface by its use of pseudoternary digital signaling. This coding scheme prevents devices from transmitting simultaneously based on TE transmission and NT echoing.

Priority Classes

Still, there needs to be a scheme to prevent one TE, or one group of TEs, from dominating the channel. Priority is assigned according to priority classes, and this is a function of LAPD. Since the D channel is defined as a signaling channel, signaling information is given top priority (class 1). Nonsignal traffic is assigned to class 2. All class 1 frames have a SAPI value of 0. All class 2 frames have a nonzero SAPI.

Within each class frames are further assigned a normal priority level or a lower priority level. These levels are indicated by a series of contiguous 1 bits that must be interpreted by a TE before it can transmit. After transmitting a frame a TE moves to a lower priority in its class.

LAPB and LAPD

CCITT standards for the ISDN data link specify that LAPB, the X.25 layer 2 protocol, may be used for packet-switching transmission on the D channel. X.25 installations predate ISDN standards, and X.25 is widely used around the world for packet data transmission. Therefore ISDN standards incorporate use of the preexisting X.25 protocols.

Besides the fact that LAPD has been designed specifically for use on the ISDN D channel, there are problems arising from the use of LAPB on the D channel.

LAPB is used on X.25 networks for setting up a point-to-point connection between a Data Communications Equipment (DCE) and a Data Terminal Equipment (DTE). There are no provisions for multiplexing X.25 circuits over the D channel such as are offered by LAPD. LAPB is used to carry X.25 layer 3 information, but it obviously isn't the most elegant method for this transmission over an ISDN interface. Layer 3 X.25 information can be placed in an LAPD frame.

The D-Channel Layer 3 Protocol

In the OSI model, functions related to addressing, routing, and delivery of information are contained in layer 3, the network layer. On an ISDN, network functions take place over the D channel, as this channel is designated for signaling between the user-network interface and the ISDN.

ISDN layer 3 deals with *signaling* procedures established between the user network and the ISDN, *call control*, and access to and control of *supplementary services.* Layer 3 protocol information is carried across the network in LAPD frames.

User-Network Signaling

An important fact in regard to user-network signaling is that D-channel signaling between the ISDN user and the ISDN is not the same as the signaling that goes on between entities internal to the ISDN. Internal network signaling is carried out by SS7 protocols, which are discussed later. Layer 3 signaling deals with signals carried from the user network or terminal to the ISDN.

Messaging

Setting up calls on an ISDN, providing call maintenance, and terminating the call are all handled by the exchange of a series of messages between the network and the ISDN user. CCITT standards (I.451) prescribe a common format for layer 3 communications, which is shown in Figure 4.7.

The *protocol discriminator* identifies the protocol for which the message is intended. *Call reference* displays a value assigned to a specific active call. There are 33 message types defined in CCITT standards, each with a specific purpose. Each type is assigned a value displayed in the message type field. Various *information elements* follow

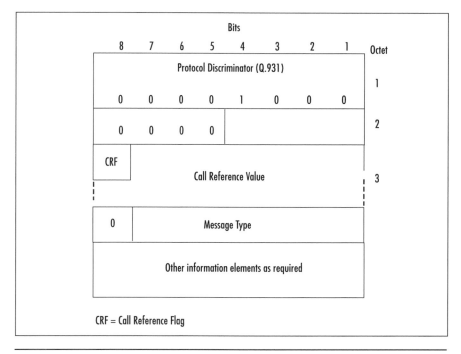

Figure 4.7   Layer 3 message format.

the message type in an order defined by standards. Following is a
brief list of possible information elements:

bearer capability	facility
called party number	information rate
calling party number	information request
channel identification	packet size
congestion level	progress indicator
date/time	

Note that the list gives only a sample. Information elements may indicate the length of the message being sent and many additional
functions.

ISDN Terminals

There are two types of terminals in the user network attached to the
ISDN. *Functional terminals* are considered intelligent devices that
can exchange messages over the interface between the user network and the ISDN. *Stimulus terminals* have only minimal signaling
capability. A stimulus message represents one particular user event
at a terminal. Stimulus terminals may trigger an event in the ISDN,
but they cannot invoke it by explicit messaging.

Circuit Mode Calls

One major use of the ISDN is for ISDN telephone service analogous
to plain old telephone service. A basic circuit mode call uses an entire B channel and is set up, maintained, and terminated by an exchange of messages between the user and the ISDN on the D
channel. The control of the call depends on the exchange of a series
of messages between the caller and the network and between the
network and the called party.

Setup

A circuit mode call connection begins with the sending of a SETUP
message from the caller to the network. The SETUP message contains information needed by the network to assign resources to the

call and begin the process of connection. The *bearer service attributes* are information elements that tell the network exactly what services are required of the network. Channel identification is also provided in an information element in the SETUP message. The channel identification tells the network the physical interface (i.e., B channel) the caller wants used to provide the bearer service.

The network will check the contents of a SETUP message and send back a SETUP ACKNOWLEDGE message to the caller. This message will trigger some type of signal to indicate a request for more information, particularly the ISDN number of the called party. The calling party enters the number required, as well as any additional information requested by the network, and forwards all the information back to the network in an INFORMATION message.

Call Setup

When the network receives its additional information, it returns a CALL PROCEEDING message back to the caller, allocates the requested channel, and begins to set up the call to the called party. At the called party end of the network, the network sends a SETUP message to the called party. The called party device's response to the SETUP message will be either a CALL PROCEEDING message, to let the network know that the message has been received and call setup is proceeding, or a simple ALERT message, indicating that the called terminal is alerting its user to the existence of the call. The ALERT message is analogous to the ringing sound a caller hears on the line when a called party's phone number is dialed.

Connection

When the called party picks up the phone, the device will send a CONNECT message back to the network. This is the signal to the network to complete the circuit over the requested B channel. At this point the network will return a CONNECT ACKNOWLEDGE message to the called party. The caller's end of the network subsequently returns a CONNECT message to the caller and the call is connected. The caller and called party can then communicate over the established circuit during a phase ISDN standards refer to as the *call information phase.*

Disconnect

Disconnection is the same as in the POTS. One or both users hang up. This will initiate a DISCONNECT message, which is relayed to the other user. The party initiating the DISCONNECT will receive a DIS-CONNECT RELEASE message from the network, and finally a RE-LEASE COMPLETE message, which will cause the user terminal to release the allotted B channel. The other party receives the same se-ries of messages and subsequently releases its end of the B channel.

Bear in mind that these level 3 messages are used for communica-tion between users and the ISDN. Messaging internal to the net-work is being handled during all phases by the SS7 signaling system used between entities inside the ISDN.

Packet Mode Connections

Three types of packet mode connections may be established by the layer 3 protocols:

- circuit mode call to a remote packet handler
- access to an ISDN packet handler over a B channel
- access to an ISDN packet handler over a D channel

For data to be transferred in packet mode, there must be layer 3 pro-tocol support during the data transfer phase of the call. Packet-switching nodes must have access to a service that can set up the virtual circuit needed for the connection.

Circuit Mode Packet Calls

Circuit mode packet-switched connections are established over the B channel in much the same way as a circuit mode call. The caller is really using ISDN services in order to gain access to a packet net-work. The called party will be an access port on the packet network called an *access unit* (AU). The AU in this case has the duties of the calling and the called party. If an ISDN terminal makes a call to the AU, the AU initiates the setup of the packet relay. If a packet node makes a call to an ISDN terminal, the AU sets up the call.

ISDN Virtual Circuits

ISDN users may use the B channel for access to a packet-switching node, which itself gives the ISDN user access to the virtual circuit service of the packet network. Recall that the D channel, as defined in standards, may also be used for virtual circuit service access.

Supplementary Service

Layer 3 messages are also used to *control* and *invoke* supplementary services. Examples of supplementary services include call waiting, call forwarding, and user identification.

Control

When a user requests supplementary services from the network, messages are exchanged between the network and user concerning the service required and the parameters of the service provision, that is, information required to handle the service. A call need not be in progress for control of supplementary services to take place.

Invoke

Invoking a service is a request for dynamic access to supplementary services. Services may be invoked by stimulus terminals or by functional terminals. Whereas a control message may not be associated with a call in progress, an invoke message is always so related. An invoked service is provided by the ISDN as it is requested.

Packet and Frame Mode Bearer Services

Standards for ISDN specify that ISDN may be the carrier for two types of nonvoice services already in widespread use. The most prevalent nonvoice services in the communications network are X.25 packet mode services and Frame Relay. X.25 networks have been in operation since the late 1960s. X.25 has considerable built-in overhead designed to deal with error identification and correction.

At the time X.25 was introduced, this level of error control was required, considering the nature of the physical links involved in telecommunications.

Original standards for ISDN call for the use of X.25 standards for packet switching of nonvoice traffic. Improvements in transmission media and protocols have since created a transmission environment with a very low level of error. ISDN standards released in 1988 recommend the adoption of Frame Relay as a substitute for X.25 packet switching. Frame Relay provides only a bare minimum of error control in the transmission. The lowering of the overhead allows a corresponding increase in the setup and speed of Frame Relay transmission.

X.25 Packet Mode Services

X.25 is a CCITT protocol suite that defines operations between devices in a packet-switching network. X.25 protocols have been used to set up a worldwide public packet-switching network. In a packet-switching network, information is encapsulated in packets that contain addressing, sequencing, and error control information as well as user or application information. The packets are transmitted over virtual channels between X.25 end user devices (DTEs) and packet switching nodes (DCEs).

X.25 standards were originally released in 1976. By the early 1980s X.25 was commonly used worldwide for data transfer, particularly between remote terminals and central. ISDN standards call for the support of X.25 networks.

X.25 Protocols

The X.25 architecture comprises three layers that correspond to the bottom layers of the OSI model:

- physical level
- link level
- packet level

At the physical layer the protocols specify the physical interface between a DTE and a DCE. X.25 physical layer standards are contained in CCITT X.21, although other physical layer standards may be substituted.

The link level is responsible for the reliable transfer of data across the physical link. X.25's link level protocol is the *link access protocol—balanced* (LAPB). LAPB is responsible for formation of frames that encapsulate data for transmission. The X.25 packet level provides for the formation of data into packets and handles the setup of the virtual circuits over which the packets are transmitted.

Virtual Circuits

X.25 is a connection-oriented protocol. Standards call for packets to be routed over a *virtual circuit* that is established by the level 3 protocol through the network before packets are transferred.

To set up a virtual circuit, a station makes a call request to the network, asking for a logical connection to another station on the network. All packets that are transferred over this virtual link are identified as belonging to this particular circuit, and they are delivered in sequence-number order.

Two types of virtual circuits are supported by X.25, the *virtual call* and the *permanent virtual circuit.* A virtual call is established as needed by a call setup and call clearing procedure. A permanent virtual circuit is, as named, a permanent virtual connection established by the network. No call setup and call clearing are necessary to use the permanent virtual circuit.

X.25 and ISDN

X.25 has been in common use for almost 20 years. ISDN standards make provisions for the incorporation of X.25 networks into the ISDN. CCITT recommendation X.31 presents the standards by which X.25 and ISDN interoperate.

Essentially, the standards allow two types of interaction between ISDN and X.25. In one standard, X.31 Case A, ISDN is able to access the services of the X.25 network. In the other, X.31 Case B, the packet-switching capability of X.25 becomes an integral part of the ISDN.

In Case A, the X.25 DTE goes through an ISDN TA to request an ISDN circuit mode connection to the X.25 DCE. The path from the DCE to the destination DTE is established using the level 3 X.25 protocols. Case A procedures cannot be used on the ISDN D channel, as D-channel signaling terminates at the LE. For this reason, Case A X.25 packet traffic must be carried only on the ISDN B channel.

In Case B, the X.25 packet-switching capability becomes a part of the ISDN. X.25 DTEs establish the virtual circuit for communication through the ISDN. The ISDN LE either has packet-switching capability or has access to the X.25 DCE. Call setup and control are handled by ISDN. Case B is the standard for ISDN in North America. This standard calls for the transfer of LAPB frames on the B channel and for the encapsulation of LAPB frames in LAPD frames for transmission on the D channel.

Frame Mode Bearer Services

As the technology has improved, communications links and switching facilities have become much more reliable. The high degree of error control and overhead necessary at the inception of X.25 is no longer required to the extent that it was 20 years ago.

New delivery services, called frame mode services, have come into common use. Frame mode services are very similar to X.25, but they eliminate the third layer of the model. Address and connection information is handled by level 2 protocols. The name "frame mode" stems from the fact that level 2 information is transported across the network in frames, not packets.

As a consequence, level 2 protocols are concerned with addressing and multiplexing in addition to the normal level 2 functions of error control and sequencing.

Asynchronous Transfer Mode (ATM)

ATM or *asynchronous transfer mode* is a technology based on cell formation and a type of multiplexing that provides users with broadband ISDN services requiring extremely high transmission rates. ATM can supply users access to this high bandwidth, as it is required, over a B-ISDN channel, where voice, data, audio, video, and network signal traffic may be fully integrated.

Standards for ISDN, defining the basic rate interface (BRI) and the primary rate interface (PRI), allow integrated transmission over the ISDN. The predefined channels of the BRI and PRI provide access to *narrowband* ISDN (N-ISDN) services.

The CCITT, which set standards for ISDN, has designated ATM as the transmission technology to provide transport for *broadband* (B-ISDN) services on the ISDN. B-ISDN standards deal with services requiring very high transmission rates, like video information services, high-speed data transfer, and real-time video teleconferencing. ATM standards deal with the organization of data into *cells* for transmission and describe the way bandwidth is multiplexed for carrying B-ISDN services.

ATM technology has been adapted for use over a seamless digital network made up of ATM devices ranging from network interface cards to high-volume digital network switches acting as backbones linking multiple LANs. In this section we take a look at broadband ISDN, present the standards for ATM, and look in to how the network and communications worlds are coming together over ATM.

ATM Overview

ATM's model is a subset of the protocol model for B-ISDN. Standards for B-ISDN result in a segmented model that maps to the physical and data link layers of the OSI stack. Figure 4.8 gives a two-dimensional look at the model for B-ISDN.

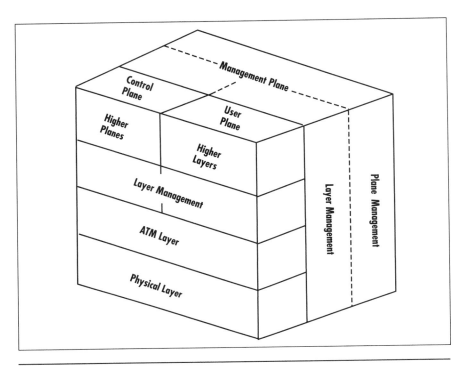

Figure 4.8   The B-ISDN protocol stack.

B-ISDN Model

Note that the B-ISDN model is made up of planes, just like the ISDN model. The control and user planes cut across the model from the higher layers right down to the physical layer. The management plane is divided in two, with a layer management plane, which manages interfaces between layers in the control and user planes, and a plane management plane, which provides a framework for the structured interaction of the protocols in the stack.

ATM Protocol Stack

In this chapter we're primarily interested in the ATM layers related to the B-ISDN planes. Figure 4.8 indicates the layers that describe

ATM function—the physical layer, the ATM layer, and the ATM adaptation layers (AALs).

Physical Layer

The physical layer is made up of two sublayers: the *transmission convergence* (TC) sublayer and the *physical medium* (PM) sublayer. The PM sublayer interfaces with the physical medium used to provide the link and passes the transmitted bitstream up to the TC sub-layer.

The TC sublayer puts ATM cells into the bitstream in frames and recovers the frames and extracts cells from the stream. These cells are either received for the ATM layer or handed up to the ATM layer.

ATM Layer

The ATM layer handles mutiplexing, switching, and control actions. At this layer the information from the ATM cell header is decoded to provide necessary information for ATM layer actions. Conversely, it is at this layer that the ATM header is created and encoded with transmission information.

At the ATM layer information is generated and interpreted that provides for the fast switching capabilities of ATM. The ATM layer protocols create the route for transmission using the Virtual Path Identifier (VPI) and Virtual Channel Identifier (VCI) fields in the cell header and direct the stream of cells over virtual channels and virtual paths. The ATM layer passes information up to the AAL layer after stripping the header and adds the header to cells passed down from the AAL.

The ATM layer generates and attaches the header for each cell passed down to the physical layer and removes the header on the receiving end.

AAL Layer

This layer is subdivided into two sublayers, which is appropriate, because this layer has two functions. One of these functions is to provide and interface with higher level applications and protocols in the B-ISDN stack. The *segmentation and reassembly (SAR) sublayer* takes packets from higher level applications and segments the information into the right length for insertion into ATM cells. Naturally, the SAR performs the converse action of reassembling high-level messages from fragmented information coming in from ATM cells. The convergence sublayer (CS) presents network services to the higher level applications and protocols.

Switched Multimegabit Data Service (SMDS)

SMDS is a connectionless switched network service implemented by telephone network carriers. It provides customers access over the user-network interface to a network carrier's digital transmission facilities. SMDS was originally implemented as a cell-based transmission service connected across the user network interface to T1 or T3 digital links. New implementations of SMDS support network access over traditional 56 Kbps analog phone loops.

The distinction is often made that B-ISDN is a standard, ATM is a technology meant to deliver B-ISDN services, and SMDS is one of B-ISDN's services. CCITT standards define SMDS.

Subscriber-to-Network Interface (SNI)

The original standards for SMDS call for transmission of 53 byte cells to the exchange carrier over the *subscriber-to-network interface*, making it the first widespread implementation of cell relay technology designed to run over ATM. The SNI marks the connection point between the user network and the SMDS carrier. The SMDS Interface Protocol (SIP) is used for communications over the SNI.

Data Exchange Interface (DXI)

Because of the high cost of using legacy packet switching equipment for SMDS, additional standards have been adopted for the inclusion of packet transmissions over SMDS. Layer 3 protocols in SMDS provide for the transmission of packets of data over the link.

SIP

SMDS is governed by its own set of protocols, the SMDS interface protocol. Layer 3 of SIP deals with the transfer of packets. Layer 2 deals with the creation of cells very similar to ATM cells. The major difference between ATM and SMDS cells is that there is no virtual connection in the connectionless SMDS service, so virtual connection identifiers are not required for transmission. SMDS is a commercial public service and its connections are predefined. Layer 1 deals with the physical requirements of SMDS.

Signaling System 7

So far, we've dealt with the kinds of transmission used for signaling between users and the network or transmissions between ISDN devices. For proper ISDN function there must be a method of signaling and messaging to provide internal control of network activity. Signaling system 7 (SS7) is designed to support digital transmission networks and is specifically designed to operate in an ISDN. SS7 is an out-of-band system used for the exchange of information between entities that make up the ISDN service provider network.

Network Signaling Systems

The establishment and maintenance of calls in a telecommunications network are dependent on some type of signaling system in operation between the different entities and devices that make up the network itself. Information about the routing of calls, information about the status of the connection, and connection control information are all carried by the signaling system. Network signaling provides three major functions to the network:

- supervision: monitors the status of the line
- routing: provides address information necessary for routing of calls
- call information: reports on call status and provides information on the progress of a call

In-Band Signaling

Before the telephone system moved to digital switching, all telephone calls were set up over the same channel as the call being made. In-band means that network signaling and voice communication both took place over the same voice band carried by the user's phone. In-band signaling adds considerable time to the call process, as it takes from 10 to 15 seconds just to set up a call. Using in-band call setup, circuits between the telecommunications network are allocated one at a time, sequentially. Trunks along the physical route of the call were allocated one at a time as needed. All network resources had to be reserved before a circuit could be established and a call could go through.

All in-band network signals must be sent over the voice band. Most in-band signaling systems are designed for use with analog voice communications. However, some early T1 lines used a single bit from each frame to carry on/off hook information. Since these bits used for signaling aren't available to the voice band, it takes some bits away from the 64 Kbps voice band channel.

Common Channel Signaling

Out-of-band signaling, in which network signals travel in a separate signaling channel, is known as *common channel signaling* (CCS). In-band signaling networks have almost all been replaced with common channel signaling systems, such as SS7.

Common channel signaling allows the exchange of information between processor-equipped switches and network facilities and allows much faster allocation of network resources. Using CCS, the average setup time for a call has dropped from 10–15 seconds to only three seconds.

The benefits of common channel signaling are significant. Bandwidth is preserved over the network because no signal traffic shares the actual transmission channels. CCS allows the addition of user services such as 800 service, credit card verification databases, and caller ID services. Perhaps most significantly, CCS brings down the costs involved in calling. In-band signaling requires separate signaling facilities for each circuit established. CCS allows the multiplexing of network signal information over one channel.

CCS networks make use of two signaling modes. *Associated signaling mode* means that signaling messages follow the same path as the associated call. *Nonassociated signaling mode* means that the path for signaling is not necessarily the same as the physical path for the call.

CCS Networks

CCS networks are made up of standard components.

- Signaling Points (SPs): processor-controlled switching offices
- Signal Transfer Point (STP): switches messages over the CCS network
- Service Control Point (SCP): databases containing information for customer services

STPs not only handle the switching of messages, they provide access to SCPs in the network.

One of the major features of a CCS network is redundancy. STPs are paired throughout the CCS network so that loss of one STP doesn't block calls. SCPs are also paired for redundancy. Several types of links are provided in the CCS network to provide redundant links.

- Access links (A-links) connect SPs or SCPs to each STP of a pair of STPs.
- Bridge links (B-links) interconnect STPS in different regions, that is, nonpaired STPs.
- Cross-links (C-links) set up a signal path between paired STPs.

All of these links are used to provide redundant links through the system and prevent network failure caused by a broken signal link.

SS7 Protocol Overview

SS7 is the CCS network designated to be used for ISDN. Like any other system for telecommunications, SS7 is defined by standards and associated protocols that describe an architecture for the system. SS7 protocols are defined in the CCITT Q.700 series recommendations.

Basically, the SS7 architecture is made up of three parts and their associated protocols (Figure 4.9).

- Message Transfer Part (MTP): MTP provides the same service and function as the bottom three layers of the OSI

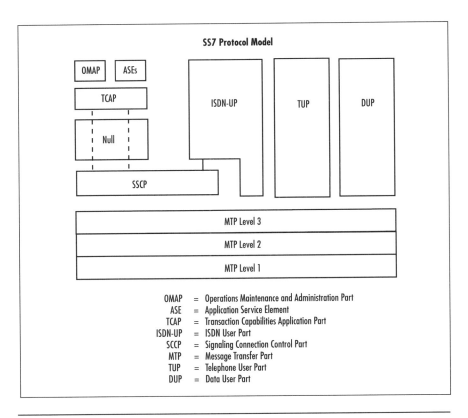

Figure 4.9   SS7 protocol architecture.

model. MTP is responsible for transfer and delivery of SS7 messages.

- Signaling Connection Control Part (SCCP): Maps to the network layer of OSI. SCCP provides addressing function and can provide for connection-oriented transfer.
- User and Application Part: Provides end-to-end signaling for switched voice and data transmission. User and application parts provide function and service analogous to layers 4–7 of the OSI stack.

MTP

The *message transfer part* can be described in three levels that correspond to layers 1, 2, and 3 of the OSI stack.

- Level 1 of MTP standards calls for full-duplex links of 64 Kbps. Rates of 1.544 Mbps may also be supported.
- Level 2 of MTP deals with the transmission of frames, called *signal units* in SS7. Error correction procedures are defined at this level, as are signal alignment procedures.
- Level 3 of MTP provides for message handling in the SS7 network and for network management. Message handling deals with the routing of SS7 messages through the network. Network management deals with the maintenance of routes through the network. MTP level 3 functions ensure that routes are maintained, link failure and traffic congestion not withstanding.

Signaling Connection Control Part

MTP layers provide connectionless services to the SS7 network. SCCP provides OSI network layer functions not supplied by MTP, such as extended addressing and connection-oriented transfer capability. MTP addressing delivers messages to a node and has limited distribution ability using its own addressing. MTP addressing has limited capability to access services and applications. The growing number of applications and services necessitate the inclusion of SCCP.

SCCP provides four classes of network service:

1. Basic connectionless class (class 0): Connectionless datagram service.
2. Sequenced connectionless class (class 1): Connectionless datagram service that provides for sequencing of messages.
3. Basic connection-oriented class (class 2): Established temporary or permanent signaling connections. Also allows segmentation and reassembly of messages.
4. Flow control connection-oriented class (class 3): Includes all class 2 services with the addition of flow control and provisions for dealing with out-of-sequence and lost messages.

User and Application Part

User and application parts are independent self-contained entities. Original standards for SS7 provide for the implementation of the ISDN User Part (ISUP), the Telephone User Part (TUP), the Data User Part (DUP), and the Transaction Capabilities Application Part (TCAP).

- The TUP deals with signaling control of telephone communications. The DUP deals with circuit mode data transactions over the network. Neither of these user parts is supported by North American implementations of SS7. ISUP is the SS7 user part concerned with ISDN signaling.
- ISUP uses transport services provided by MTP or SCCP, depending on requirements. ISUP messages are exchanged to provide for the setup and maintenance of an ISDN circuit that will carry user information.
- TCAP provides application layer services to the SS7 network. TCAP can carry special billing instructions and information, provide customer network control, and support database queries over SS7.

SS7 Services

A topic worthy of its own book might be the different types of SS7 services available. There is an extensive list of SS7 services. They can be loosely grouped into access or data-based services and CLASS services.

CLASS

SS7 signaling allows an array of services on the ISDN. The most widespread services allowed by SS7 are called Custom Local Area Signaling Services (CLASS). Many of these services are now in use. In a given area, the services offered depend on the equipment in use and on the network provider's allocation.

The basic CLASS service is called automatic number identification (ANI), also known as caller ID. ANI displays the number of the calling party to the called party during the setup phase of an SS7-directed call. Debate over the implementation of ANI has taken on social and political as well as technical implications. Readers will be familiar with the controversy surrounding implementation of ANI. Some hold that ANI protects users of the phone network from invasions of privacy. Customers may use ANI to set up a blocking procedure on their line, not allowing connections from specific numbers returned by ANI. The opposing view is that ANI takes away privacy from the calling party, which can lead to a number of problems.

Luckily, there are less controversial implementations of CLASS services that don't involve the capture and display of the caller's number.

1. Automatic callback: Places a return call to the last incoming caller's number.
2. Automatic recall: Monitors a busy line until the call is completed and then notifies the caller that the line is open.
3. Computer access restriction: Allows access to computer systems only from a predefined list.
4. Customer-originated trace: Even a customer without ANI could send the number of a harassing caller to the local exchange carrier.
5. Selective services: Allows the customer equipment to be set up to allow calls to be blocked, forwarded, or accepted from predefined lists.

There are many more types of CLASS service. All of these services can be provided through SS7 messaging if SS7 is available to the LE.

Data-Based Services

Data-based services deal with provision of services or routing of calls through a distributed network. A list of data-based services includes:

- Service: Implementation of SS7 allows portability of 800 numbers from carrier to carrier and implements faster switching of 800 calls.
- Automatic call distribution: An organization can use automatic call distribution to route certain types of calls through the ISDN to their destination automatically. A call over an 800 number requesting information could be routed anywhere in the ISDN where that information is available.
- Enhanced 911: One major feature of this would be that the caller's ID number and address are displayed to the 911 operator. Additional database services such as information about availability and location of service equipment and personnel could also be displayed.
- Line Information Data Base (LIDB): Can provide detailed information about line usage and billing information. LIDB databases could validate credit card charges on line.
- Citywide Centrex service: Allows PBX services to be provided to business locations by the network provider.

Many other network information databases and services can be accessed using SS7 networks: online telephone directories and online dialing services, for example.

Intelligent Networks

Telecommunications network providers have been working to move from centrally controlled network services to distributed services linked by SS7 access. Distributed signaling networks that can provide customized network services to users require the implementation of more intelligent equipment on the network.

Standards for this implementation are provided by CCITT Recommendation I.312. These standards provide for the establishment of so-called *intelligent networks.*

Intelligent networks allow users of the network to access a variety of network services directly. That's the basic concept of an intelligent network. Users take over control of service access. User control of an intelligent network allows the implementation of more user-specific services on the network.

A logical extension of SS7 signaling is the formation of these distributed service networks. Standards in the United States that deal with this extension define what is called the Advanced Intelligent Network (AIN). The goal of the AIN is to allow every end user access to and control of every service on the network.

At present, the telecommunications networks implement services through switches in the network. Specific services are available only to subscribers who use the associated switch. To justify the cost involved in implementing new switches, network providers must keep services as broad as possible to attract enough users to justify the expense of the upgrade. Intelligent networks will provide a common platform for development of these services, allowing users to develop applications tailored to their specific needs.

As intelligent networks give users and user organizations direct control of network services, they also provide a common platform for the development of these services. Establishment of a common development platform will result in services designed for more specific user functions than are now available.

Broadband B-ISDN

So far, we've been talking about models, standards, and protocols that define what's known as narrowband ISDN (N-ISDN). Many applications, particularly multimedia and video services, need a lot more bandwidth than the standard BRI and PRI. Companies that want these services over ISDN can contract for a user interface that can provide the needed bandwidth. But this can be a wasteful activity. By nature, traffic on communications lines is bursty. Companies contract for communications services based on the bandwidth provided. A company that contracts for enough bandwidth to handle peak loads may find that peak loads occur only about 20 percent of the time. Nobody wants to pay for bandwidth that goes unused.

As part of the ISDN standards, the CCITT has issued standards for broadband ISDN, or B-ISDN. Broadband ISDN is said to provide "bandwidth on demand," with the customer paying only for the bandwidth actually used. One key to understanding B-ISDN is to recognize that the B-ISDN interface is not broken out into channels like the BRI and the PRI.

Broadband ISDN services, defined in CCITT standards, are characterized by their need for high bit rates in transmission. B-ISDN is differentiated from the original narrowband ISDN by its need to meet the high-bandwidth requirements as they occur.

The BRI offers a considerable degree of functionality to ISDN users, and the PRI multiplies available bandwidth by a significant amount. Standards for BRIs and PRIs define what is now known as narrowband ISDN (N-ISDN). ISDN standards calling for high-bandwidth services define a new category of ISDN, broadband ISDN (B-ISDN).

Most B-ISDN services call for much higher transfer rates than the PRI can provide. B-ISDN services such as high-speed data transfer and real-time desktop videoconferencing need lots of bandwidth, as much as 25 Mbps for compressed high-resolution video. A customer requiring these services would need a bundle of PRIs to provide available bandwidth, and transfer of all that information would monopolize a standard N-ISDN channel. Conversely, when high-bandwidth services aren't being accessed, lots of interface bandwidth is unused.

Customers using N-ISDN are paying for available bandwidth. B-ISDN customers have similar requirements for N-ISDN services but require high levels of bandwidth at some times to allow transfer of services unique to B-ISDN. B-ISDN channels must still handle different tasks such as packet transfer and telephone calls, but standards also call for the integration of bandwidth-intensive services over the same access loop. So the B-ISDN channel must be *scalable.* This means that the channel must allow high-bit-rate transfers for B-ISDN services when needed, so that the customer using a B-ISDN channel pays for bandwidth that is used, not predefined bandwidth supplied by N-ISDN channels.

Asynchronous transfer mode (ATM) is the technology defined in the standards to be the bearer of ISDN services. The B-ISDN channel is multiplexed using ATM to provide a single channel over which traditional N-ISDN services and B-ISDN services may be integrated.

Architecture

The architecture for B-ISDN is shown in Figure 4.10. Note that the B-ISDN model is made up of planes just like the ISDN model. The control and user planes cut across the model from the higher layers right down to the physical layer. The management plane is divided in two, with a layer management plane, which manages interfaces between layers in the control and user planes, and a plane management plane, which provides a framework for the structured interaction of the protocols in the stack.

Broadband Services and Standards

Some ISDN services will need transmission speeds greater than those that can be delivered by a single PRI. These services are to be delivered by broadband ISDN. The B-ISDN services are loosely divided into two main groups, communications services and distribution services.

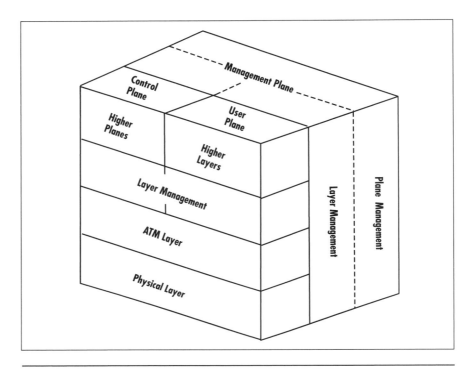

Figure 4.10   B-ISDN model.

Communications Services

Communications services include all of the services delivered over the traditional analog telephone network, as well as conversational, messaging, and retrieval services.

- Conversational services are two-way real-time communications between remote user stations. Videoconferencing is one major service made possible by B-ISDN.
- Messaging services enable the transfer of user-to-user mail applications including voice, video, and document services in any combination.
- Retrieval services offer users the ability to access databases of information stored as video, text, images, documents, or data.

Distribution Services

Distribution services will provide users of the B-ISDN access to network services such as high-density television, pay-per-view television, video libraries, interactive multimedia applications, and news services. They are defined as being or not being *user controlled*. Access to online video databases might be described as user controlled, because users can choose when they want access and what they want access to at any given time.

Services outside user control would be high-density television (HDTV) programming, which can be understood as analogous to present-day TV programming. The network provides broadcasts of programs and information at scheduled times, and users may choose to access them or not.

Requirements

To implement and utilize the B-ISDN there are certain criteria, or *requirements*, that must be met for proper operation. These criteria deal with the bandwidth requirements of B-ISDN services and with the levels of quality in presentation that are required by users. For example, the metal customer loops that connect user sites with the ISDN are supported by N-ISDN standards but will be unable to carry the bandwidth required for some B-ISDN services. These loops must be replaced, probably by optical fiber loops, in order to enable B-ISDN at the customer site. Limitations imposed by circuit-switching technology also present the requirement for the adoption of ATM cell relay switching to enable many B-ISDN services.

Bandwidth

All of the services of an N-ISDN, plus additional services with very high bandwidth requirements, are to be supplied by the B-ISDN. High-resolution video, a B-ISDN service, requires a channel of approximately 150 Mbps. To support multiple B-ISDN services, an interface must have an aggregate channel rate of 600 Mbps. Optical fiber local loops will support these high bandwidths, giving rise to the possibility that N-ISDN services may continue to be supplied over the metal-based local loop and that high-bandwidth B-ISDN services will be supplied over an additional fiber loop. Inside the ISDN, all of these bandwidths must be supplied as requested to enable B-ISDN.

Summary

An overview of the technical aspects and requirements associated with the ISDN gives us a fairly comprehensive look at the current state of communications and data processing technology. The mutual dependence of these two technologies has produced advances and developments at a rapid rate.

Standards for ISDN were developed years ago as communications and computer researchers realized a need for and an understanding of the eventuality of the convergence of the two fields. ISDN standards were a response to the perceived need to channel new developments toward a common goal of end-to-end digital connectivity.

The ISDN model is designed to display the multiple channels of an ISDN connection and the function provided by each channel. Through the BRI and the PRI, point-to-point and point-to-multipoint connections are possible.

The BRI and the PRI are offered today by most ISDN access carriers as solutions to business needs. In the creation of their standards an effort was made to anticipate the requirements for communications and to provide for them.

The BRI, with its 2B + D channel configuration, is the standard interface between the ISDN and a small business or home user. The BRI provides service that is the equivalent of basic telephone service combined with data service capability, and it can be configured to provide a higher level of service to users than is available over the analog local loop.

The PRI gives a much wider selection of channels and configuration choices. Medium to large businesses and organizations contract for the PRI, or a bundle of PRIs. The much higher aggregate bandwidth of the PRI not only provides an organization more channels for communication but also may enable high-bandwidth transmissions over combinations of B channels.

The key to ISDN functionality is in its channel structure. D-channel signaling for setup and control of calls eliminates overhead on the bearer channels (B channels). Control messages are relayed in LAPD frames. LAPD frames may also contain packetized data, allowing use of the D channel as a packet transmission channel.

Public data transfer services offered by telephone service providers are supported by the ISDN. Layer 3 signaling over the D channel allows the setup of frame mode bearer services. ISDN can provide a link to X.25 packet switching networks by setting up a communications channel to an X.25 gateway or by carrying X.25 information in an LAPD frame.

Standards for broadband ISDN (B-ISDN) provide a flexible interface between users and the network. B-ISDN supports applications with very high bandwidth requirements over an interface that is not provided in channels as in the BRI and the PRI. B-ISDN standards call for the use of ATM, a cell relay technology, as the carrier for B-ISDN services.

ATM will provide layer 1 and layer 2 network services over a cell switched network at very high speeds. ATM is designed as a transmission structure to carry multimedia applications, video, high-quality voice, and high-speed data transfer. A public data transfer service already in place, the switched multimegabit data service, provides layer 3 packet capability and will adapt to run over ATM.

ISDN data link and layer 3 signaling on the D channel define the standards for user-to-network and for network-to-user messaging. Messages between internal network stations are provided by an *out-of-band* signaling system called SS7. SS7 carries user messages across the ISDN. SS7 has its own protocol structure and internal messaging format and creates an *intelligent network* that can respond systematically to user requests as well as calls from other internal network devices.

Part II

Current PC ISDN Hardware and Software

The hardware and software ISDN offerings available for the PC are surprisingly varied and numerous. In this part of the book, we'll examine how to determine your ISDN hardware needs. Then we'll proceed to examine a number of different kinds of hardware and software offerings that you might use to connect your PC, or a small network of PCs, to an Internet service provider (ISP) using ISDN.

The number of options for internal and external interfaces, built-in or external terminal adapter equipment, and other aspects of ISDN hardware can sometimes be confusing. That's why we concentrate on explaining what items of hardware and software are necessary to establish and use a working ISDN connection. That's also why we try to contrast and compare the various options and to explain the pros and cons of particular implementations or approaches.

In this, the second part of the book, we start you off in Chapter 5 by presenting a questionnaire that can help you to determine your ISDN hardware and software needs. In Chapter 6, we examine the various options available for internal ISDN PC adapters, with discussions of the leading vendors and their ISDN interface products. In Chapter 7, we shift our emphasis to examine external terminal adapters and network termination equipment. Then, in Chapter 8, we review the various kinds of bridges and routers (generally for Ethernet networks) designed to attach small local area networks (LANs) to an ISDN link. In Chapter 9, we change direction to examine the various kinds of ISDN software available, with special emphasis on interoperation with standard network drivers and stacks like Novell's Open Datalink Interface (ODI) and Microsoft's Network Device Interface Specification (NDIS). Finally, in Chapter 10, we take a quick look at the options available to bring voice and data through your ISDN link, as we examine the offerings for native ISDN phones and the widgets that will let your plain old telephone service (POTS) phones work over an ISDN link.

Our goal in Part II is to arm you with information about what kinds of ISDN products are available for your PC, to expose you to the various vendors who participate in this marketplace, and to try to share with you our own experiences (and the experiences reported by others) in using this equipment and software. We feel that you'll be much better equipped to purchase and configure what you really need if you understand what's available and what kinds of trade-offs you must make to pick one product over another.

5

Determining Your ISDN Needs

So You're Serious about ISDN?

If you've skipped Part I of this book and started here, that's OK. The idea here is to explain briefly only what you need to know to decide whether ISDN is for you without causing your eyes to glaze over. If you don't understand an acronym or buzzword, you can check the glossary or return to Part I for the details.

Today, ISDN is one of the "Top 10" buzzwords that's sweeping the computerized world. You may be thinking seriously about Integrated Services Digital Network for personal or business use, or you may only recently have found out what the acronym stands for. Even now, you may still not be sure what it *really* is, how it *really* works, or if it will be *really* cost effective. Not to worry: You're way ahead of the pack, just by being curious enough to buy this book! Here, we'll help you learn more about if, and how, ISDN might benefit you.

Deciding whether to jump into the world of digital telephony (ISDN) from the analog telephony world—or POTS (plain old telephone system), as it's irreverently called by ISDNers—isn't really as complicated as it looks from the outside. Sure, a multitude of different ISDN products are available and more keep popping up every day. All we can say is, "Welcome to the bleeding edge of electronics!" Thankfully, this variety of good products ensures enough competition to cover your needs with reasonably priced and well-supported products. As recently as the first half of 1995, this was not the case.

Our advice is, don't let the plethora of available ISDN products overwhelm you. You need only one or two of them to get your connections up and running, and we'll help you choose the ones that are right for you.

Thankfully, most telephone companies are now fairly well educated in the intricacies of ISDN, or at least some of their employees are. As one person (who must remain nameless) has cogently said, "All of the ISDN workers went to the same classes, but not all of them stayed awake, nor did they all walk out with the same knowledge." At least you'll be able to call your local telephone service provider, ask for ISDN assistance, and eventually find a person who knows what ISDN means. This is generally true if you live in an urban area in the many parts of the United States. Rural areas will have to wait for ISDN service a while longer.

How Do You Decide?

The very first step in deciding whether ISDN is right for you is to answer the following questions truthfully.

Do I really need high-speed, digital phone service?

For personal use at home, the only compelling reason to install ISDN is for fast access to the World Wide Web (WWW) and other Internet or online services. If you have the desire and can afford the associated costs, you'll find the speed highly appealing. If you're an online worker, you'll find those added costs will quickly be repaid by the savings in connect time and productivity improvements.

For business use at home or in a one-person office, the primary reason to install ISDN is also to obtain speedy access to the WWW and other Internet or online services. Second, you'll also get two phone numbers as part of your connection and will be able to use computerized fax services and digital telephony (answering via computer and digital telephones) just like the big companies do. The cost of a single ISDN line may be less than or equal to the cost of two business lines to your home or office; this alone may make the switch worthwhile!

For small businesses, if you have an office with two or more people, each of whom needs fast access to the Web and other Internet or online services, ISDN may be an appropriate way to go for voice, data, and multiple ISDN phones. If your computers are already connected via a network, installing ISDN will be more complicated, but it may also allow sharing your ISDN lines and services using the network. In other words, users will able to access the Internet from their desktop machines, through a specialized ISDN access device that connects directly to the network.

Small business owners or operators may find that the costs of equipment, ISDN line installation, and monthly fees are offset by increased productivity of their employees. However, if you aren't confident about running your own network without ISDN, you may find it advisable to hire an ISDN consultant who is familiar with your type of network, to suggest the appropriate equipment for your particular needs and to install and maintain the associated equipment. Although they can be expensive up front, consultants can save you money by keeping you and your employees working, rather than wasting time fooling around with your network and ISDN problems. Take our word for it—we learned this firsthand!

Can I afford phone company installation costs?

The cost of installing a single basic rate interface (BRI) (2B + D) ISDN service varies from $0 to $600 in the United States. The average installation fee is in the $150 to $250 range. Our own local Regional Bell Operating Company (RBOC), Southwestern Bell, offered a promotional test fee structure that went from no cost for installation if you signed a three-year contract to $585 with no contract, with incremental charges for one- or two-year contracts. By the time you read this, they will have changed these rates again, as will many of the other regional phone companies. Call yours and ask for the current installation charges; ask around and find out if there's any competition in your area, too. You may find an even better deal just by shopping around! Be sure to ask about any special promotions or long-term commitment "deals" they may offer; these can save substantial sums.

Can I afford the monthly phone company service fees?

The RBOCs and other ISDN providers seem to be constantly changing their tariffs and, therefore, their rate structures. Maybe they're not as bad about it as the airlines are about ticket prices, but sometimes it's hard to tell. Rates in the United States currently run from a monthly fee of $25 to $92.50 with no per-call charges to between $19.50 and $70 per month with per-call usage charges of $0.0042 to $0.15 per B channel per minute.

Service charges for basic rate ISDN vary across the United States for each common carrier, but generally speaking, the monthly (recurring) charge for local (exchange) ISDN access is typically close to twice the cost of a standard business or residential analog line charge, plus a usage charge (approximate costs are provided in Table 5.1; usage charges are per B channel in the ISDN local calling area, which may differ from the analog local calling area).

Table 5.1   Approximate costs for basic rate ISDN.

Service Provider	Installation	Monthly Charge	Usage
Ameritech	$100–$150	$35–$95	Varies by state
Bell Atlantic	$100–$170	$30–$50	$0.02/minute; $0.01/minute evening
BellSouth	$200–$230	$90–$100	None
NYNEX	$55–$60	$25–$30	Varies by location
Pacific Bell	$125	$25–$30	$0.01–$0.14/minute; $0.01/minute evening
SNET	$265	$50	$0.035/minute
Southwestern Bell	$450–$560	$60 ($105 unlimited)	$0.04/minute
US West	$65–$110	$35–$90	$0.04 first minute; $0.15 additional minutes

In cases in which usage charges apply, until monthly utilization exceeds 60–100 hours of connect time, the monthly charge for use of a single B channel (64 Kbps) compares favorably with that of PVC-based services such as Frame Relay and private lines.

The factors that determine whether a particular wide area service is appropriate for residential use, telecommuting, or a small business or remote office should include the following:

- the number of computers (PCs) at the remote location
- the bandwidth required to support applications to be operated across the wide area network (WAN) connection
- anticipated number of hours of connect time per month over the WAN link
- number of local area networks (LANs) at the remote location
- whether servers on the remote LANs must be accessed by client applications at the other sites via the WAN link

If bandwidth is the primary consideration, and if bandwidth requirements fall between 64 Kbps and approximately 350 Kbps (achievable through compression for ISDN and Frame Relay), both must be considered as alternatives.

Frame Relay typically has a higher fixed monthly charge than ISDN, but no usage costs are associated with this service. Fixed monthly charges for 64 or 128 Kbps Frame Relay service vary depending on the service provider, the number of permanent virtual circuits required, the distance from a service provider's central office or point of presence (POP), and the prevailing committed information rate (CIR) subscription charges.

ISDN becomes less attractive and Frame Relay more so as the number of hours of WAN connect time increases, because ISDN is generally offered as a metered service (pay per minute). Because per-minute rates vary from provider to provider and different rates are available for business and residential service, and because rate plans vary and change frequently, it can be difficult to identify the precise point at which Frame Relay service becomes attractive, but we recommend that if connect time exceeds 60–100 hours per month, it is generally more economical to use Frame Relay service.

Can I afford ISP installation or setup costs?

The going rates for ISPs (Internet service providers) to set up an individual, nonbusiness ISDN account using SLIP or Point-to-Point Protocol (PPP) varies from $25 to $200 across the United States. Most ISPs charge more for business account setup with multiple users. In their defense, it takes a knowledgeable network person upward of 30 minutes per user in setup time. In fact, this process is far from automated at most ISPs. Some of this cost theoretically goes toward the labor involved in the setup process; the remainder is usually intended to help defray the provider's up-front hardware costs.

Can I afford the monthly ISP fees?

ISPs usually offer competitive ISDN rates; therefore, they frequently change their rate structures. Without going too far out on a limb, we've observed that most ISPs offer two different classes of

ISDN service: dedicated and dial-up (sometimes called "on demand"). Most such connections use the PPP protocol and depend on the provider's own server software and its ability to measure and bill for connect time.

Dial-up PPP rates generally range from $30 per month with 45 hours of one B channel connect time included, with additional hours charged at $1 per, to $49 per month with unlimited hours of one B channel connect time included. Using both B channels together for a 128 Kbps pipe usually costs between one and a half to twice as much.

Flat rate monthly charges for a continuous ISDN call (also called a nailed-up line) or unlimited time on a dedicated access port (because nobody can use the connection you're using if you use it all the time, it's often called a dedicated line) range from $150 for a single uncompressed B channel to $400 for two compressed, BONDed (Bandwidth ON Demand) B channels. Rates for dedicated lines appear to vary, at least in our immediate vicinity, more than rates for dial-up lines, so you'll want to shop around as much as you can stand to when looking for such service.

It's also important to remember that ISDN equipment takes less than one second to "connect" to your ISP. Therefore, if you are being billed for "connect" time, you may be able to keep your charges quite low by setting your time-out to a few idle seconds (this is discussed in detail in Part III). In general, when buying ISDN connections, you should expect to pay your ISP at least $30 per month and possibly as much as $60 to $100, even if you spend as little as three hours per day on line.

If you're serious about establishing a dedicated line, be sure to ask prospective ISPs about the kinds of pricing alternatives they offer. Based on our investigation of ISPs of all kinds nationwide, these alternatives can include:

- bundling ISDN equipment and service charges

Some ISPs offer pricing structures that forgo up-front equipment purchase costs (for equipment at your site and theirs, both of which are required to create a working ISDN connection) in exchange for higher monthly service fees that amortize the costs of the equipment over time. If cash flow is easier to manage than the initial outlays, this might be the right option for your operation.

- host- versus LAN-based ISDN access

Just because you can attach an ISDN router to your LAN doesn't mean you should; it may be cheaper to set up a single machine with a built-in ISDN connection, and force your users to obtain Internet access through that machine, than to make LAN Internet access available. If monthly costs are a concern, be sure to explore this option with your ISP candidates.

- access-only versus service bundles

Many ISPs will want to provide other services for you, in addition to providing Internet access. This can include for-a-fee access to Web server hosting, file transfer protocol (FTP) access, e-mail accounts, and other services that your organization might find worthwhile. If you're interested in this kind of bundle, you'll be spending more money with an ISP anyway; this should translate into bigger discounts on individual elements of the bundle, including ISDN access, as the size of your monthly bill increases. For instance, by locating a server at an ISP and combining those charges with the charges for ISDN and dial-up accounts, an IP address pool, and domain name registration services, the authors were able to save nearly 35 percent of the total costs involved through a creative bundling deal.

Appendix A includes a reasonably comprehensive list of ISDN-equipped ISPs in the United States (for the most up-to-date version of this information, please visit our Web document on this subject at http://www.corecom.com/html/isplist.html).

Can I afford the ISDN equipment for my PC or LAN?

For an individual PC, the cost of an adapter card, bridge, router, or ISDN "modem" with an internal or external NT1 ranges between

$200 and $1500. Some manufacturers have marketing agreements with local telephone service providers or ISPs whereby you can purchase the hardware in a package deal with the service. It is possible to get a combined ISDN adapter and NT1 for as little as $100 in some package deals.

Generally, you should expect to pay between $300 and $400 for an ISDN adapter card with built-in NT1 and a POTS port. A separate NT1 costs between $100 and $250 with power supply (and sometimes a built-in battery backup). External ISDN bridges or routers generally range between $500 and $1500, depending on the features provided.

The bottom line is as follows: An adapter card is about half the cost of a separate NT1 and bridge or router combination.

Internal Versus External ISDN Adapters

Today, there are two kinds of ISDN adapters—internal interface cards, usually called "ISDN adapters," and external, serial-port attached interfaces, sometimes called "ISDN modems"—in common use for single PC connections. Although the distinction may seem a little arbitrary, it's important to understand the trade-offs involved in using one or the other type of connection on your machine.

External ISDN adapters are easy to set up and configure but will often impose limits on the bandwidth available through the resulting connection. That's because even "fast" serial ports on most PCs (those serviced by 16550-class UARTs), top out at a bandwidth of 115,600 bps. Even though this may seem close enough to the raw bandwidth available from two ISDN B channels, 128,000 bps, it also means that even if your ISP offers compression schemes that can bring up the effective bandwidth of your ISDN connection to as high as 304 Kbps, you may not be able to use all that bandwidth because of the limitations on external serial ports for most PCs.

On the other hand, provided that an internal ISDN adapter supports a compression scheme that's compatible with your ISP, you may be able to use every bit of this bandwidth with this type of connection.

But while it may be faster, adding another internal adapter to a PC that's already loaded with an SVGA card, a LAN card, an SCSI controller, and a multimedia adapter can be challenging, if not downright difficult.

Thus, you'll be faced with a clear trade-off between convenience and ease of installation and use for external ISDN adapters and higher performance (but difficult installation) for internal ISDN adapters. If you're in a hurry, don't have much experience working with PCs, or don't need maximum throughput, an external ISDN adapter is probably right for you. But if you've got the time to spend (or the money for a consultant to handle installation for you), and the inclination to wring the maximum performance out of your ISDN connection, then an internal adapter is right up your alley.

Connecting a LAN to the Internet via ISDN

For remote sites requiring ISDN-supportable bandwidth for two, three, or more PCs, a bridge or router may be used. A bridge connects two local area networks together by forwarding LAN (Ethernet) frames across a wide area network connection. For example, LAN traffic generated from a PC attached to an Ethernet LAN at a remote office may be forwarded across an ISDN connection by a bridge at the remote office to a second bridge at a corporate office, where the traffic is then forwarded across a second LAN to a corporate LAN server. The decision to forward frames across the ISDN connection is based on the LAN frame addressing information (e.g., a 48-bit Ethernet address).

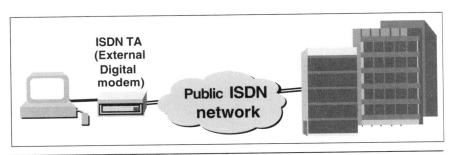

Figure 5.1   LAN to Internet Connection.

A pair of routers can perform a similar forwarding function, but as opposed to forwarding frames based on LAN frame addressing information, routers selectively forward network protocols (e.g., TCP/IP, Novell/IPX, AppleTalk), based on the network protocol type and network protocol addressing. Whereas a bridge may be configured to restrict traffic that is forwarded across a WAN connection to a particular (set of) network protocols, routers can be configured to restrict traffic to particular sources and destinations for each "routed" network protocol.

A cost analysis often justifies the selection of a remote access bridge or router over a terminal adapter. The formula is simple:

1. Multiply the cost of a terminal adapter by the number of PCs that require a dedicated TA.
2. Multiply the one-time charge for installation of ISDN basic rate service for each ISDN subscription required (typically one per TA).
3. Multiply the recurring monthly charges for ISDN basic rate service by the number of PCs that would require individual terminal adapters and ISDN service (e.g., $40 per month, plus an estimate of usage per PC per month for both RBOC and ISP).
4. Compare the total cost of items 1–3 against the cost of deploying a router or bridge, which is the sum of a single ISDN basic rate subscription (one-time and recurring charges), the cost of a remote access bridge or router, and the cost of a pocket Ethernet hub.

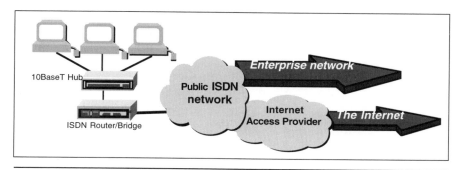

Figure 5.2   ISDN connections to the Internet and an enterprise network.

Assume a street price of approximately $200 to $400 per TA, a $150 ISDN installation charge, and $40 per ISDN subscription per month recurring charges (or consult the table of approximate ISDN charges). The $1100 mean price of an ISDN router and bridge, plus $100 for a pocket hub, compares favorably even for two PC configurations, provided ISDN is used for one year.

Many ISDN routers and bridges can also be deployed in single-PC configurations. An Ethernet cross-connect cable can be used to connect the PC to the router/bridge, which eliminates the need for (and defers the expense of) a hub. In this scenario, although the initial outlay for a router or bridge is higher than for a terminal adapter, it is a practical alternative if the number of PCs at the remote site is expected to grow. Certain ISDN routers and bridges have both an ISDN basic rate interface and a high-speed serial port capable of supporting Frame Relay service. These units will provide an upgrade path from ISDN to Frame Relay and can prove even more cost effective over time.

Can I afford the time required to deal with my local phone company?

Most RBOCs and other ISDN service providers have ISDN order lines with reasonably knowledgeable personnel to help you with your needs. However, this does not mean that everything will progress smoothly, rapidly, or without close supervision.

Here's some of what you'll encounter on the way to ISDN nirvana. If your location is near an ISDN-equipped CO, there may be unused phone wire pairs available to you; if not, you may have a long wait for the necessary hookup. If your wiring is less than 10 to 15 years old and the local phone company isn't swamped with installations when you call, you may get lucky and have to wait only a couple of weeks for installation. Otherwise, it can take up to six weeks or more, even if your location meets most of these conditions. During this period you will be spending your valuable time on your POTS phone to more than one phone company employee trying to get things going or to figure out what, if anything, is happening.

Please note also that there's a distance constraint of 1.5 miles from the network termination to the central office (CO) ISDN equipment. If you're unfortunate enough to be farther away from the nearest CO than that distance, the telephone company must install one or more repeaters between the CO and your location. This adds to the installation lead time and can contribute to the installation expenses involved. It's also too often true that the nearest CO may not be ISDN enabled and will require the phone company to run a so-called foreign exchange (FX) line to a properly equipped CO to bring you your ISDN connection. This, too, can add to the time and expense involved.

Finally, it may not be immediately obvious, either to you or to the phone company, whether you will be charged at local call rates or intra-LATA (local access and transport area) call rates to use your ISDN connection. Since this can raise per-minute connect charges from 1 to 2 cents per minute to 8 to 10 cents a minute, it can add significantly to usage charges (and may make ISDN uneconomical). This is especially unfortunate when, as is the case for several of the book's authors, their ISP is only one mile away, but because that ISP's ISDN line is FXed from a more distant CO, intraLATA call rates do apply. The moral of this sad story is that you need to factor the calling costs to access your ISP into the overall monthly charges that you figure for an ISDN connection!

Because ISDN to residential locations is relatively new, there will be more problems than you have with your current analog system. When an ISDN service goes down, you don't get a weak or buzzy line, you get a big, fat nothing! Zip, zero, nada!

ISDN service is either up and working or it's stone-cold dead. So, if you lose power to your NT1 device, your ISDN service will be cut off (that's why battery backup is nice during the occasional power outage). This "dead or alive" characteristic is quite different from POTS, which draws its power from its own sources, not from your house or office wall plug. However, that same plug is exactly where your NT1 or computer gets its power. So, if you do elect to drop POTS connectivity in favor of ISDN phones, you'll want to obtain an uninterruptible power supply (UPS) with significant battery backup capabilities to keep your ISDN phone running in the event of a power failure. We use both kinds of phones ourselves and rely on POTS to get us through power failures.

Can I afford the time necessary to install the ISDN equipment myself?

Assuming you are a knowledgeable computer user who feels comfortable installing cards inside your computer, but not an electrical engineer or hotshot programmer, it can take you from a day to a week to get your ISDN equipment installed and running properly.

Using an external NT1 with a serial ISDN modem-type device, you may get lucky and have it all running in a few minutes. If you try to install an ISDN adapter card that behaves like a network card in a computer that already has another network card installed, and you try to get it all running under Windows for Workgroups or NetWare, and the provisioning (setup) on your ISDN line isn't exactly what you ordered, it may take a bit longer.

However, the introduction of Windows 95 with its plug-and-play capabilities and ISDN support has made what used to be a trying task merely tedious. If you're bound and determined to do the ISDN thing yourself, you can ensure a successful experience if you'll simply rely on Windows 95 to handle behind-the-scenes configuration. That means, of course, that you'll want to select plug-and-play compatible hardware from the Windows 95 Hardware Compatibility List (available through the Microsoft Web site at http://www.microsoft.com/).

The time frames we mention here can include several hours on the phone to the customer support personnel of your chosen ISDN adapter card, to Microsoft or Novell for networking advice, to your telephone service provider for switch and provisioning information, and to your Internet service provider for connection testing and debugging. It can also involve seemingly endless changes to your PC's configuration if Windows 95 and plug-and-play are unable to handle the hard work for you.

Warning! These are by no means the worst-case ISDN horror stories. Unfortunately, a certain amount of thrashing around happens all too frequently, given the variety of new cards and other hardware in PCs today. This sort of thing happens much less frequently in the Macintosh world, because of the standardization of the operating system and its interface managers for add requirements. In any case, be aware that it may take you longer than you anticipate to get everything up and running smoothly. If you plan for this, and arrange for expert help to be on tap if and when it's needed, you'll lose a lot less sleep during this potentially excruciating process.

Can I afford to hire a consultant to install the equipment in my location?

If you're getting ISDN for a profitable business that needs your time to keep it profitable, seriously consider hiring a qualified consultant. Do a quick cost/benefit analysis comparing your lost time and lessened efficiency versus the consultant's fees. Keep in mind that a good consultant can assist you in choosing the proper equipment for your business, both now and when you need to expand.

If you are getting ISDN for personal use only and, like most of us, have more time than money, keep on reading and do it yourself. As the working wife once said to the out-of-work husband, "Honey, your time is valuable but not costly." Choosing the right ISDN equipment and ISP and knowing how to deal with the phone company should make your initial ISDN experience less of an ordeal than you may expect.

What do you want to do?

Are you still with us? Good! That means you're either committed to getting your own ISDN service or you should be committed ... or both. To aid with your tasks, find the section that follows that best describes your situation and read it completely and thoroughly. In each of these sections, we've condensed the answers to the previous questions and customized them for the specific group it addresses.

Home/Personal Use (ISDN Internet via Computer + POTS Phone)

Here, you already have a computer at home and simply want to get ISDN service so you can access the Internet and other online services faster and better. You wouldn't mind the extra telephone line either, since your kids/wife/housemates are always griping about you tying up a line with your modem. You aren't really a hardware type, so installing complicated boards doesn't appeal to you. You already have an Internet account and your ISP offers ISDN PPP dial-up accounts, or you're willing to switch to another ISP for an ISDN account; perhaps your modem is getting old and you want a faster connection.

For this scenario, you need the following:

1. ISDN service from your local telephone company. Installation averages $150–$250. Monthly fee averages around $30.
2. External serial port ISDN modem, $300–$400.
3. PPP software and TCP/IP stack. Freeware or shareware.
4. ISDN service from your Internet service provider, $50 setup plus $30–$60 per month.

Bottom Line   The total installation and hardware cost is between $500 and $700. The monthly fees will run approximately $120.

Home Office/Personal Use (ISDN Voice and Data + POTS Phone)

You are a work-at-home consultant or have a one-person office. You already use a modem with your Internet account and CompuServe, America Online (AOL), etc. You have three POTS lines for voice, your computer, and your fax machine. You want to install an ISDN service to replace the data and fax phone lines and to increase your online speed and bandwidth.

You feel comfortable installing cards in your PC and are enough of a hacker to alter your I/O address and interrupt setup without calling tech support. You will either leave your computer on all of the time for your fax machine or you'll not worry about it after business hours. You have enough time to spend doing it yourself and want to keep the initial cash outlay to a minimum.

For this scenario you need the following:

1. ISDN service from your local telephone company. Installation $150–$250. Monthly fee $30.
2. Combined NT1/TA internal adapter card with POTS port, $400.
3. Built-in ISDN support from MacOS, Windows 95, or Windows NT.
4. ISDN service from your Internet service provider, $50 setup, plus $30–$60 per month.

Bottom Line   The total installation and hardware cost is about $700. The monthly fees will run approximately $60–$90. Eliminating two business lines saves you about $60 per month in phone charges, so you break even on the phone service. Your ISP charges jumped from $20 to $60 for a net increase of $40 with ISDN over POTS usage for all lines, plus local telephone usage charges.

Small Business Office (ISDN Voice and Data, Multiple ISDN Phones)

Your office is relatively high-tech with you and your partner using PCs in a Windows 95 Ethernet network. Each of you has a separate POTS line for dialing out. You have separate voice lines, with no receptionist and no intercom functions. You both want faster access to Internet and other online information services, which will undoubtedly be offering ISDN connections in the near future. You also want to be able to e-mail more easily to your clients and send/receive large files more quickly. If you grow even a little, you'll need a receptionist and a small key-based phone system. You are adept at working with your hardware and feel comfortable with the amount of your time it will take to get the job done.

You are at the point where you need to determine carefully whether you need an ISDN and/or network consultant or really want to do it yourself. Presuming you want to do it yourself, here is the least expensive and simplest scenario.

For this application you need the following:

1. ISDN service from your local telephone company. Installation $250. Monthly fee $120, including per minute usage charges.
2. Combined NT1/TA internal adapter card with POTS port, two at $400.
3. ISDN service from your Internet service provider, two at $50 setup, plus $60–$120 per month.
4. All the software and drivers you need are included with Windows 95.

Bottom Line   The total installation and hardware cost is about $1150. The monthly fees will run approximately $120–$180. If you replaced one POTS line for each person with an additional ISDN number, you saved approximately $60 per month. Your ISP charges probably increased from about $40 to $120 per month. This results in a net increase due to ISDN of $160. You could further lower this by $30 by using one of the ISDN ports for your fax machine.

You could replace all of your POTS lines with the two ISDN services (four numbers total) if you installed a separate NT1 and used TAs without built-in NT1s in your computers. You could plug your POTS phones into the NT1 as well as your fax. You would need a substantial uninterruptible power supply for your NT1 to keep your phone lines up and going if the power goes out, so the cost would stay about the same for the hardware. The monthly service could be lowered another $30 to $60 depending on how many POTS lines you currently have. This should make the monthly costs for your phone lines less with ISDN but your ISP charges will still be more, so it isn't a completely break-even situation. However, you are getting the benefit of the ISDN speed and bandwidth.

What Do You Need?

As you have undoubtedly gathered, there are certain elements that are essential for your ISDN service installation to succeed. At a minimum, you will need the following items, information, or services to connect to the Internet and make voice calls via your ISDN telephone service:

1. A properly provisioned (set up) and operational ISDN line from the phone company.
2. A properly configured ISDN HOST or LAN-ISDN account with an Internet service provider.
3. For ISDN host connections, PC software to link you with the ISP or enterprise network (PPP usually). For LAN-ISDN connections, you will need TCP/IP host software for each PC on the LAN to provide connections to the Internet. For remote LAN-ISDN connections to enterprise networks, you may require either TCP/IP or NOS protocol (IPX) software for each PC.
4. An NT1 device, properly installed and tested at your location (which will be built into many of the ISDN hardware components you'll be considering), if NT1 capabilities are not provided in the digital modem, bridge, or router you purchase.
5. A TA (terminal adapter) device, router, or bridge, properly installed, configured, and tested in or attached to your computer. If you are connecting a PC LAN, you need LAN NIC cards and drivers for each PC and a multiport repeater or hub.
6. A computer (perhaps lots of them).
7. A POTS (analog) telephone or an ISDN (digital) phone.

Part III explains the procedures involved in obtaining, installing, and getting all of these elements working properly. The rest of this chapter and the rest of Part II discuss the currently available hardware and software from which you may choose.

What Are Your Choices?

Your hardware choices will vary greatly, but they can be divided into three major groups as indicated in Table 5.2.

Table 5.2   ISDN hardware.

Product Type	Adapter Cards	ISDN Bridges/Routers	ISDN Modems
Description	Internal TA or TA/NT1 bus-attached cards that communicate directly (no serial chip use) via TCP/IP, NDIS, ODI, or other protocol drivers. They act as network cards.	External network devices used to connect one or more computers via Ethernet LAN cabling and hubs to external networks (e.g., the Internet) via ISDN.	Internal cards or external devices that communicate with your computer via its serial chip, like an analog modem. May have TA only, TA/NT1, or TA and analog modem capabilities.
Advantages	Faster throughput than ISDN modems. May have POTS plug and built-in NT1 at lower price than modems, bridges, or routers. Can use BONDing for 128 Kbps throughput.	Faster throughput than ISDN modems. Often have POTS plug and built-in NT1. Can use BONDing for 128 Kbps throughput. Higher throughput possible using compression.	Connect easily to external or internal serial port. Set up like a standard modem using standard COM port and existing software. Talk to both analog and ISDN devices.
Drawbacks	Some difficult to set up and configure, especially with other network cards in same computer. Windows 95 plug-and-play eases this pain and suffering. No direct interoperability with analog devices. Requires one TA per user.	Requires Ethernet card in each computer and cabling (hub or Ethernet crossover) between computers and router/bridge. Requires each host be configured as well as router/bridge. Some routers/bridges difficult to set up and configure. No direct interoperability with analog devices.	Slow performance. One B channel, 64 Kbps or less, with slower UART. BONDing less common. May require V.120 to communicate with other ISDN devices.

Table 5.2   Continued

Product Type	Adapter Cards	ISDN Bridges/Routers	ISDN Modems
Examples	3COM Impact ISA Adtran Express Digiboard DataFire Hayes Accura ISDN ISDN*Tek Commuter Plus US Robotics Sportster 128K	ACC Congo Proteon Globetrotter Cisco 1004 Farallon Netopia Livingston PortMaster Office Router	3COM Impact IQ TA Cardinal IDC1001 Motorola Bitsurfr Pro US Robotics I-Modem

Summary

If you're still with us, you really, really are set on getting yourself deeply into this ISDN thing. Don't worry too much about the myriad acronyms, products, and unintelligible jargon. If you can understand what we've presented in this chapter, you can purchase, install, configure, and use your own ISDN equipment on your own computer.

Generally speaking, the adapter cards with built-in NT1 and POTS plugs are the most cost-effective for personal and individual business use, provided that you have the time to hassle with installing and configuring them. ISDN modems are the easiest to install and configure but provide the least amount of functionality at possibly a higher price than the adapter cards. The ISDN bridges and routers are the most expensive but possibly the most versatile of all three categories: They are reasonably easy to install and configure, provided you already have an Ethernet card in your computer.

If you want to replace your existing POTS phone system with ISDN, you'll want to get a separate NT1 with its own UPS or you'll be without phone service whenever the power goes out. Even then, keeping one POTS line in service is good insurance. And don't forget those pesky per-minute usage charges for outgoing local calls—if you place many local POTS calls, this could add up over an ISDN line. In the next chapter, you'll move onward to grapple with the specifics of ISDN hardware and software.

6

Internal ISDN PC Adapter Cards

ISDN Internal Adapter Cards

ISDN adapter cards are essentially network cards. They plug into your computer and must be installed as network devices, complete with drivers and protocols. This means you must know more than you probably want to know about IRQs, hardware interrupts, input/output (I/O) addresses, and SRAM buffers. If some or all of this is completely foreign to you, you're not alone. You should either understand these things reasonably well or get your handy hardware vendor/consultant/local guru to install and configure your adapter card for you.

If you decide to plunge in yourself, be prepared to spend some time deciphering your Windows 95 control panel, MSD (Microsoft System Diagnostics) output, or other hardware system configuration program's printouts regarding your system's interrupts and RAM usage while you try to choose among the remaining available interrupts, I/O base addresses, and static RAM buffer spaces for your adapter card on your system. Then you can get on with configuring your computer with the appropriate network drivers for TCP/IP, presuming you're going to use your ISDN to connect to the Internet, or whatever other protocols you intend to use.

If this sounds difficult, you're catching on quickly: When it comes to pre–Windows 95 systems (running DOS 6.22 or lower, Windows 3.1 or 3.11, or Windows for Workgroups), it is difficult. Until the release of Windows 95, there was no such thing as "plug and play" for ISDN adapter cards. But even if you're constrained to use a pre-95 version of Windows, take heart: These configurations are not impossible to install and manage, they're just difficult at best for inexperienced networkers. If Windows 95 is indeed an option on your systems, allow us to recommend using it whenever possible (and we swear, there's no relationship between us and Microsoft at work here, either!).

This chapter discusses the most popular ISDN adapter cards available. Please keep in mind that many of these cards were on the market only a few months before this book went to press. When we examined and tested them, only a small crew of intrepid users had experience with each card, and then only with a few computer systems for a handful of uses. Since interoperability (which is the buzzword for one ISDN card being able to communicate with another ISDN system) is a primary concern, more experience and testing will be necessary before all of the potential problems surface for each card. All known interoperability problems are discussed with each card (but it's always the unknown or unexpected ones that get you in the end). These cards are discussed in alphabetical order by vendor name.

For completely up-to-date discussions of ISDN issues, please subscribe to the Internet newsgroup, comp.dcom.isdn. For the most complete list of ISDN information on the World Wide Web (WWW), connect to Dan Kegel's fantastic site at http://alumni.caltech.edu/~dank/isdn/. If you can't find the ISDN information you need from Dan's site, it probably doesn't exist. We also recommend going to the Microsoft Web site to get more information on the plug-and-play architecture at http://www.microsoft.com/win32dev/base/pnp.htm.

Prices and availability fluctuate wildly and frequently, so the following information may have changed by the time you read this. Your best bet is to check the WWW site of each manufacturer, using Dan Kegel's page as a starting place, for price and feature changes when you're ready to buy. For those of you who can't conveniently use the Word Wide Web, a complete list of manufacturers along with their addresses and phone numbers is located in Appendix B of this book.

Considerations in Selecting Digital Modems versus Access Cards

Subscribers should consider several issues before recommending, purchasing, or providing ISDN digital modems. With digital modems, the effects of conversion from asynchronous-PPP to synchronous-PPP must be understood. That is, when using a digital modem, data is first serialized and sent using asynchronous PPP, where each 8 bits (octet) of data are framed with one start bit and one stop bit. The digital modem converts each 10-bit datum into 8 bits (octet) before it transmits the datum over an ISDN B channel. This results in a 20 to 25 percent decrease in maximum available throughput from the maximum 56 or 64 Kbps the subscriber may expect. A second issue to consider is that most external digital modems require a high-speed/high-IRQ serial I/O card (a 16550AF Universal Asynchronous Receiver/Transmitter is most often recommended, but even faster devices like the DigiPort card are available today).

Nearly all 386-based PCs and many early 486-based PCs are not configured with a fast serial card, the cost of which must be factored into the purchase of a digital modem (for approximately $50 to $75, at street prices). It has been our experience that installation of high-speed serial cards is sometimes quite frustrating with MS-DOS/

Windows 3.x. As with ISDN itself, this is much easier to accomplish using Windows 95.

The availability of ISA cards that are Windows 95 compatible is now widespread. We have had more difficulty ascertaining the availability (and acquiring evaluation units) of industry standard architecture (ISA) cards that run under MS-DOS/Windows 3.x, but have included two in our tests. The downside of ISA cards is that they must be installed in an internal expansion slot. Removing the casing and installing a card are likely to be intimidating for many users, but such cards and their associated drivers may also be installed by professional and qualified PC service companies or individuals. There is also the possibility that some users may discover their PCs do not have an expansion slot or IRQ available for an ISA card. For that reason, newer extended ISA or PCI machines with a wealth of expansion slots may be preferable in cases in which ISDN connectivity is a must-have.

WinSOCK Stack Considerations and Concerns

ISDN internal ISA adapter cards for Win 3.x require the WinISDN driver supported by TCP/IP software such as OnNet 2.0. Neither of the ISDN internal ISA adapter cards for Win 3.x that we tested was compatible with the older OnNet software. However, this was not a problem for external digital modems.

A survey of the December 1996 Computer Library lists 86 internal ISDN adapters, ranging from ISA (58), to PCI (8), to EISA (8), to PCMCIA (Personal Computer Memory Card International Association) (12). Reading these products' specifications indicates that Windows 95 compatibility in this population is high but that coverage for third-party WinSOCK stacks (1.1 or 2.0) needed for Windows 3.x support is only spotty. Since Microsoft's TCP/IP installs with Windows 95 itself (typically, for the residential user, this is done at the factory), and since its performance appears to compare favorably with that of competing stacks, we believe that few PC owners will choose to spend time or money on a replacement stack.

Larger organizations are also likely to focus on Microsoft TCP/IP as a means of reducing technical support. We believe that, eventually, Microsoft TCP/IP will be to the PC what TCP/IP kernel software is to UNIX workstations.

Comparative Analysis

Table 6.1 provides a summary comparison of the ISDN adapter card products that we tested. A check mark (✔) indicates that the product provides the feature or satisfies the criteria. Numeric values are interpreted as follows: 1 = superior, 2 = good, 3 = lacking. An asterisk (*) indicates that the feature was available but not evaluated. An O indicates that the feature is optional. Please note the following:

1. Diva for Windows 3.x and PCMCIA card are also available.
2. DOS Client or Windows for Workgroups 3.11 is available, but no Windows 3.11.

U.S. Robotics Sportster 128K Terminal Adapter

Model tested:
    Sportster 128K, ISA/EISA, Integrated NT-1 and U-Interface for PC

Other models:
    Sportster 128K, ISA/EISA S/T Interface (external NT-1) for PC

Estimated price:
    Suggested list price $399. Street price (e.g., DataComm Warehouse) approximately $299.

System requirements:
    Intel 386 SX or better, 4 MB RAM (DOS), 8 MB RAM (Windows)

Table 6.1   Comparison of ISDN adapter card products tested.

ISA Card	Internal S/T	Integrated NT1	Analog Port	PPP Support	Multilink Support	Multiple Adaption Rate Protocols Support	Analog Modem Support	Quality of Diagnostic Utilities	Usability of Configuration Utilities	Windows 95 Compatible	MS-DOS/Windows 3.x	Microsoft TCP/IP, Dial-up Networking Compatible	OnNet 2.0 Dialer Compatible	Ease of Installation, Configuration	Documentation Quality	Quality of Support
U.S. Robotics	✔	✔	2	✔	*	*		1	1	*	✔		✔	1	1	*
Diamond Multimedia NetCommander ISDN	✔	✔	1	✔	*	*		1	1	✔		✔		1		
Eicon Diva for Windows 95 (Note 1)	✔		0	✔	*			2	3	✔		✔		3	3	1
Digi International DataFire-U (Note 2)	✔	✔	0	✔	✔			3	1	✔		✔		1	2	*

OS requirements:
  MS-DOS/MS Windows 3.x or MS Windows 95 using the Win-ISDN interface

WINSOCK stacks:
  Microsoft TCP/IP for Windows 95, OnNet 2.0 (FTP software) and Chameleon v4.5 (NetManage) for Windows 3.x

Test environment(s):
  Intel 486/50 DX2 PC, MS-DOS/MS Windows 3.11 (WinISDN interface), OnNet 2.0 WinSOCK TCP/IP stack (see Table 6.2)

Table 6.2 Test details: U.S. Robotics Sportster 128K terminal adapter.

Features	Support	Comments
ISDN BRI with integrated S/T/U	✔	RJ-45 connector
Analog port	✔	RJ-11 connector
Telephony API	✔	TAPI
Integrated analog modem		Not available
PPP support	✔	Also supports ISC (proprietary) and PPP-ML (multilink)
Multilink support		TurboPPP configuration option, not tested
Compression	✔	STACker, Microsoft, or Ascend
Diagnostic capabilities	✔	System diagnostics, call logger, and protocol monitor provided through Sportster ISDN 128K Manager utility
Software supplied	✔	Sportster ISDN 128K Manager utility for Windows 95, MS-DOS/MS Windows 3.x, and MS-DOS/MS Windows Remote LAN access (bridge Ethernet packets across ISDN to remote LAN)
Accessories	✔	One RJ-45 cable for ISDN access (supplied), NT1 backup kit (optional), external ring generator (optional)
Additional drivers supported	✔	Windows NT and Novell Connect (from USR) drivers can be purchased for an additional $150 each. UNIX driver developed by third-party vendor (CDA-IAC) is $195.

Hardware description:
Internal digital modem card mounted in 16-bit ISA/EISA slot. It has an RJ-45 connector for ISDN U termination, an RJ-11 analog port for analog voice/facsimile equipment. I/O base address and IRQ values are set automatically by the software configuration utility if the jumpers on the adapter card are left at factory settings (the only reason to change these is that an external NT-1 must be used).

Software configuration interface:

The Sportster ISDN 128K Manager Utility provides a very straightforward and uncomplicated configuration process for configuring the internal modem card.

Documentation:

An Installation Guide and a copy of *Discover the World Wide Web with Your Sportster* are included in the package. An offer for one month of unlimited access from PSINet is included. The Installation Guide gives an excellent description of ISDN and how to order service from the telephone company. Very clear instructions are also provided for physical installation, but the manual relies entirely on the strength of the Manager Utility for installing software for Internet access, directing the user to "follow the instructions on the install screens."

Diagnostics and monitoring:

The Manager Utility provides an excellent set of configuration and management tools. A *Configuration settings* window is used to modify current parameter settings. *System diagnostics* can be run to check system and card integrity and can be scheduled to be performed at startup. A *Call Logger* facility records detailed information for every call placed (see sample). A *Protocol Monitor* is also provided. HyperText Help is available for all utilities. One section of the window graphically displays ISDN connection status.

Usability for target environment:

It is well suited for residential and business use. The Manager Utility is not the least bit intimidating.

Kudos and/or complaints:

Very easy installation (kudo). Documentation is spotty (complaint), but Manager Utility more than compensates (kudo). NT and Novell drivers are expensive options. Can assign password to safeguard ISDN configuration (kudo).

Diamond Multimedia NetCommander ISDN

Model tested:

NetCommander ISDN, ISA, Integrated NT1 for PC

Other models:
    None available

Estimated price:
    Suggested list price $299. Street price approximately $289.

System requirements:
    MS Windows 95 capable PC, fast Intel 486 or Pentium processor, recommend 8 MB RAM

OS requirements:
    MS Windows 95 using the Windows 95 drivers; NT 4.0 drivers also available

WINSOCK stacks:
    Microsoft TCP/IP

Test environment:
    Aptiva Pentium 150 PC, Windows 95, ISDN Accelerator Pack for Windows 95 by Microsoft, Microsoft TCP/IP (see Table 6.3)

Hardware description:
    An internal digital modem card mounted in 16-bit ISA slot. Has an RJ-45 connector for ISDN U termination, an RJ-11 analog port for analog voice/facsimile equipment. One status LED.

Software configuration interface:
    Extremely user-friendly interface. Integrated nicely with Windows 95. Treated as a multipurpose adapter card.

Documentation:
    The NetCommander Installation Guide provides brief but accurate step-by-step illustrated instructions. The SETUP software is so easy to use, and online documentation is so accurate, you would think you were using a Macintosh.

Diagnostics and monitoring:
    AutoISDN is a superior GUI-based utility. The *Connection Status* window provides a real-time ISDN line/channel monitor

Table 6.3   Test details: Diamond Multimedia NetCommander ISDN.

Features	Support	Comments
ISDN BRI with integrated S/T/U	✔	RJ-45 connector
Analog port	✔	RJ-11 connector
Telephony API		None mentioned
Integrated analog modem		Not available
PPP support	✔	PPP/CHAP through Win95 dial-up networking or equivalent WinSOCK stack PPP dialer
Multilink support		Not tested
Compression	✔	IP header compression through Win95 dial-up networking or equivalent WINSOCK stack PPP dialer
Diagnostic capabilities	✔	AutoISDN is an exceptionally well-conceived, graphical user interface (GUI)-based utility.
Software supplied	✔	Supra NetCommander ISDN Setup diskette, Microsoft ISDN Accelerator Pack for Windows 95, Microsoft Internet Explorer v2.0
Accessories	✔	One RJ-45 cable for ISDN access (supplied), one 6-inch RJ-11 cable for analog device
Additional drivers supported		Windows 95 plug and play, NT 4.0

and provides easy to understand error messages with online hypertext help. The *Connection Log* records call number, time, duration, direction, and destination. The *Preferences* and *Configuration* windows can be used to edit configuration information. The *Diagnostics* window is used to test the analog phone port and to enable logging.

Usability for target environment:
Extremely well suited for residential use.

Kudos and/or complaints:
Superior setup and installation utility (kudo). Superior diagnostics utility (kudo). At list price of $299, this is an exceptional value. Limited set of supported IRQs may hamper configuration in some PCs (complaint).

Eicon Diva for Windows 95

Model tested:
Diva ISA card for Windows 95

Other models:
Diva PCMCIA card for Windows 95; Diva ISA card for MS-DOS/Windows 3.x

Estimated price:
Suggested list price $495. Street price approximately $495.

System requirements:
MS Windows 95 capable PC, fast Intel 486 or Pentium processor, recommend 8 MB RAM

OS requirements:
MS Windows 95, MS-DOS/Windows 3.x

WINSOCK stacks:
Microsoft TCP/IP

Test environment:
Intel 486 DX2/50 PC, Windows 95, Microsoft TCP/IP (see Table 6.4)

Hardware description:
An internal digital modem card mounted in a 16-bit ISA slot, requires an external NT-1. Tested using Tone Commander Model NTIU-100TC. Has an RJ-45 connector for ISDN U termination. No LEDs.

Software configuration interface:
The Diva for Windows 95 installation process is driven largely by extensions to the Windows 95 Network applet in Control Panel. As described, the installation process requires several PC shutdown and restart sequences, which was not the experience with other ISA cards tested.

Table 6.4   Test details: Eicon Diva for Windows 95.

Features	Support	Comments
ISDN BRI with integrated S/T/U		Card currently available requires External NT1; integrated NT1 available 3Q96, RJ-45 connector
Analog port		None
Telephony API		None mentioned
Integrated analog modem		Not available
PPP support	✔	Through Windows 95 dial-up networking
Multilink support		Available, not tested
Compression		None mentioned
Diagnostic capabilities	✔	DOS applet for extracting ISDN events from card's maintenance ring buffer
Software supplied	✔	Diva for Windows 95 software
Accessories	✔	One RJ-45 cable for ISDN access (supplied)
Additional drivers supported		Support for circuit- and packet-switched data

Documentation:

A pamphlet-length Installation Guide falls short of adequate. Minimum description of AT commands may cause novice user problems; advanced user could pick correct string as a consequence of understanding remote access service, modems, and ISDN.

Diagnostics and monitoring:

DOS command-line logging utility records the maintenance driver ring buffer contents in ASCII text. The resulting LOG file is useful in diagnosing problems.

Usability for target environment:

A good product, but compared to other products tested, more challenging to install; requires an external NT1.

Kudos and/or complaints:

No integrated NT1 (complaint). No analog port (complaint). Must set I/O port address using DIP switches, whereas IRQ is

set by software, would be nice if both could be software configured (complaint). RJ-45 cable is of highest quality and very long
(kudo). Logging available only via DOS utility (complaint). Documentation fails to mention that external NT-1 is required and
does not adequately discuss required AT command for modem
initialization (complaint).

Digi International DataFire-U

Model tested:
DataFire-U, ISA, Integrated NT-1 for PC

Other models:
DataFire-S/T, ISA, requires external NT-1; DataFire/4-S/T, ISA,
4 BRIs, requires external NT-1

Estimated price:
Suggested list price $595. Street price approximately $400.

System requirements:
DOS- or Windows-capable PC, no requirements specified

OS requirements:
MS Windows 95 using the Windows 95 ISDN drivers DOS Client
with PROTMAN drivers; Windows for Workgroups 3.11 or Windows NT with RAS driver

WINSOCK stacks:
Microsoft TCP/IP

Test environment:
Aptiva P150 PC, Windows 95, ISDN Accelerator Pack for Windows 95 by Microsoft, Microsoft TCP/IP (see Table 6.5)

Hardware description:
An internal digital modem card mounted in 16-bit ISA slot. Has
an RJ-45 connector for ISDN U termination.

Table 6.5   **Test details: Digi International DataFire-U.**

Features	Support	Comments
ISDN BRI with integrated S/T/U	✔	RJ-45 connector
Analog port	✔	RJ-11 connector
Telephony API		None mentioned
Integrated analog modem		Not available
PPP support	✔	Not mentioned
Multilink support	✔	Not mentioned
Compression	✔	Not mentioned
Diagnostic capabilities	✔	Simple DOS programs supplied for line status and trace
Software supplied	✔	For Windows 95, must download Microsoft ISDN Accelerator Pack and DataFire drivers from http://www.microsoft.com/windows/software/isdn.htm. No other configuration software is provided or required.
Accessories	✔	One RJ-45 cable for ISDN access (supplied)
Additional drivers supported	✔	DOS client using PROTMAN, Windows for Workgroups 3.11 and Windows NT using RAS drivers

Software configuration interface:

Extremely user-friendly Configuration Wizard requires only two steps. No other configuration utilities provided. Integrates nicely with Windows 95. Treated as a Network Adapter (same as LAN card).

Documentation:

Although software was provided for other environments, Windows 95 support only recently added, and the only documentation provided was a README file. Quality of other documentation appeared to be thorough but oriented toward more sophisticated users.

Diagnostics and monitoring:

Two DOS programs provided for determining line status and protocol traces. Programs not documented and difficult to run using Windows 95 DOS emulation (programs run in a DOS window, which closes before it is possible to read the output—can be corrected by running programs from batch file). Diagnostic output is cryptic but can be invaluable in diagnosing ISDN line problems.

Usability for target environment:
Well suited for residential use because Windows 95 software and documentation are packaged with the product. Model with four BRIs might be suitable for small enterprise or ISP use.

Kudos and/or complaints:
Superior setup and installation utility (kudo). Internet access required to download drivers (complaint). Cryptic diagnostics (complaint).

Interesting Items from the "Untested" Pool

In our perusal of available hardware and related systems, we found some interesting products that we didn't have time to test in preparing the second edition of this book. Nevertheless, we feel the following products are worth a quick check, if only to see if their features prove them worthy of further investigation, if not some testing of your own.

Combinet EVERYWARE 1000

Plugging directly into the PC's ISA bus, the EVERYWARE 1000 looks like an Ethernet adapter card to the PC's software. The EVERYWARE 1000 is compatible with popular network operating systems, including Windows and Novell NetWare as well as TCP/IP-based applications.

The EVERYWARE 1000 series is available in the four models listed below, with data compression and integrated NT1 options. With the compression hardware, file transfer rates of up to 512 Kbps are achieved on the two aggregated B channels of the ISDN basic rate line. All models have a DTE-side S/T port for use with an ISDN phone, fax machine, or other ISDN devices.

PC-1030: ISDN BRI PC Card
PC-1040: ISDN BRI PC Card with NT1
PC-1050: ISDN BRI PC Card with Data Compression
PC-1060: ISDN BRI PC Card with NT1 and Data Compression

EVERYWARE 1000 Features

- no separate Ethernet NIC, cables, or hubs required
- data compression (on some models)
- built-in NT1 (on some models)
- on-demand dialing
- supports ISDN phone, fax
- software upgradable
- authentication and callback security
- remote management
- ODI and NDIS drivers included

EVERYWARE 1000 Specifications

- PC bus: ISA, single-slot, 2/3 length, 16-bit
- PC desktop compatibility 386, 486, Pentium
- PC software compatibility ODI and NDIS 2.01 drivers
- compatibility tested with NetWare 3.x, 4.x, Windows 3.1, Windows for Workgroups 3.11
- no additional memory required
- Data Compression Stac hardware, Lempel Ziv algorithm (models 1050 and 1060 only)
- operates on two B channels, 128 Kbps (precompression) management
- text-based menu through COM port emulation (9600 baud)
- Combinet remote login over Ethernet or ISDN (UDP/IP)
- DIP switches 2 for COM selection (1, 2, 3, 4)
- ISDN switch types compatibility: AT&T 5ESS, Northern Telecom DMS 100, National ISDN-1 (NI-1)
- NET3/5 (Europe, Singapore, Hong Kong), 1TR6 (Germany), VN3/4 (France)

- ISDN line interfaces ISDN BRI S/T RJ-45 (models 1030, 1050) or ISDN BRI U RJ-45 (models 1040, 1060)
- compatible with data, voice, or voice/data B channels
- multipoint configuration
- ISDN terminal device interface
- S/T port for ISDN phone/fax support

EVERYWARE Software

Combinet EVERYWARE software is included with each Combinet on-demand networking access unit and can be upgraded simply by downloading a diskette file. EVERYWARE access units give users remote access to all applications and data resident on an enterprise network. Combinet software benefits include:

- software upgradable for investment protection
- simple installation and maintenance
- interoperable with all Combinet products
- efficiently manages telephone connections to minimize usage charges
- compatible with standards-based ISDN BRI, switched 56 telephone service and Ethernet LANs
- computer, network operating system, and application transparency
- extensive security options

Comments

Combinet's ISDN bridges and routers have been solid industry workhorses for several years. Hopefully, the EVERYWHERE 1000 carries on this tradition. None of the models seems to include a POTS plug, and the compression is useful only if it is compatible with the compression technique used by the device on the other end of your ISDN connection and the device has compression turned on.

Intel: RemoteExpress ISDN LAN Adapter

According to Intel, the RemoteExpress adapter is a ready-to-use solution. Board configuration is automatic and there are no switches or jumpers to set and no IRQs. The RemoteExpress adapter comes with built-in drivers for most popular networks. In addition, three levels of security protect the network every time a remote computer tries to log on. First, a unique MAC-level address identifies the remote user's personal RemoteExpress adapter, making sure it's registered and authorized. Second, the remote user PC name protects against entry by unauthorized computers. And third, the network password must be supplied correctly.

Requirements

- ISDN BRI S/T phone line (available through local phone company)
- Intel 386 SX-based computer or higher, 4 MB RAM, DOS 5.0 or higher
- NT1 with power supply
- product: RemoteExpress ISDN LAN Adapter
- order number: PCIS9500

Prices

RemoteExpress ISDN LAN Adapter PCIS9500, $499
BellSouth region (5) PCIS9500, $399
GTE region PCIS9500, $199
NYNEX region PCIS9500, $199
Pacific Bell region PCIS9500, $199
Other regions PCIS9500, $499
RemoteExpress ISDN Bridge Pack PCIS9501, $2199
BellSouth region (5) PCIS9501, $2199
GTE region PCIS9501, $2199
NYNEX region PCVD9501, $2199
Pacific Bell region PCIS9501, $2199
Other regions PCIS9501, $2199

Comments

Marketing relationships between Intel and the telephone companies listed above may qualify you for lower prices when purchasing

RemoteExpress products in conjunction with new ISDN service. Contact an Intel Advanced Network Reseller for details. Or, for a list, request FaxBack document 8212. To find out if there's ISDN service in your area, call Intel at (800) 538-3373, extension 208. Currently not available outside North America.

Little information is available from Intel about this product; however, according to ISDN Systems, Inc., the RemoteExpress card is Intel's version of the ISC SecureLink ISDN Adapter card discussed next.

ISDN Systems, Inc.: ISC SecureLink ISDN Adapter

The SecureLink II ISDN Adapter was designed to work with the same familiar software used in the office LAN environment. The SecureLink II includes NDIS, ODI (for IPX), Packet Driver, and TAPI drivers, so it can be used with the most popular, off-the-shelf software packages.

The SecureLink II ISDN Adapter is equipped with an RJ-11 (POTS) jack, so you can use your analog telephone to communicate over the digital network. Dynamic bandwidth allocation, compression, PPP, Multilink PPP, Integrated NT1, RJ-11 analog phone jack, Internet access, security via a SecurID card, and TAPI provide a complete solution for a wide variety of communications applications.

When used in conjunction with the SecureLink II ISDN Server, the SecureLink II Adapter offers unparalleled security. Multiple levels of security protect your LAN from unauthorized access. For an extra measure of security the SecureLink II works in conjunction with the SecurID card from Security Dynamics.

Shipped with card, Quick Start Up Guide, Reference Guide, RJ-45 cable, SecureLink driver installation disks, and Microsoft Windows Telephony (TAPI) installation disk.

The price is $199 to $595.

Requirements

- ISDN BRI phone line (available through local phone company)
- PC 386 CPU-based or higher, 4 MB RAM, DOS 5.0 or higher

Specifications

- PPP and Multilink PPP
- TCP/IP or IPX routed
- NetBEUI, 802.3 or 802.5 bridged
- all major LANs supported
- ISA or EISA
- DOS
- Windows 3.1 and 3.11
- Windows 95 and Windows NT 3.5
- TAPI on-screen dialing
- simultaneous voice/data
- two S/T interface plugs
- U interface
- RJ-11 for POTS
- built-in NT1
- inter-switch at 56K
- single B at 56K
- combined 2 B (112/128)
- V.120
- NDIS, ODI (NetWare), Packet Driver, TAPI, WinISDN
- bandwidth on demand
- compression
- SecurID from Security Dynamics
- Softset card (no jumpers)

Comments

The SecureLink ISDN adapter card plugs right into your computer and contains all of the functions you could want from an ISDN adapter card priced under $600 retail. It comes with professionally written user manuals and well thought-out installation, driver, and utility software. The ISC support staff is very responsive to customer's needs and will even call you back to see if everything is working well. They were more experienced with Novell and ODI drivers than with Windows and NDIS systems, but they learned quickly.

The original SecureLink cards sometimes had problems with shared SRAM address space in the computer in which they were installed, so the new SecureLink II cards contain onboard RAM space that is supposed to remedy this problem. Personal experience has shown that the SecureLink card works well in a Windows for Workgroups environment, once the SRAM conflicts are diagnosed and avoided. This is one of the best buys in the ISDN adapter card market today.

ISDN*tek CyberSpace Freedom Series Internet Cards

All the CyberSpace Freedom Series (Internet, Commuter, and Enterprise) adapter cards provide a WinISDN driver that can be addressed by application software through the industry standard WinISDN interface. Cards are available for Internet access, telecommuters, and demanding enterprise environments. An integral NT1 version is also available for each type of card.

CyberSpace Internet Card

The CyberSpace Internet Card is designed to provide low-cost ISDN access to the global Internet, with simplicity of installation and reliability as key features. The WinISDN application programming interface (API) provides Windows and WinOS/2-based PCs with an easy standard interface to ISDN-ready TCP/IP software. The Internet is then accessed through routers maintained by service providers. Because typical Internet access does not support voice calls, the Internet card does not possess voice call capabilities. The CyberSpace Internet card at $395 supports a 56 or 64 Kbps data call on either B channel and requires an external network termination (NT1). It can share the ISDN line with other ISDN hardware.

The CyberSpace Internet+Plus card features an onboard NT1 at $495 and can be connected directly to the phone company's wall jack. This configuration eliminates the external NT1 and dedicates the ISDN line to this card. The card also supports either one-channel or two-channel data calls. When used with appropriate multilink PPP software, the user can obtain up to 128 Kbps data rates.

Features

- PC (ISA-bus) hardware
- Windows drivers
- 56K/64K data call over one B channel
- 128K data call over two B channels using MPPP software
- compatible with Internet software and routers
- versions for S or U ISDN connections
- Japanese INS64 version available

CyberSpace Commuter Card

The CyberSpace Commuter card is designed to provide a fully digital telecommuting solution. The Commuter card supports both B channels of the ISDN connection, which can be used for voice and data or for up to 128 Kbps of data. It retains all the features of the Internet card, in that it can support a 56K to 64K data call on either B channel, and data on both B channels can be aggregated to 128 Kbps using appropriate Multilink-PPP (MPPP) software. The card continues to support Internet access software and to communicate with Internet routers.

The significant new feature of the Commuter card is voice call capability. Not to be confused with analog voice service, the Commuter card uses a standard headset or handset, thereby eliminating the need to purchase an expensive digital telephone. The telephony functions normally found on the telephone keypad are handled by the supplied dialing application running on the computer. The telephone line can be configured so that when the computer is not powered, incoming calls are automatically routed to a telco-maintained voice mail system or back to the corporate office.

The Commuter card requires either a standard handset or an amplifier-equipped headset to support voice. It is a 100 percent digital ISDN product, does not have an analog phone port, and does not support fax, modem, or analog phone sets. It does, however, include the ability to send Touch-Tones for accessing automatic call distribution (ACD) and credit card data entry equipment.

The CyberSpace Commuter card, at $495, requires an external NT1 and can be used with other ISDN equipment. The CyberSpace Commuter+Plus card, at $595, includes an onboard NT1, which can be connected directly to the phone company's wall jack. Using this configuration with a headset eliminates all other external equipment such as an NT1 and desktop phone set and dedicates the ISDN line to this card.

Features

- PC (ISA-bus) hardware
- Windows drivers
- 56K/64K data call over one B channel
- 128K data call over two B channels
- voice call over one B channel
- simultaneous voice and data calls over the two B channels
- sends Touch-Tone DTMF while call is active
- streaming data mode for rerouting voice
- voice capture mode for answering machine applications
- versions for S or U ISDN connections
- four-wire headset or handset compatible voice jack
- compatible with Internet software and routers

CyberSpace Enterprise Card

The Enterprise card is a superset of the Commuter card and offers several logical channels of X.25 connectivity over the D channel of the ISDN basic rate interface. Voice and data connections are similar to those for the Commuter card. In addition, the Enterprise card supports DTMF Touch-Tone detection, so incoming calls may be

automatically routed or recorded messages can be retrieved remotely from disk.

The X.25 or packet connections can be used for sending small messages or control signals from the computer to remote equipment.
Simple messages to the host system or another peer, such as a code
to call back with file information on a customer, can be sent while
both B channels are active with other duties. This allows an incredible variety of network connections for enterprises, particularly
home-based enterprises of the twenty-first century.

Features

- PC (ISA-bus) hardware
- Windows drivers
- 56K/64K data call over one B channel
- 128K data call over two B channels
- voice call over one B channel
- simultaneous voice and data calls over the two B channels
- several logical channels of X.25 over D channel
- generates and detects Touch-Tone DTMF while call is active
- supports call hold, conference, and transfer
- streaming data mode for rerouting voice
- streaming video mode
- video capture for surveillance
- voice capture mode for answering machine applications
- supports ISDN U connections
- four-wire headset or handset compatible voice jack
- compatible with Internet software and routers

The Driver Software The WinISDN.DLL driver supports synchronous PPP (Point-to-Point Protocol) and HDLC from the Windows-based TCP/IP stack mentioned earlier. It works with Service
Provider's ISDN routers when used with any WinISDN-based PPP
software. It supports FTP, Ping, e-mail, Gopher, Mosaic, and so

forth when used with appropriate TCP/IP software. Driver support for peer-to-peer connectivity, messaging, file transfers, streaming data, and voice connections is also included. The voice product includes a dialer/phone book miniapplication. A Software Developer's Kit for easy interface to Visual Basic or C programs is also available.

Comments   ISDN*tek's six offerings are professional looking, including the user manual and packaging. They come complete with installation and testing software. You have to set dip switches on the card, but the installation software runs on your computer and helps you determine what settings will be required before you plug the card into your computer.

The use of a regular telephone handset or headset with the Commuter and Enterprise cards to achieve digital telephony is an added plus. The lack of NDIS and ODI drivers for the cards and the lack of Windows NT drivers will make many potential users skip these products in favor of others until the drivers are available. If you have the correct hardware to use the ISDN*tek cards, they are a good buy and should be considered reasonable competition for the ISC SecureLink II card.

Summary

As you can see from the impressive group of ISDN adapter cards, you need not be limited by a lack of good hardware choices. Of the cards we tested, the Diamond MultiMedia NetCommander has the most user-friendly and feature-rich interface. At $299 (list price), this is the best price-performance product tested. The Digi DataFire and USR Sportster are nearly as easy to install and configure. Of the cards we describe but did not test, the ISC SecureLink II and Intel RemoteExpress (which is the same card as the SecureLink II) are the front runners in hardware functionality, software, and relative ease of installation.

Our best advice regarding ISDN adapter cards is to be sure you really want their benefits, despite their current costs and their drains on your time and sanity. Part III of this book provides detailed instructions on setting up a home office using an ISC SecureLink card, as well as case histories of other installations. If you read on and still want to install an ISDN adapter card yourself, you're either as crazy as we are or you know more about ISDN than we did. Either way, you'll probably succeed. Good luck!

7

ISDN Modems and NT1s

ISDN "Modems"

If your guiding principle is KISS (keep it simple, stupid!), then don't ignore the simplicity of so-called ISDN modems. Although they may not be quite as fast or as loaded with features as ISDN adapter cards or ISDN bridges and routers, they certainly can produce the desired results. And they're a lot easier to use.

Some of these ISDN modems are as easy to install as plugging them into your wall power outlet, attaching an RJ-45 cable (supplied with the unit) into your ISDN wall jack, and connecting the modem to your serial port with a standard DB-25 cable (not always included). Some can be configured by plugging your plain old telephone service (POTS) phone into the RJ-11 jack on the modem and setting it via the telephone keypad. Others offer DOS or Windows setup programs.

All of the ISDN modems bypass the major installation and configuration problems found with the ISDN ISA adapter cards. That is, they let you avoid the problems common to setting shared memory buffers, I/O addresses, IRQs, and network drivers. To your computer, the ISDN modem is just another modem, accessible through the RS-232 serial port and its associated UART (or even through its own built-in UART).

The best of these modems use ISDN standard protocols when communicating with other ISDN devices and use standard Hayes AT commands for communicating with your computer and other analog devices. Using one of these devices is really like using a much faster modem. In fact, some of them can even sense the type of incoming call and use the appropriate analog or digital protocols automatically.

All of these ISDN modems are subject to the constraints of your computer's serial UART chip. If you're using a newer computer with a 16550A UART, you may be able to attain transmission rates of 57.6 Kbps; otherwise, you'll be limited to about 19.2 Kbps. If you have an older computer, you may need to install a new serial interface card with a high-speed UART. Some of the ISDN modems on the market today support 2 B channel BONDing (for example, the Motorola BitSURFR Pro), so you may gain some benefits from a higher speed serial interface card (like the DigiPort family of products from Digi International, Inc.).

On the positive side, most of the ISDN modems are external devices, so you don't have to uncase your PC to hook them up. Some include built-in NT1s (network terminations), and others don't. In any case, they all are powered by their own power cables, which draw power from your AC wall outlet. This means that if the ISDN modem has a POTS jack for your analog phone, you can use it with your computer turned off. Some even have an internal battery backup in case your electricity goes off. Of course, the ISDN modems with internal NT1s and battery backup are more expensive, but the extra features may be worth the additional costs, depending on how you plan to use them.

Several high-quality ISDN modems are discussed in this chapter. All work well, but none are completely equivalent because they all have different feature sets. Because the industry is still in its infancy, standardization is nonexistent; each of these new products is trying to carve out a new market niche, and every manufacturer is constantly trying to "outfeature" the competition.

You would be wise to check the latest trade magazines and Internet newsgroups (like *comp.dcom.isdn* or *comp.dcom.modems*) before purchasing an ISDN modem. You should also check with your Internet service provider and local telephone service provider to make sure your choice works with their systems. If it doesn't, it won't matter how much you like the equipment; if it doesn't work, you'll have to find something else!

Network Termination 1000 Devices (NT1)

If the ISDN modem (or ISDN ISA adapter card) doesn't contain an internal NT1 (network termination 1000) device, you must purchase one separately. NT1s range from small, simple-looking devices with a couple of RJ-45 jacks (one for a cable to the ISDN wall jack and the other to your TA [adapter card or ISDN modem] and power cord jack [if it doesn't have its own power supply]) to the full-featured IBM 7845 NT1 Extended with its programmable interface and multiple S/T and analog output jacks. Some NT1s are designed to be used with external uninterruptible power supplies (UPSs). These are very useful when you have several analog and digital devices that need to run continuously, even when your computer is off.

Choosing a good NT1 is much simpler than choosing an ISDN TA. Check with the manufacturer of your chosen TA (adapter card or ISDN modem) to ensure compatibility with the NT1, but virtually all are interoperable. Whether the NT1 has a battery backup or a

UPS for power failures may be very important to you as well. If you are simply looking for an external NT1 to link your ISDN modem to your ISDN line with no analog (POTS) phone jack in the NT1, purchase the simplest and cheapest. If you want more features, look at the IBM 7845 or others that will undoubtedly be on the market soon, or consider getting an ISDN bridge or router with a built-in NT1 that offers the features you need.

All of the NT1s discussed in this chapter should provide good service if you follow the checklists and purchase the model that suits your needs. The listed manufacturers are reliable and stand behind their products. Always double-check their warranties and keep your receipts, however; most vendors require proof of purchase before they're willing to admit they owe you anything at all!

Meet the ISDN Modems

Table 7.1 provides a summary comparison of the ISDN products that we tested. A check mark (✔) indicates that the product provides the feature or satisfies the criteria. Numeric values are interpreted as follows: 1 = superior, 2 = good, 3 = lacking. An asterisk (*) indicates that the feature was available but not evaluated. An O indicates that the feature is optional. Please note the following:

1. ISA card for Windows 3.x is available; ISA card for Windows 95 is also available.
2. ISA card with advanced Windows drivers is available.

Motorola BitSURFR Pro Terminal Adapter

Model tested:
BitSURFR Pro Terminal Adapter, Integrated NT1 for PC

Other models:
BitSURFR Terminal Adapter
BitSURFR ISA Card for PC

Table 7.1   Comparison of ISDN products tested.

	Internal S/T	Integrated NT1	Analog Port	PPP Support	Multilink Support	Multiple Adaption Rate Protocols Support	Analog Modem Support	Quality of Diagnostic Utilities	Usability of Configuration Utilities	Windows 95 Compatible	MS-DOS/Windows 3.x	Microsoft TCP/IP, Dial-up Networking Compatible	OnNet 2.0 Dialer Compatible	Ease of Installation, Configuration	Documentation Quality	Quality of Support
ISDN Terminal Adapters																
Motorola BitSURFR PRO (Note 2)	✔	✔	2	✔	*			2	2	✔	✔	✔	✔	2	1	*
3Com/Impact Gateway (Note 1)	✔	✔	1	✔	✔		O	3	2	✔	✔	✔	✔	2	2	2
ZyXel Elite 28641	✔	✔	1	✔	*	✔	✔	2	3	✔	✔	✔	✔	2	3	1

Estimated price:
Suggested list price $495. Street price approximately $399.

System requirements:
Intel 486 or Pentium processor, 8 MB RAM, high-speed (UART 16550AF) serial port recommended

OS requirements:
MS-DOS/Windows 3.x using TurboCom/2 drivers; MS Windows 95 using built-in drivers

WINSOCK stacks:
Microsoft TCP/IP

Table 7.2   Test details: Motorola BitSURFR Pro Terminal Adapter.

Features	Support	Comments
ISDN (BRI) with integrated S/T/U	✔	RJ-45 connector
Analog port	✔	Two RJ-11 connectors
Telephony API		
Integrated Analog modem		
PPP support	✔	Also supports V.120 rate adaption, V.25bis dialer
Multilink support	✔	Multilink PPP available but not tested, also supports asynch inverse multiplexing between PCs using async protocols
Compression		
Diagnostic capabilities	✔	Status window in Configuration Manager
Software supplied	✔	BitSURFR Configuration Manager utility, HyperAccess Lite (a PC communications applet), NetManage Chameleon WinSOCK TCP/IP software
Accessories	✔	One RJ-45 cable for ISDN access (supplied), one 6-inch RJ-11 cable for analog device
Additional drivers supported		TurboCom/2 advanced serial port drive for MS-DOS/Windows 3.x

Test environment(s):

Aptiva P150 PC, Windows 95, Microsoft TCP/IP stack; Aptiva 486/66 PC, MS-DOS/MS Windows 3.11, OnNet 2.0 and PCTCP 1.x TCP/IP stacks (see Table 7.2)

Hardware description:

An external digital modem card with very small footprint and external power supply. It has an RJ-45 connector for ISDN U termination, two RJ-11 analog ports for analog voice/facsimile equipment, DB-25 connector for serial cable. Six light-emitting diodes (LEDs) to indicate ISDN line state (LS), voice port 1 and 2 status, data call port status, receive data and transmit data.

Software configuration interface:

Windows graphical user interface–based Configuration Manager provides menus for (a) configuration of ISDN switch type, SPIDs, directory numbers; (b) rate adaptation protocol selection V.120, PPP (single or multilink, using async-to-sync conversion or AIMux), and associated parameters (e.g., single or multichannel operation); (c) calls; and (d) operation.

Documentation:

The BitSURFR Pro Getting Started Guide provides an introduction to ISDN, the BitSURFR terminal adapter, and a high-level description of physical installation and configuration of the TA. A User's Guide provides complete details for the AT command set that may be used through VT100 terminal emulation to configure the BitSURFR. A TurboCom/2 User's Guide describes installation procedures for the advanced serial port driver for MSDOS/Windows 3.x provided with the digital modem. Guidelines for ordering ISDN are also provided.

Diagnostics and monitoring:

Adapter Status window under the Configuration Manager provides graphical (green and red light) indicators of ISDN connection status, can be used to determine whether service profile IDs (SPIDs), switch types, and terminal endpoint identifiers (TEIs) are correctly configured.

Usability for target environment:

Suitable for residential and small office use.

Kudos and/or complaints:

The Configuration Manager holds the COM port and you cannot dial while the status window is in use (complaint).

3Com Impact ISDN Digital Modem

Models tested:

Gateway 3C871 external digital modem for PC

Other models:
Gateway 3C872 external digital modem for PC with integrated analog modem
3C861 ISA card for PC (MS-DOS/Windows 3.x and Windows 95)

Estimated price:
Suggested list price $499. Street price is approximately $399.

System requirements:
386, 486, or Pentium, 16550AF UART recommended but not required

OS requirements:
DOS 3.1 or later, Windows 3.x, Windows 95

WINSOCK stacks:
Microsoft TCP/IP, FTP Software OnNet 1.1 or later

Test environment(s):
Aptiva P150 PC, Windows 95, Microsoft TCP/IP stack
Aptiva 486/66 PC, MSDOS/MS Windows 3.11, OnNet 2.0, and PCTCP 1.x TCP/IP stacks (see Table 7.3)

Hardware description:
Includes external digital modem, $10 \times 7 \times 1.5$ inches, external power supply. Also has RJ-45 connector for ISDN U termination, one RJ-11 analog port for analog voice/facsimile equipment, DB-9 connector for serial cable. Five LEDs indicate power, test, D- and B-channel status.

Software configuration interface:
The Windows (GUI)–based Configuration Dialog Box provides menus for configuration, testing (tools), and online help. DOS-based install also available. GUI configuration menu requires entry of switch type, telephone numbers, and SPIDs. Check box enables/disables multilink. AT modem commands must be entered separately if any other nondefault configuration parameters are needed; for example, enter ATS84=0 to enable CHAP (PAP is default). Other parameters configurable only via modem commands include B-channel data rate (56 or 64), dynamic bandwidth alloca-

tion, B-channel protocol (quick select, async-sync PPP, or V.120), V.120 frame type/size, and multilink parameters. Windows 95 wizards can add the modem and configure a dial script, using 3Com drivers included on the DOS/Windows Install diskette.

Documentation:

The 3Com/Impact ISDN External Digital Modem User Guide describes both Macintosh and DOS/Windows 3.1 installation, configuration, and troubleshooting. The appendices provide an AT modem command set overview, register descriptions, values, result codes, and several alternatives for obtaining technical support (bulletin board, Web site, CompuServe Ask3Com e-mail support, automated fax support, and the obligatory human help desk support). Quick Start Instructions provide abbreviated configuration instructions and ISDN line configuration recommendations. A separate win95.txt file provides instructions for configuration via Windows 95, and a separate readme.txt file documents recent release features (including CHAP support,

Table 7.3   Test details: 3Com Impact ISDN digital modem.

Features	Support	Comments
ISDN BRI with integrated S/T/U	✔	RJ-45 connector
Analog port	✔	RJ-11 connector
Telephony API		
Integrated analog modem	✔	Available, but not on model tested
PPP support	✔	Async-to-synch conversion of PPP; also supports V.120
Multilink support		
Compression		
Software supplied	✔	Configuration utility diagnostic, Zmodem application, plus Microsoft Internet Explorer
Diagnostic capabilities	✔	Configuration utility has one diagnostic test (call number or receive call)
Accessories	✔	One RJ-45 to RJ-11 cable for ISDN access (supplied)
Additional drivers supported		TurboCom/2 advanced serial port drive for MS-DOS/Windows 3.x

not described elsewhere). A TurboComm/2 User's Guide and software are also included for DOS/Windows 3.1.

Diagnostics and monitoring:
Configuration Dialog Box includes a Tool button that invokes a diagnostics menu that supports firmware download, configuration save/reload, test call originate/receive, and display of control messages during test calls. Dialog Box main menu provides constant display of layer 1 status, SPID status, and TEI values. However, the Dialog Box cannot be active when dialer application uses the modem to place calls. Instructions also cover using Windows 95 modem diagnostic tools.

Usability for target environment:
Suitable for residential and small office use.

Kudos and/or complaints:
When default settings are appropriate, this box is incredibly simple to install and configure. Requiring the user to interpret and enter Hayes modem commands for nondefault configuration is somewhat unfriendly but is at least well documented. Windows 95 instructions are plug and play and require no prior knowledge of Windows 95 itself. Inability to run the Dialog Box during dialer scripts makes it difficult to diagnose CHAP/multilink negotiation problems.

ZyXel Elite 2864I

Model tested:
NetCommander ISDN, ISA, Integrated NT-1 for PC

Other models:
None available

Estimated price:
Suggested list price $699. Street price approximately $499.

System requirements:
MS Windows 95 capable PC, fast Intel 486 or Pentium processor, recommend 8 MB RAM

OS requirements:
> MS Windows 95 using the Windows 95 drivers, MS-DOS/Windows 3.x, IBM AS400/RS6000, Novell

WINSOCK stacks:
> Microsoft TCP/IP, MS-DOS/Windows 3.x TCP/IP stacks and dialers

Test environment(s):
> Aptiva P150 PC, Windows 95, Microsoft TCP/IP stack, Aptiva 486/66 PC, MS-DOS/MS Windows 3.11, OnNet 2.0, and PCTCP 1.x TCP/IP stacks (see Table 7.4)

Hardware description:
> An external digital modem, external power supply, RJ-11 analog port for analog voice/facsimile equipment, and parallel port. LEDs for link status, both B channels, transmit/receive, and analog (V.34) signals, voice and fax indicators. Data/Voice and Originate/Receive push buttons on front.

Table 7.4   Test details: ZyXel Elite 2864I.

Features	Support	Comments
ISDN BRI with integrated S/T/U	✔	RJ-45 connector
Analog port	✔	RJ-11 connector
Telephony API	✔	CAPI
Integrated analog modem	✔	Facsimile and data at V.34/V.42 bis
PPP support	✔	Also supports V.120, V.110, X.75 and proprietary bonding rate adaption protocols
Multilink support		Standards-based multilink
Compression	✔	
Diagnostic capabilities	✔	ISDN protocol analyzer available via terminal emulation to modem
Software supplied		
Accessories	✔	One RJ-45 cable for ISDN access (supplied), one RJ-11 cable for analog device, one shielded RS-232 cable
Additional drivers supported	✔	Variety of drivers for different rate adaption protocols

Software configuration interface:
None provided. User accesses modem using VT100 terminal emulation and configures modem using extended AT command set.

Documentation:
User's Manual and ISDN User's Manual provided. These contain a wealth of information that is challenging for an advanced user and completely overwhelming to a novice. We found the documentation to be insufficient to install this modem successfully.

Diagnostics and monitoring:
ISDN D channel and B channel protocol analyzer can be enabled through terminal emulation. When enabled, the contents of the maintenance buffer can be viewed through terminal emulation. AT commands can be used to examine all registers, attempt calls, modify configurations. Full-featured but too complicated for a novice user.

Usability for target environment:
Suitable for residential use if documentation were simplified and some type of setup/install script was provided. The modem is actually quite simple to configure.

Kudos and/or complaints:
Documentation attends to minutiae, but fails to provide novice users with what turns out to be a simple setup procedure (complaint). Remarkably full-featured modem (kudo).

Network Termination Devices (NT1s)

This section describes stand-alone NT1s. The network termination 1000 (NT1) device provides the connection between the telephone company ISDN jack in your wall and the ISDN terminal adapter (TA) device, which in turn connects to your computer. As you may have already seen in the previous sections, many TAs have built-in NT1 devices. This is popular in the United States, where the consumer must usually purchase an NT1. In Europe, the NT1 is considered part of the telephone company's equipment; therefore, all European TAs are sold without NT1s.

The following listing and brief discussion of NT1s are provided primarily for those of you who want an external device for your ISDN TA device(s) and possibly for your analog phones (that is, if the NT1 has a POTS jack). External NT1s may be powered by UPSs with battery backups to keep your telephone service up and running for up to eight hours during AC power outages. They also allow you to keep your phones and fax equipment turned on continuously without keeping your computer on.

As this section was written, the list prices for NT1s ranged between $200 and $350, but some sales prices were as low as $175. These prices should continue to fall in the United States, following increased usage from individuals installing ISDN lines in their homes and businesses.

Since the NT1 has been exclusively a business item until recently, little sales literature or other consumer information is available for most of the models listed in the following. They have been treated more like "black box" devices than feature-filled consumer items by virtually every manufacturer (except for IBM; IBM has added a considerable number of features to its 7845 NT1E for those of you who want more than a plain NT1).

Your best bet will be to call around immediately before you purchase an NT1 to make sure you're getting the latest model with the desired features at the best price. A list of NT1 manufacturers and vendors is included in an appendix to this book.

ADTRAN ISDN Network Termination (NT1 ACE)

ADTRAN NT1s support the ANSI 2B1Q line coding and multiple switch vendors including AT&T, NEC, Northern Telecom, and Siemens.

NT1 ACE

This small, plastic, stand-alone unit is appropriate for desktop use. It can be powered by external power supplies such as the ISDN PS2 or the NT1 power supply kit.

ISDN PS2 Power Supply

This unit is designed to complement the NT1 ACE; the PS2 provides up to 12 watts to the NT1 ACE and terminal equipment. It provides 9.5 seconds of reserve power to terminal equipment to bridge AC power interruptions.

NT1 Power Supply Kit

The power supply kit is a low-cost alternative power supply for the NT1 ACE. The kit includes a basic unregulated wall-mount power supply (at 10 watts), a T adapter, and an RJ-11 cable that links power to the NT1.

Alpha Telecom, Inc. UT620
ISDN NT1 Network Termination Device

The UT620 is an affordable ($225) and compact ISDN network termination (NT1) device that provides both an ISDN telephone and a terminal adapter port for access to the ISDN network. The UT620 NT1 device is designed to conform to the ANSI T1.601 (1992), T1.605 (1992), and ITU/CCITT I.430 standards and to industry standard 2B1Q line code for the U-interface. The UT620 is easy to install as a desktop or wall-mounted unit for the office environment.

Features/Specifications

- network U interface
- line: two-wire, full duplex
- data rate: 144 Kbps available to customer
- line code: 2b1Q per T1.601 (1992)
- O/P amplitude: 2.5 V, zero to peak
- connector: one RJ-45 or one RJ-11

- automatic ANSI (American National Standards Institute) maintenance functions
- terminal S/T interface
- line: four-wire, full duplex
- data rate: 144 Kbps available to customer
- line code: AMI, 100 percent duty cycle
- conforms to ANSI T1.605 (1991) TX source impedance, RX impedance, receive sensitivity
- connectors: two RJ-45
- supports point-to-point and point-to-multipoint
- DIP switch
- S/T interface termination resistance
- S/T bus timing mode
- PS2 power selection
- stand-alone desktop
- wall mount
- rack mount
- $1.3 \times 3.93 \times 5.7$ inches
- 0.97 pound
- two-year warranty

AT&T NT1 L-230 Network Terminating Unit

AT&T has added an additional network terminating unit to its NT1 product line. Called the in-line NT1 L-230, the new unit is smaller and lower in cost than previous models. The shirt pocket–sized unit can be attached under a desk to save space. The new terminating unit features LED status indicators and provides multipoint data connections. It has a manufacturer's suggested retail price of $230.

IBM 7845 Network Terminator Extended (NT1)

The IBM 7845 ISDN Network Terminator Extended is a programmable, stand-alone device that allows a personal computer or a workstation equipped for basic rate ISDN and standard analog telephone lines to share a single digital phone line into the home or office. The Network Terminator (NT) Extended provides the connection between the telephone company jack and the ISDN TA. It will also connect standard analog telephone equipment to the ISDN network over the same ISDN basic rate service. This allows customers to replace their existing analog telephone service with one of the ISDN B channels while continuing to use their existing phone equipment.

The analog telephone function of the NT Extended offers several key custom calling features similar to those offered by the telephone companies as options with regular telephone service.

Features

- speed dialing
- redial of last number dialed
- repetitive redialing of the last busy number
- return of the last incoming call
- call hold, call retrieve
- call waiting
- call blocking
- three- or six-way conferencing
- a rechargeable battery, included with the NT Extended, to provide backup power to the analog phone service should a temporary power outage occur

For more information on the IBM 7845 NT Extended, refer to IBM's Hardware Announcement 194-252, dated July 26, 1994.

Motorola: NT1D

Network termination 1 (NT1) unit providing interface between ISDN network and ISDN terminal equipment in both point-to-point and multipoint configurations.

Specifications

- line rate: 192 Kbps
- line interface: 8-pin modular (RJ-45); U interface, ANSI T1.601-1992
- maximum length: 18,000 feet on 26-gauge wire

- customer interface: 8-pin modular (RJ-45); S/T interface, ANSI T1.601-1991
- size: 6 (w) × 5 (h) × 1.5 (d) inches; weight 2.5 pounds
- power: 120 V AC; 5 watts
- supplied: wall-mount transformer; RJ-11c to RJ-45 cable (6 ft) for U interface
- Motorola NT1-D, $225 list
- order number 6457503600010 network termination 1 device

Summary

The list of ISDN modems is impressive, but it can also be confusing. Their veritable plethora of features—that most of us will never use—look good in theory, but will they help us to "get the job done"? Some of them undoubtedly will help, but others may not.

The bottom line on these devices it to check your requirements carefully against the list of features and the price of the ISDN modems. If you're not careful, you'll spend more for a slower digital modem device with a lot of features you don't really need than you would if you purchased an ISDN adapter card. But if you want simplicity and ease of installation, you're looking in the right place when considering an external ISDN modem with a built-in NT1.

The list of NT1s is short but contains known producers of quality products. Check the extra features and give one a try if you're in the market for a stand-alone NT1. The IBM 7845 appears to have the most features but may also have the highest price. However, you can probably find it for less than $300, and that makes it only about $100 more than the lowest priced NT1.

A final note: You may be happier with your entire ISDN system if you get an external NT1 even if you get an internal adapter card, because you won't have to keep your computer running to use your ISDN phone number, either via an ISDN phone or your analog phone plugged into the POTS jack on the NT1.

8

Ethernet ISDN Bridges and Routers

What Are Ethernet ISDN Bridges and Routers?

Bridges and routers are both network devices that pass local area network (LAN) packets of information from one network node or machine to another. They differ in that bridges pass along LAN packets without looking at the network addresses in the packets, whereas routers pass the packets to the proper network address (or to other routers it believes are closer to that address). In the simplest sense, bridges merely link two network devices, but routers distribute the information they receive more intelligently.

Routing functionality is key to advanced functions that are frequently important to larger business users. Simple Network Management

Protocol (SNMP), security protocols, call management, and TCP/IP traffic management are some of the functions necessary for successful telecommuting, Internet access, and business-to-business networking applications for multiple users at the same location.

Both bridges and routers connect to an existing network, most commonly Ethernet (but support many other topologies, including token ring, ARCnet, and FDDI). This section provides information on several currently available Ethernet bridges and routers that include ISDN capabilities. Bridges and routers are higher priced and more complex than either ISDN adapter cards or ISDN modems, but as we explained in earlier chapters, allow many PCs to share ISDN access.

ISDN-capable Ethernet bridges and routers, although the most versatile and powerful of the ISDN devices discussed in this book, are designed more for small-business and remote office connectivity use than for individuals seeking to connect to the Internet via an ISDN line or to make a few phone calls with an analog phone plugged into the POTS jack of the ISDN device. For pointers to the World Wide Web (WWW) pages for each of the manufacturers (and much more detailed information on each device), we suggest you check out Dan Kegel's ISDN WWW site at http://alumni.caltech.edu/~dank/ isdn/ or that you contact these manufacturers directly, using the information in the book's appendices. The following information is listed by manufacturer. Please note also that the lowest priced ISDN bridge is about $1000.

When to Bridge? When to Route?

Bridging can offer a practical alternative when IP address conservation is important and additional subnetting for remote locations is undesirable. Bridging is useful where enterprise topology and administrative concerns are best met by having remote and central locations operate as if they were a single LAN and where protocols other than IP (especially nonroutable protocols like NetBEUI or DLC) are to be used between locations.

Connections to the Internet are typically routed. An Internet service provider (ISP) assigns an organization one or more class C IP network numbers or, more commonly, a small piece or a "splinter" of a class C IP network number, depending on the organization's needs. The only routing decision an ISDN remote router is required to perform in single-LAN configurations such as these is whether or not it should forward packets addressed to destinations other than those on the same LAN across the ISDN interface to the ISP.

If more than one LAN is to be supported at a remote location, then whether it's necessary to use routing or bridging at the remote site requires additional consideration. IP routing at a remote site will be strongly influenced by the methods used to assign IP network numbers and addresses. Where a remote site is provided with several class C network numbers, that site can use Routing Information Protocol (RIP) version one routing or static routing. But if a remote site is provided with a single class C address (or a splinter of a class C address suitable for further subnetting) and it is to be divided into multiple LAN subnets, then RIP version one cannot be used, because it does not support classless addressing or variable-length subnet masks (VLSMs). In such cases, RIP version two, Open Shortest Path First (OSPF), or proprietary routing protocols, such as Cisco EIGRP (Enhanced Interior Gateway Routing Protocol), must be considered. For most remote sites, static routing is typically an expedient and manageable alternative, because the number of routes a remote location must know and select from is small (typically one default route across the ISDN basic rate interface and routes to the individual LAN subnets at the remote location) and routing table changes are infrequent.

You can use this rationale to help you decide whether bridging or routing is necessary for your configuration. Fortunately, many ISDN devices that route can also bridge (and it's rare to find such devices that can bridge but can't route).

Comparative Analysis

Table 8.1 provides a summary comparison of the products tested. Please note the following:

Price:
     Approximate retail price for unit with IP software only. Sometimes, units tested were more expensive.

Minimum criteria:
     ✔, the unit met all minimum criteria

Footprint:
     S(mall), M(edium), L(arge) when compared with other units

Power supply:
     I(nternal) or E(xternal)

Configuration:
     Overall ease of configuration via command line (1 = easy, 2 = moderate, 3 = difficult)

Diagnostic usability:
     Overall support for problem diagnosis (1 = easy, 2 = moderate, 3 = difficult)

Documentation audience:
     Target audience for product documentation: U(ser) or A(dministrator)

Documentation quality:
     Overall quality (usability, accuracy, completeness) of documentation (1 = good, 2 = fair, 3 = poor)

Support:
     Quality of support services received during analysis (1 = good, 2 = fair, 3 = poor)

Additional features:
     ✔, unit supports the feature (may require additional software); see detailed report

—, feature is available but was not tested for this unit; see detailed report

Compression:
✔, unit operates with using Stac or VJ compression
P , unit supports Lempel-Ziv-Welsh (LZW) or proprietary compression only

Multilink support:
✔, unit operates using standard multilink
P, unit supports proprietary multilink only

GUI config. utility:
C, unit is supplied with an additional graphical user interface (GUI) Windows configuration utility
M, unit can be configured by a separate network management product sold by this vendor

Additional ports:
A(pple Local Talk), D(TE async/sync), C(onsole/Modem for Dial Access), and H(ublet)

Table 8.1   Comparison of ISDN bridges and routers.

	Price	Minimum criteria	Footprint	Power Supply	Configuration Ease-of-use	Diagnostic Usability	Documentation Audience	Documentation Quality	Quality of Support	Compression	Multilink Support	Classless Routing	Extended Diagnostics	IPX Routing	Other Protocol Routing	Tunneling (foo in IP)	Multicast Routing Support	GUI Config. Utility
		Subjective Evaluations								**Additional Features**								
Small Office/Home Office (SOHO) Only																		
ACC Congo	$900	✔	S	E	1	1	U	3	1	P	✔		✔	✔				—
Farallon Netopia	$1299		L	I	1	3	U	1	1		✔			✔	✔			
Livingston PortMaster	$1195	✔	M	I	3	2	A	2	1	✔	—		✔	✔				—

continued

Table 8.1   Continued

	Price	Minimum criteria	Footprint	Power Supply	Configuration Ease-of-use	Diagnostic Usability	Documentation Audience	Documentation Quality	Quality of Support	Compression	Multilink Support	Classless Routing	Extended Diagnostics	IPX Routing	Other Protocol Routing	Tunneling (foo in IP)	Multicast Routing Support	GUI Config. Utility
Subjective Evaluations										**Additional Features**								
SOHO/Remote Office/Branch Office (ROBO)																		
Cisco 1004	$1595	✔	S	E	3	1	A	2	1	✔	P	✔	✔	✔	✔	✔	✔	
Proteon Globetrotter	$995	✔	S	E	1	1	A	2	1	✔	✔	✔	✔	✔	✔		✔	M

Cisco 1004

Cisco 1004 is a remote access router and bridge, equipped with one ISDN basic rate U-interface, one console port, and one Ethernet port (10BaseT connector). Unit evaluated was operating Cisco IOS 11.1 in 4.0 MB dynamic random-access memory (DRAM) and 2.0 MB Flash. Unit measures 8.0 × 8.0 × 1.5 inches with external power supply. Power supply has cord on both ends. Includes an internal PCMCIA (Personal Computer Memory Card International Association) slot for software upgrades. Metal case, no on/off switch. Front panel status lights for power, system integrity, B channel 1 and 2, separate LEDs for LAN transmit, receive, collision, and link status.

Target environment:
    SOHO, ROBO

Estimated price:
    $995 for unit, add $600 for IP routing image or $1000 for IP, AppleTalk, IPX routing image and 2 MB RAM, or $1200 for IP, AppleTalk, IPX routing image and 4 MB RAM

Configuration:
IOS 10.3(6), includes basic Internet + desktop software (see Table 8.2)

Table 8.2   Configuration details: Cisco 1004

Minimum Criteria	Support	Comments
ISDN BRI with integrated S/T/U	✔	
Ethernet 10BaseT interface	✔	
Variable subnet masking	✔	
Static route support	✔	
PPP/CHAP encapsulation	✔	
IP packet filtering	✔	Input/output filters, multilevel, multiprotocol support
Nominal diagnostic capabilities	✔	PING, traceroute
Telnet remote management	✔	
SNMP agent	✔	IOS 10.3 includes Cisco enterprise ISDN Management Information Base (MIB) support

Additional Features	Support	Comments
PPP compression	✔	STAC or Predictor compression algorithms
Multilink (use two Bs)		Able to raise but unable to maintain second B channel using IOS 11.0.(4)
Dynamic (classless) routing	✔	Interior Gateway Protocol (IGRP), Enhanced IGRP, OSPF, Border Gateway Protocol (BGP4)
Extended diagnostic capabilities	✔	Extensive debug command set provides packet monitoring and trace.
Multiprotocol routing	✔	IPX, AppleTalk
Tunneling	✔	GRE, Multicast Backbone (MBONE)/DVMRP tunnels
Bridging	✔	
IP multicast support	✔	DVMRP, PIM (sparse and dense modes) Core-based trees
Analog port(s)		
Other LAN/WAN interfaces	✔	Console port can be configured as async dial WAN port
Other software packages available		Desktop software package includes AppleTalk, IPX, Clicknet Web configuration utility

Software configuration interface:

Prompt-driven setup program creates initial configuration file. Mostly English command-line interface used to modify configuration file. Context-specific help available by entering "?" at any time. Configuration files can be copied to/from remote host using RCP or TFTP. The command set is consistent (but not identical) across product line. Scrolling status and debug messages displayed to console; inability to pause/suppress debug output to console can be annoying when entering configuration commands.

Documentation:

The *Router Product Command Summary* handbook and online *UniverCD* are aimed at experienced network administrators. *ISDN Application Note and Troubleshooting Guide* (available via anonymous FTP, at ftp://ftp.Cisco.com/shamilto/isdn95.doc) provides excellent configuration file and debug examples. Authorized Cisco user access provides additional documentation, patches, new software releases, etc.

Diagnostics and monitoring:

Extensive multilevel debug capabilities. Must generate IP traffic (e.g., PING) to test BRI. Ability to monitor ISDN events at multiple levels. Remote Telnet and SNMP v1/v2 management support provided, including Cisco proprietary ISDN MIB. Syslog support.

Usability for target environment:

Suitable for single/home office or branch office with traffic load that can be supported by single BRI, or branch office requiring sophisticated routing or multicast support. Network administrators will appreciate extensive debug and management hooks. Command file configuration complexity may intimidate novice ISDN users. Extensive IP routing capabilities desirable for enterprises with large ROBO ambitions and need/desire to use classless or policy-based routing.

Support services:

Toll-free phone technical support. Web access to software upgrades, documentation, and MIBs available to registered Cisco customers.

Availability of additional features:
> IOS version 11.0 supports additional features (e.g., standards-based multilink, EZ setup utility). Asynchronous dial access can be supported by configuring console port. PCMCIA card can be used to load updated Cisco IOS images or configurations.

Kudos and/or complaints:
> The SETUP utility supports skeleton configuration, but additional configuration commands (remote ISDN number, CHAP username and secret) must be entered manually. Initial configuration is easy to perform by following *ISDN Application Note and Troubleshooting Guide*. Availability of debug commands and thorough examples in this *Guide* are indispensable in diagnosing CHAP compatibility problems. LAN routing capabilities exceed those provided by other SOHO products.

Livingston PortMaster Office Router

The Livingston PortMaster Office Router is a remote access router, equipped with one ISDN Basic Rate U-Interface, one manager port, and one Ethernet port (AUI and 10BaseT connectors). Unit evaluated was operating PortMaster version 3.4.2L 28X in 512 KB NVRAM and 1.0 MB RAM. Unit measures 10.0 inches × 8.5 inches × 1.75 inches with metal case, power on/off switch, and internal power supply. RJ-45 serial port for console, can be paired with V.34 modem for remote dial access. The unit has three dip switches (diagnostics boot on/off, boot flash or remote, Ethernet network type), front-panel lights for System (diagnostics, self-test, and power on), Ethernet Link integrity, Ethernet traffic (one LED), NT1 self-test and telco circuit integrity LED, and a separate LED for each B channel.

Target Environment:
> SOHO

Estimated Price:
> $1195

Configuration:
PortMaster Office Router OR-U, single BRI, single Ethernet model (see Table 8.3)

Table 8.3 Configuration details: Livingston PortMaster Office Router

Minimum Criteria	Support	Comments
ISDN BRI with integrated S/T/U	✔	
Ethernet 10BaseT interface	✔	AUI Ethernet port as well as 10BaseT
Variable subnet masking	✔	One netmask per network, not per subnet
Static route support	✔	
PPP/CHAP encapsulation	✔	
IP packet filtering	✔	Input/output filters on source/destination IP addresses, protocol, port, established sessions. Filters can also be used to perform packet traces or to cause a log event.
Nominal diagnostic capabilities	✔	PING and traceroute from router
Telnet remote management	✔	rlogin, PortMaster rlogin, and netdata (TCP clear channel) supported as well as Telnet.
SNMP agent	✔	
Additional Features	**Support**	**Comments**
PPP compression	✔	VJ and STACker
Multilink		
Dynamic (classless) routing		
Extended diagnostic capabilities	✔	Only debug facilities for PPP negotiation and ISDN events are documented.
Multiprotocol routing	✔	IPX RIP
Tunneling		
Bridging		
IP multicast support		
Analog ports		
Other WAN/LAN ports		
Other software packages available		Livingston Office Router Wizard, a Windows 95 GUI application, and PMConsole, a UNIX/Windows-based GUI configuration utility. Other UNIX applets provided for retrieving configuration, supports RADIUS authentication.

Software configuration interface:

Livingston Office Router Wizard is an excellent example of an easy-to-use configuration utility. Other means of configuration include a command-line interface through VT100 terminal emulation, or PMConsole GUI available for UNIX and Windows platforms. Command-line interface has online help, but help commands do not always provide sufficient syntax details. Most aspects of command-line configuration are similar to those of other units tested with same configuration style. PMConsole is useful configuration, remote management utility, more full featured than other GUIs tested.

Documentation:

Hardware Installation Guide, PMConsole for Windows Administrator's Guide, and Configuration Guide for PortMaster Products included with unit. Configuration Guide gives good details about all aspects of PortMaster product configuration, but descriptions do not identify exact command(s) necessary to perform individual tasks, forcing the reader to match descriptions against list of commands provided at back of guide.

Diagnostics and monitoring:

Debug facilities available but poorly documented. (Example: Guide mentions that "Debug 0x55" turns on PPP negotiation, but full list of hexadecimal values and corresponding debugging facilities is not provided. Livingston support offered to send a description of debug facilities when we asked.) Interface and connection statistics available through console.

Usability for target environment:

Appropriate for SOHO environment.

Support services:

Toll-free and toll voice/fax support, e-mail support, and user groups. Marketing staff helpful. Technical support response excellent. Web site contains white papers on filtering, FTP site contains upgrades and new releases.

Availability of additional features:
Supports RADIUS, extensive packet filtering.

Kudos and/or complaints:
Excellent set of configuration and management utilities. No time-out for console login (security concern). Console output of the Location table displays password in clear text (security concern). Internal power supply and NT1 (kudo).

Farallon Netopia Internet Router

The Farallon Netopia is a remote access router equipped with one ISDN basic rate U-interface, one AUI Ethernet port, and two Ether-Wave 10BaseT connectors, which can be used in daisy chain configurations instead of a hub. The unit we evaluated had a molded plastic case and measured 2.5 inches by 12.5 inches by 9 inches. The Netopia has an On-Off switch, and 8-pin DIN Console connector, on LocalTalk/PhoneTalk connector, and LEDs for Ethernet (receive and link status for each EtherWave port, Transmit and Collision LEDs, and LEDs for the ISDN D, B1, and B2 channels.

Target environment:
SOHO

Estimated price:
Netopia 440 ($1699), model 630 ($1299 five-user IP only, no Apple-Talk/LocalTalk, KIP), model 640 (630 with unlimited IP, $1599)

Configuration:
Netopia 440 (see Table 8.4)

Software configuration interface:
Easy-setup is a simple and straightforward menu-driven interface. DHCP server support is attractive for installation at novice user sites. Attractive set of ISDN connection scheduling options (day of week, time of day, call duration, and called party).

Table 8.4   Configuration details: Farallon Netopia Internet Router.

Minimum Criteria	Support	Comments
ISDN BRI with integrated S/T/U	✔	Integral NT1 (U interface)
Ethernet 10BaseT interface	✔	Two EtherWave and one AUI
Variable subnet masking	✔	
Static route support	✔	
PPP/CHAP encapsulation	✔	
IP packet filtering	✔	Input/output filters on source and destination address, address mask, protocol, and port.
Nominal diagnostic capabilities		ISDN switch loopback test, dial "connection" utility, no PING or traceroute support from unit.
Telnet remote management	✔	
SNMP agent	✔	Diskette supplied with formatted and compiled Internet Engineering Task Force (IETF) and Farallon enterprises MIBs

Additional Features	Support	Comments
PPP compression	✔	VJ and STACker
Multilink (use two Bs)	✔	Not tested
Dynamic (classless) routing		
Extended diagnostic capabilities		LAN/WAN and (ISDN) event histories. PPP and WAN event statistics (counters), ISDN and Device Event histories. PPP and WAN trace.
Multiprotocol routing		IPX routing, AppleTalk
Tunneling	✔	IP in AppleTalk (AURP)
Bridging		
IP multicast support		
Analog ports		
Other LAN/WAN interfaces	✔	Two EtherWave (hubless) and one LocalTalk ports
Other software packages available		Units come with Internet Host Software for Mac or Windows, terminal emulation program. Unit acts as address server using DHCP. *Up and running guaranteed!* package includes PCMCIA (modem) card, allows Farallon support direct access to router via analog phone for configuration and management, includes twin-pack Timbuktu Pro. New software supports network address translation.

Documentation:
User guide provides basic description of ISDN and Internet services and explains how to go about ordering ISDN and Internet service. Guide includes worksheets to assist in configuration. Pocket installation guide for client software.

Diagnostics and monitoring:
The limited nature of the diagnostic and monitoring features hampers an otherwise thoughtfully conceived unit. Statistics and event histories can be useful, but unit needs a PING feature.

Usability for target environment:
DHCP support is a nice feature for novice customers. This would be a good unit to install at single-LAN customer sites where no Internet expertise is present.

Support services:
Toll-free voice, fax, and e-mail customer service. Technical support 800 number responded quickly. *Up and running guaranteed!* support provides customers with Netopia technical assistance via PCMCIA-installed modem and guaranteed configuration resolution plus one year of support.

Availability of additional features:
Standard on 430/440: single-client license of Netscape Navigator/ NTS's TCP Pro (WINSOCK)/Telnet/Eudora Lite/Win95 jumpstart (network license), PING. For Macintosh (440) Netscape/ MacTCP/Eudora Lite/Telnet/PING. Router can be configured to act as DHCP server.

Kudos and/or complaints:
No idle time-out for console login (security issue). Extremely limited diagnostics (complaint). User can view AppleTalk routing table but not IP table/ARP cache (complaint). Excellent AppleTalk support (kudo). PCMCIA card for analog modem useful for Farallon dialin (kudo); could be more useful if it could be used to support remote access to ISDN network for roaming employees (complaint). Periodic console screen refresh is distracting (complaint). Excellent support (kudo).

ACC Congo

The ACC Congo Voice Router is a remote access bridge and router (brouter), equipped with one ISDN Basic Rate U Interface, one 10BaseT Ethernet port, and two analog ports. The unit we evaluated was operating software version 8.2.3 in 1.0 MB Flash and 1.0 MB RAM. The unit measures 1.25 × 8.5 × 6.0 inches, has a molded plastic case, on/off switch, small (wall-jack) external power supply, 8-pin DIN console port, 10BaseT and ISDN BRI-U interfaces, two RJ-11 analog ports, front-panel status lights for power, status, ISDN (B1, B2, Mode, Link status), and LAN (transmit/receive, collision, link status).

Target environment:
SOHO

Estimated price:
Congo IP (S/T, requires external NT1) $995
Congo IP (S/T and U) $1195
Congo Voice Router (IP/IPX, unlimited LAN devices) $945
Congo Voice Router (data only, no POTS) $845
Congo Voice Router Personal Edition (four LAN devices, IP only) $645
Congo IP/IPX, add $400 to S/T or S/T and U configurations

Configuration evaluated:
Congo Voice Router (one BRI, One 10BaseT Ethernet) in January 1997

Software configuration interface:
Express ACCess easy configuration provides a question and answer method of configuring the unit that is simple and complete. Even multilink (dynamic bandwidth allocation) worked using the default (standards) multilink selection. Only additional configuration requirement if not running RIP on unit is to add a static route; if running RIP, unit is operational with no additional configuration.

Web Wizard Configuration Tool for the Congo and Congo Voice Router ACC provides a browser-based configuration tool

Table 8.5   Configuration details: ACC Congo

Minimum Criteria	Support	Comments
ISDN BRI with integrated S/T/U	✔	Unit evaluated required external NT1.
Ethernet 10BaseT interface	✔	
Variable subnet masking	✔	
Static route support	✔	
PPP/CHAP encapsulation	✔	
IP packet filtering	✔	Filters can be used to prioritize, restrict, or discard incoming or outbound IP packets according to source destination IP addresses and UDP/TCP ports or ranges of ports.
Nominal diagnostic capabilities	✔	Ping
Telnet remote management	✔	Telnet server only (cannot initiate telnet from router)
SNMP agent	✔	MIB-II and Enterprise SNMP MIB supports Traps, GETS, and SETs

Additional Features	Support	Comments
PPP compression		Only proprietary algorithm supported
Multilink (ability to use 2 Bs)	✔	
Dynamic (classless) routing		
Extended diagnostic capabilities	✔	Syslog messages, statistics via console/telnet commands, syslog support.
Multiprotocol routing	✔	IP (RIP) and IPX (RIP and SAP)
Tunneling		
Bridging	✔	
IP multicast support		
Analog ports		Congo model with 2 analog ports available
Other LAN/WAN ports		Yukon model can swap ISDN and Frame Relay cards.
Other software packages available	✔	TFTP and serial (ZMODEM) download of configuration files and system image. ACC Congo units come with Web Wizard Software for Windows 3.x/Windows 95-based PCs. Unit acts as an address server using DHCP, and performs network address translation. Congo units by default look for BOOTP server on Ethernet LAN.

for Windows 3.x and Windows 95-based PCs called the Web Wizard. The Wizard runs on the PC as a combination BOOTP/HTTP server, TFTP client and SNMP manager. From a Web browser such as Mosaic or Netscape Navigator, the user opens a URL to the PC's IP address to access a the Wizard's HTTP server. The BOOTP server of the Wizard automatically provides the Congo with its Ethernet Address. From the Wizard home page, the user can read a mini-tutorial on ISDN, view a step-by-step pictorial description of the hardware installation process, and then configure the Congo. The configuration is downloaded to the unit via TFTP. A guide to troubleshooting and a glossary are also available.

Documentation:

We were provided with Software Version 9.5 documentation (Quick Start and Update Booklet). The Quick Start is very useful for novices. It is a step-by-step introduction to configure the Congo router using Express ACCess interviewer and Web Wizard. The Update Booklet contains an overview of new features, configuration guidelines, and a description of new commands (DHCP, Named IP filters, etc.).

Diagnostics and monitoring:

Extensive SNMP trap messages (event and trace messages, ACC Enterprise specific), similar to UNIX syslog messages, are displayed as ASCII strings to a local console or telnet window and are available for troubleshooting configuration, monitoring remote user access, ISDN and PPP call, and protocol behavior. These can be sent to a logging host as well as displayed on console. Display commands provide useful IP (IPX) and ISDN statistics. Routing, ISDN call, and access tables can also be displayed.

Usability for target environment:

Congo is well-suited for SOHO environment. The easy installation, coupled with the presence of two analog ports on the Congo Voice Router, make it a superior unit for the teleworker. The unit is also attractive for small business and remote office; here, Dynamic Host Configuration Protocol (DHCP) is a very useful feature, as the PC client IP addresses need not be configured nor remembered. A default address/address range is supplied to the router and each client can acquire an address. The client that needs to communicate with the router only needs to have DHCP enabled in the PC TCP/IP control panel/configuration.

A second feature, Network Address Folding (NAF), provides a way to fold an entire range of LAN IP address onto a single IP address. As a result, several hosts on the LAN can access the public Internet or enterprise network simultaneously, using only a single, public (or enterprise-unique) IP address.

Support services:

Web site, 1-800 technical support. Knowledgeable and helpful marketing and field staff assisted evaluation process. Prompt engineering response to inquiries regarding operation.

Availability of additional features:

Remote login available to other (ACC) routers. Flexible Ping command.

Kudos and/or complaints:

Telnet and traceroute cannot be initiated from router. Console login has no timeout (security issue). Web Wizard is very easy to use (kudo). Web Wizard settings are presented as one large scrolling page which makes it difficult to capture (complaint). Splitting these settings into groups by using either frames or links would be helpful. All these settings can be saved to a text file (kudo). DHCP support and NAF support on the Congo improve an already impressive product.

Proteon GlobeTrotter 70

The Proteon GlobeTrotter 70 is a remote access router and bridge, equipped with one ISDN Basic Rate U Interface, one manager port and one Ethernet port (10BaseT connector). The unit we evaluated was operating OpenRoute 2.1 [A1] in 2.0 MB DRAM and 1.0 MB Flash. The molded plastic unit measures $7.25 \times 6.38 \times 1.25$ inches,

Diagnostics and monitoring:

Current configuration of physical ports, interfaces, protocols, destinations, users, SNMP, and general parameters are available through the command interpreter. Traffic and error counters are provided for interfaces and protocols (IP, PPP-LCP, PPP-CHAP/PAP, PPP-IPCP, SNMP, compression protocol, ARP). Routing and ARP tables as well as memory and buffer allocation information are also provided. ISDN calls in progress are monitored for duration of call. Accounting statistics are available from the command line. The Event Logging System process can be configured to have logging messages displayed at the router console (Telnet window). Events that can be monitored include data transmission and reception.

Usability for target environment:

Two levels of online help make the GlobeTrotter Setup Utility a particularly friendly configuration management system for the SOHO environment. The GT72 supports features such as IPX routing, Multilink, and enhanced diagnostics, which also make it suitable for the ROBO environment.

Support services:

Toll voice support, e-mail support, and user groups. Web site contains information on bridging, IP, ARP and IPX, AppleTalk Phase 2, and SNMP. It also contains detailed configuration and the Event Logging System Guide. FTP site contains drivers, documentation, software fixes, etc.

Availability of additional features:

GT 72 provides IPX, Appletalk 2 routing and bridging.

Kudos and/or complaints:

The setup utility and QuickConfig are easy to use and understand (kudo). The option to export the configuration created using setup over the LAN is not available until the unit had already been enabled for IP and write privileges are enabled for SNMP from the local terminal (complaint). Help is available for the command-line interface and the command interpreter provides access to an extensive set of monitoring and diagnostics features (kudo). Like other command interpreters, this form of interface may be challenging for an inexperienced end user. The software guide or CD-ROM is required if you really want to take advantage of the command interpreter.

Summary

If you already have an Ethernet card in your computer and you understand your network reasonably well, one of the ISDN bridges and routers listed in this chapter will undoubtedly give you the best ISDN connection possible. Keep in mind that each of these products has a list of features and specifications that are too complex for all but network-aware persons to fathom. This is but a sample of the products available. The best advice to you is to do it yourself only if you're highly knowledgeable about your network hardware and software, or you are working from a remote location for a business that has a knowledgeable network administrator who will either physically help you at your location or at least remotely configure your bridge or router when you get it attached to your network card.

Check Dan Kegel's ISDN WWW site at http://alumni.caltech.edu/~dank/isdn/ for the WWW pages of each manufacturer or contact the manufacturers directly via the information in the appendices for the latest products and prices before you order.

9

ISDN Software

An Overview of ISDN Software Requirements

All of the ISDN hardware devices discussed in this book come with their own installation software or a physical method of setting the configuration via Dual In-line Pin (DIP) switches or telephone keypad commands. The software discussed in this chapter includes those additional programs you may need to get your chosen ISDN device to work with your computer system (configuration utilities and network driver software), to help you make ISDN voice phone calls (telephony software), and to connect to your Internet service provider (ISP). The amount of additional software you will need to implement your ISDN system depends on the type of hardware you decide upon.

What Is "Configurability"? What Constitutes "Ease of Use"?

The ISDN products included in this book address home, small business, and branch office remote access needs. Users who have little or no prior knowledge of the intricacies associated with installing, operating, and maintaining a local area network (LAN) and associated network operating system represent a considerable portion of this marketplace. Specifically, many users may at most be familiar with the user aspects of Internet applications such as e-mail clients and Web browsers, or NOS-specific applications that facilitate file and printer sharing, having installed such software on a PC at home or in the office. Route configuration, addressing and subnetting, and ISDN configuration can be burdensome and intimidating experiences.

ISPs and enterprises deploying a remote office ISDN solution can adopt several strategies when addressing the issue of remote office equipment installation, configuration, and daily administration:

1. Train subscribers and employees on specific equipment and empower them with the knowledge required to configure and maintain their remote LAN site.
2. Have user or field staff physically install equipment at a site and connect an analog modem to the administrative or console port of the equipment so that configuration and facilities verification can be performed remotely by operations personnel.
3. Centralize configuration and control by preconfiguring equipment prior to site installation. The user or field staff is then responsible for on-site installation, host configuration, and ISDN facilities verification.

Each of these practices has its share of operational difficulties, and each has been deployed with varying degrees of success. Ultimately, the users must take some responsibility for the daily operation and maintenance of the equipment, as problems with ISDN facilities, LAN cabling, and host and router/bridge software are inevitable.

Configuration management systems are elements critical to the successful deployment of ISDN products. Choosing equipment that offers a configuration management system that is easy to use and that provides useful and meaningful diagnostic facilities can help an organization in many ways. If the system is easy to use, end users and subscribers are less likely to be intimidated by the system and may be more inclined to attempt to correct or at least isolate a problem before reporting it to the help desk and daily operational staff. If the system has useful diagnostic capabilities, both end users and daily operational staff will have access to the kinds of information that are required to isolate the problem to a particular facility or equipment or configuration and correct it.

We consider ease of use and the presence of diagnostics equally important aspects of remote access products. Ease of use prompts attempts to bring the aspect of "plug and play" to such products, but it is our experience that configuration of ISDN products, particularly ISDN routers, remains an error-prone activity for the following reasons:

- Routing, bridging, and ISDN technology are relatively new to a considerable part of the marketplace addressed by this equipment. Aspects of configuration that are seemingly simple to an engineer or advanced Internet user—for example, the dotted decimal notation for Internet addressing and binary and hexadecimal numbers required to interpret a subnet mask—are not intuitive and contribute to erroneous data entry.
- Idiosyncrasies remain among ISDN switches and software, and configuration of ISDN switching type, service profile IDs (SPIDs), and directory numbers can be tricky.
- Connectors and cabling are quirky. ISDN, administrative console, 10BaseT Ethernet "straight-through," and Ethernet "crossover" cables may all have RJ-45 terminations, and most users cannot distinguish among them (even in situations in which an ISDN provider uses RJ-11 terminations, these may be confused with RJ-11 terminations for analog ports on a router or bridge).
- Information required for proper configuration can, in many cases, be immediately diagnosed by a configuration management system as incorrect in syntax (e.g., an

Internet protocol [IP] address with a dotted decimal value in excess of 255), but it is not possible for the system in certain cases to know that a value is semantically incorrect (e.g., an invalid ISDN SPID).

For example, a user can enter a syntactically correct IP address, but it may already be assigned to another device on the LAN, or it may be an inappropriate address for that LAN. Incorrectly typed subnet masks can be even tougher to diagnose!

For these and many similar reasons, we believe diagnostic capabilities are critically important features of remote access products. Following are some of the diagnostic capabilities that prove to be most useful:

- ISDN event monitoring/logging: Notifications such as terminal endpoint identification failure, loss of or no data link signal, and SPID registration failure are useful in determining whether the ISDN basic rate interface (BRI) is correctly connected and configured (either by the user or the telephone company).
- Wide area network (WAN) link level monitoring: Error counters for frames transmitted and received over the ISDN BRI, including bad cyclic redundancy check (CRC) and frame discards (short frames, long frames, underruns), are useful in determining whether the signal quality provided by the telephone company is suitable for data. Such errors can also assist a user in isolating the cause of unusually poor performance.
- Ethernet LAN monitoring: Transmit/receive counters and error counters (bad checksums, collisions, short frames, long frames) are useful in determining whether some component of the LAN environment (a connector, a cable, a hub port, a transceiver/NIC) is not working or connected properly.
- Traffic utilization monitors: The ability to determine how "busy" an ISDN interface is can be helpful in determining whether additional channels or compression should be

added or whether ISDN no longer satisfies the needs of a remote LAN environment. Ethernet utilization information is helpful in determining whether LAN segmentation, microsegmentation, or faster LAN technology is required to meet the needs of a remote LAN environment.

- PING client: PING uses Internet Control Message Protocol (ICMP) echo request/reply packets to test IP level connectivity between hosts and routers. PING can be used to test on-demand ISDN circuits by causing your ISDN TA, router, or bridge to place a call. It can also be used to verify IP configurations and routing (especially in the absence of a traceroute facility).

- Trace (traceroute): Traceroute is a utility that sends a sequence of IP packets to a target host or router, eliciting a response from each router along the path to some target host or router. Traceroute uses the IP address from each response to construct the route a packet takes to a network host. Traceroute is useful in determining whether IP routing is correctly configured (specifically, to isolate the system with incorrect routing information or a point in the topology where connectivity has been lost).

- Point-to-Point Protocol (PPP) and higher level real-time packet level monitoring: The ability to view PPP negotiation is helpful in determining whether PPP, LCP, IPCP, and authentication information exchanges are proceeding as expected. For example, remote and access server compatibility issues and incorrectly configured PAP/ CHAP passwords can be isolated in this manner.

- Higher level packet level monitoring (e.g., IP, TCP, routing protocols): This is helpful in situations in which links are functioning correctly but other aspects of internetworking are not.

In the following section we describe the configuration and management features of some of the products that are currently available. We provide an overview of the types of configuration management systems offered and describe the factors considered during evaluation.

Configuration Management Systems

ISDN products offer four basic types of configuration interfaces:

1. For external devices (digital modems, bridges, and routers), a menu- and forms-driven configuration system, accessible via a direct console (management) port via a VT100 terminal emulation program (e.g., Windows TERMINAL, Win95 HyperTerminal, ZTerm for the Macintosh), or over an Ethernet using the Telnet application.
2. For external devices, a command-line interpreter, accessible via a direct console (management) port or via the Telnet application.
3. For both internal and external products, a graphical user interface (GUI) that may be operated from a PC or UNIX workstation under a windowing system such as Windows 95, Windows 3.x, or an X Windows System (or derivative).
4. For external routers and bridges, a HyperText Markup Language (HTML)–based browser interface, accessible via a PC running a Web client application and a TCP/IP protocol stack on the same LAN as the router/bridge.

Each of these configuration utilities has advantages and disadvantages.

Menu-Driven Configuration Utilities

The menu- and forms-driven configuration utilities available primarily for external ISDN devices present the user with one or (more frequently) a series of menu screens. The screens display configuration parameters and the user is expected to either type a parameter value or select one from a list of values.

Menu-driven configuration utilities are typically easy to read and fairly intuitive. However, terminal emulation programs must be configured with the appropriate window and session parameters or the menus are not presented properly (a command-line interpreter is more forgiving in this respect). Navigation of screen-based management systems can be awkward; if arrow keys are not supported (or not available on the user's keyboard), tab keys and return keys must be used to traverse through menu fields. On some systems, control-character sequences must be used to navigate between screens. Either method can be awkward, depending on what the user is accustomed to using.

Some menu hierarchies are neither intuitive nor consistent, and it may be necessary to traverse several menus before one arrives at the menu required to configure a single parameter. To see the results of multiple commands—for example, to display a statistics window (e.g., ISDN call history) or to display the IP routing table— the user typically must refresh a forms-based screen.

It is difficult, if not impossible, in some cases to display both, or to "scroll" between the two forms-based screens on the terminal window. Some vendors use special characters to frame and format areas of the screen. These may be difficult to print, depending on screen and printer fonts available on a PC. Proponents of menu-driven configuration systems will note that a user does not have to know or "peck and seek" the correct command syntax for what can be a large set of commands and that the learning curve for navigation is faster than for a command-line interface.

Some configuration management systems use numbered menus, whereas others invoke submenus by alphabetic commands. Menu systems that use numeric values require fewer keystrokes to navigate from menu to menu, but the user must remember the association between the number and the configuration task to be performed. Several vendors offer a hybrid of alphabetic menu- and command-driven configurations. Menus are used for configuration, but alphabetic commands may be entered to navigate from screen to screen. In some cases, commands may be abbreviated and concatenated to expedite navigation.

For example, a configuration system may have a parent screen (Configure) from which subsequent screens for more specific options may be chosen (i.e., configure IP, configure ISDN parameters, and so on); these menus in turn have options (e.g., configure IP routing, configure IP filters). On certain configuration systems, users can "jump" to a specific submenu using the first two or three letters of each screen name (i.e., of the form "CO IP RO").

Command-Line Interpreters (CLIs)

CLIs use textual messages as input to a configuration system. Commands typically consist of one or more *keywords*; for many commands, a set of one or more parameter values must be provided. For example, to add a static route to an IP destination, one must typically enter the IP destination, the associated subnet mask, the next-hop address, and a routing metric. A representative command line syntax of this form is

```
add ip route entry ip-address next-hop ip-metric
```

If 10.0.0.0 is reachable via a next-hop address of 128.128.50.5 and it is three hops away, the command entered following this syntax would be

```
add ip route entry 10.0.0.0 255.0.0.0 128.128.50.5 3
```

Many command-line interpreters offer context-sensitive or other forms of online syntax help to assist the user in constructing a command or correcting a command syntax error.

CLIs are popular among network administrators because they often provide access to the very advanced configuration and monitoring capabilities of a router or bridge. In our evaluation, we observed that systems with CLIs offered the broadest range of real-time packet monitoring and access to system and event logging facilities and utilities (such information is displayed or scrolled on a console or Telnet window in response to a *display, show* command, or in the case of real-time monitoring, it may be displayed as the event occurs).

Although such features are valuable to network administrators, they may be quite intimidating to a home or small office user. CLIs are, in our opinion, overly challenging for initial configuration. Many vendors seem to have arrived at the same conclusion. To make initial configuration less intimidating, several vendors participating in this evaluation offer *interviewers*, a simple question-and-answer facility that is invoked when an ISDN product is first configured. The interviewers are designed to collect sufficient information from the user to build a minimum working configuration. Interviewers do not require the user to understand the command-line syntax unless the user wishes to construct a more advanced configuration.

Configuration Management Applications

Some vendors provide a configuration management application that may be operated from a PC or UNIX workstation under a windowing system. To use such applications, the PC must be connected to either the serial or console port of the router to be configured or the same Ethernet segment as the router to be configured (in this scenario, the ISDN product must be connected to the Ethernet and ISDN service).

In most instances, the configuration management application allows installation or download of the configuration to the ISDN device. Configuration of an ISDN router across the Ethernet requires that the router software and the PC application have some means of addressing each other. Sometimes, vendors require that the router be configured with a valid IP address through a console interface. Other vendors have been more creative, preconfiguring the router with a default IP address (e.g., 1.1.1.1), or they use media access control (MAC) addressing or protocols that can be operated using MAC or IP multicast or broadcast addresses.

The windows-based applications offer "point and click" methods for configuring routers and bridges and in many cases provide hypertext links to help files. These applications collect configuration information input by the user through windows, icons, menus, and forms.

Like interviewers, these applications gather sufficient information from the user to build a working configuration. Once the configuration information is entered, the application establishes communication with the ISDN device, downloads the configuration, and for external devices reboots the router, bridge, or modem. In some cases, the application will reestablish communication with the device and "dry run" the configuration by attempting to place a call to the configured remote destination; if a failure occurs, the application will identify failure reasons and assist the user in reconfiguration.

In addition to providing an initial configuration facility, some windows-based utilities offer access to many of the diagnostic features otherwise available through a command-line interpreter; diagnostic information is typically displayed in a subwindow of the main management application.

Browser-Based GUI Configuration Managers

Some vendors have begun offering a *browser-based graphical user interface* tool based on HTML, a language on which the World Wide Web is constructed. Users install a utility and access this through their Web browser. Tools of this form collect configuration information input by the user through radio buttons and HTML forms, then download the configuration to the router using TFTP, BOOTP, Dynamic Host Configuration Protocol (DHCP), or some other (proprietary) means. Typically, the router must be connected to the same Ethernet segment as the PC on which the browser is operating.

This form of configuration management offers the user a point-and-click method of configuring routers and bridges using a GUI, with which many users will already be familiar. These tools are very attractive for home and small office applications, in which familiarity with Web browsers may exist but routing and bridging expertise may be limited or nonexistent. Certain vendors provide additional Web pages to provide background information, definitions, information about ordering ISDN service, and forms to request diagnostic information. Like Windows-based utilities, some browser management tools offer access to diagnostic features otherwise available through a command-line interpreter.

Internet Protocol and Connection Software

The primary Internet protocol software you will need for your PC running DOS or Windows is the TCP/IP stack. The core TCP/IP protocols are Transmission Control Protocol (TCP), Internet Protocol (IP), User Datagram Protocol (UDP), Address Resolution Protocol (ARP), and Internet Control Message Protocol (ICMP). This suite of Internet protocols provides a set of standards for how your computer will communicate with the Internet. Various TCP/IP stacks are available as shareware or freeware or are included in commercial Internet packages. Your ISDN device will need to be compatible with your TCP/IP stack to connect with the Internet.

As noted in Chapter 6, Windows 95 and Windows NT 4.0 are shipped by Microsoft with a built-in TCP/IP stack, and typically do not require any additional software (other than perhaps ISDN drivers) for use with ISDN products. Windows 3.1 and Windows for Workgroups require an add-on stack. The most common of these are Trumpet, Microsoft (MS) TCP/IP-32, and NetManage's TCP/IP. All of these run under Windows 3.1, WfW (Windows for Workgroups 3.11), or Windows NT 3.5. The Windows Sockets application programming interface (API) was developed to provide a standard application interface to different vendors' protocol implementations. The official name for the dynamic-link library (DLL) used for Windows Sockets 1.1 support is WINSOCK.DLL. All of the TCP/IP stacks just mentioned support the Windows Sockets 1.1 API, allowing common Windows Internet applications, such as Netscape, Mosaic, Chameleon, FreeAgent, and Eudora, to run.

If you choose an ISDN adapter card or digital modem, you will probably also need PPP software to create a dial-in connection to an ISDN ISP. Although there is little difference between SLIP and PPP from the user's standpoint, it seems that the ISDN hardware manufacturers have provided only PPP software, for both the remote (user) end and the server (ISP) end. Most, but not all, of the ISDN hardware products discussed in this book have PPP software included in the package, or the product is PPP compatible. Those that don't undoubtedly will have it available soon or they will be out of the market. Most are going toward MPP (Multiple Point-to-Point Protocol) in the future, so check for this feature in the specs of your chosen ISDN device. SLIP is also included with

Windows 95 as an option that must be installed through Add/Remove programs.

ISDN Modem Software

If you choose an ISDN modem to replace your current analog modem for your Internet connection, you shouldn't need to change any of your software. ISDN modems respond to the Hayes AT command set, so you should be up and running very quickly.

ISDN PC Adapter Card Software

Choosing a PC ISDN adapter card will create the need for network driver software to link the card with your computer's operating system and interface program (Windows, for example). This gets you into the various layers of operating system programs, interface programs, network drivers, and LAN packet drivers. Some of the drivers you will see on PCs are NDIS (Network Device Interface Specification), ODI (Open Datalink Interface), TCP/IP, NetBEUI, and NetBIOS. Your chosen ISDN hardware manufacturer should provide the appropriate drivers if the device needs drivers other than those that are normally included with DOS, Windows, Windows 95, or OS/2 and Warp.

You may still need to obtain a different TCP/IP "stack" if your system doesn't like the one you're currently using. For example, if you're currently using Trumpet Winsock with WfW and SLIP to connect to the Internet, you may need to switch to Microsoft's TCP/IP-32 instead of Trumpet because the NDIS drivers may not be able to connect between Trumpet and the ISDN card. This isn't all that painful, since MS TCP/IP-32 is free from Microsoft. But all of this acronymspeak does give you an idea of how complicated the software is for an ISDN network adapter card, and how much simpler life can be with a Windows 95 plug-and-play device.

ISDN Ethernet Bridge or Router Software

The final level is the ISDN bridge or router that connects to your existing Ethernet plug, assuming you have an Ethernet card in your computer with a network up and running. You will have driver questions to answer with your Ethernet card that are similar to those of the network adapter cards. However, if you're not actually installing another network card, you shouldn't have to install any additional network driver software to get your computer to communicate with the bridge/router.

Still, this isn't as easy to do as it might look here, because you must reconfigure your network to recognize the additional device. If you're on a Novell or other "serious" network, you'll need the help of your network administrator to do this properly, or without causing trouble for something else on the network. You will also have to install TCP/IP software to let your ISDN bridge/router dial and connect to your ISP.

Shareware and Freeware

The few current shareware programs available are primarily TCP/IP packet drivers and router software. Much of this is being produced by people in Germany for the European MS-DOS/MS-Windows and UNIX markets. Some has been tested on products available in the United States. These packages are discussed later in this chapter.

Most of the shareware and freeware Internet application software has a built-in PPP client. These include Trumpet Winsock and MS TCP/IP-32. You may need what is called a "shim" to put between Trumpet and your device's internal software to initiate the ISDN connection. Shim software is usually freeware from someone who has figured out the solution and is willing to give it away. Of course it isn't "supported," so you're on your own using it. Shims generally slow down the transmission and aren't the optimum way to go. But sometimes a shim is the only way to get things working.

Commercial Software

Other than the software provided with your ISDN device, most PC-based ISDN systems need only a TCP/IP stack to connect to an ISDN ISP. Microsoft is giving its MS TCP/IP-32 away free for WfW

3.11 users. Windows 95 comes with its own TCP/IP ISDN software and drivers. OS/2 Warp also provides its own TCP/IP stack and Internet software. All of these have adequate documentation for installation and start-up. It is helpful if you can get your ISP to help you with some of the settings that may be specific for their ISDN server equipment (generally an ISDN router).

ISDN Shareware/Free Software

ISDI: An MS-DOS NDIS-Driver for ISDN Access

ISDI is a (real mode) NDIS-MAC driver for IP-Routing or remote Ethernet bridging over ISDN on Windows-based PCs. ISDI communicates with the ISDN card using the ISDN API 1.1 specification (a standard defined by German ISDN card manufacturers and the German Telekom). Because of this, ISDI is completely hardware independent and has been tested successfully with many active or passive ISDN cards.

ISDI was developed for Internet access over ISDN from WfW 3.11 and MS TCP/IP-32. ISDI has successfully been tested with Win95 beta releases. ISDI is also known to work with other NDIS-based TCP/IP packages for DOS and Windows, such as Chameleon.

ISDI was written for use with ISDN BRI PC cards and has been tested with the Teles.S0, one of the cheapest ISDN cards in Germany; NCP cards; AVM A1 and B1; Creatix S0/16; Diehl Diva; SCOM and S0Tec; Loewe ISCOM C100; MIRO; mbp Solis; NCP P16 and A; and Dr. Neuhaus NICCY 1000 PC.

ISDI supports the LAPB, Frame Relay, PPP, SLIP, and Cisco-HDLC protocols for communication with ISDN routers or servers. ISDI can communicate with the following commercial systems: Ascend Routers, Biodata ISDN Router, Cisco Routers, Conet S2M Router, INS/CLS Banzai ISDN Router, netCS ISDN Router, RzK SLIP Bridge, SGI Indy ISDN 1.0, Spyder Routers, SunLink ISDN 1.0, and SunLink ISDN 1.0.2.

Some protocols conserve the protocol type over point-to-point lines (multi-LAPB, Frame Relay, Cisco-HDLC). These protocols are able to do multiprotocol routing. For PPP, only IP support is implemented at the network configuration layer.

The current version of ISDI supports two independent active connections at a time. Alternatively, a connection can use both B channels for load sharing. ISDI can be loaded more than once, if more than two simultaneous connections to different sites are desired. Load sharing can be configured as static or dynamic (bandwidth on demand). Dynamic load sharing can be used concurrently with a second independent connection. Load sharing over two channels is implemented using simple round-robin scheduling, because IP doesn't require the original packet sequence.

ISDI shareware by Herbert Hanewinkel is available from ftp.biochem. mpg.dein/pc/isdn.

ISPA: MS-DOS Packet Driver for TCP/IP over ISDN

ISPA is an Ethernet-type (class=1) packet driver for IP-routing or remote Ethernet bridging over ISDN. ISPA communicates with the ISDN card using the ISDN API 1.1 specification (a standard defined by German ISDN card manufacturers and the German Telekom). Because of this, ISPA is completely hardware independent and has been tested successfully with many active or passive ISDN cards.

ISPA was initially developed for use with PCROUTE as a cheap Ethernet-ISDN router. However, more and more, it is used to connect a stand-alone system to the Internet using ISDN. ISPA has been tested successfully with a wide range of commercial, shareware, and public domain TCP/IP packages, such as FTP PCTCP, Sun PC-NFS, Novell's LAN WorkPlace and PDETHER, WATTCP-based IP programs, NCSA and CU-Telnet/ftp, UMN gopher and popmail, Trumpet Winsock, and XFS.

ISPA supports a large set of protocols for communication with other vendors' ISDN routers or servers. Among these protocols are LAPB, Frame Relay, PPP, SLIP, and Cisco-HDLC.

ISPA can communicate with at least the following commercial systems: Ascend Routers, Biodata ISDN Router, Cisco Routers, Conet S2M Router, INS/CLS Banzai ISDN Router, netCS ISDN Router, RzK SLIP Bridge, SGI Indy ISDN 1.0, Spyder Routers, SunLink ISDN 1.0, and SunLink ISDN 1.0.2.

ISPA was written for use with ISDN BRI PC cards and has been tested with the Teles.S0, one of the cheapest ISDN cards in Germany, NCP cards, AVM A1 and B1, Creatix S0/16, Diehl Diva, SCOM and S0Tec, Loewe ISCOM C100, MIRO, mbp Solis, NCP P16 and A, and Dr. Neuhaus NICCY 1000 PC.

The current version of ISPA supports two independent active connections at a time. Alternatively, a connection can use both B channels for load sharing. ISPA can be loaded more than once, if more than two simultaneous connections to different sites are desired. Load sharing can be configured as static or dynamic (bandwidth on demand). Dynamic load sharing can be used concurrently with a second independent connection.

Load sharing over two channels is implemented using simple round-robin scheduling, because IP doesn't require the original packet sequence. It's completely hardware independent. It works the same way as Cisco, in that it implements load sharing over to X.21 interfaces. We have tested ISPA with a Cisco Router and two Philips TAs. Load sharing will not double the performance this way.

ISDA shareware by Herbert Hanewinkel is available from ftp.biochem.mpg.dein/pc/isdn.

INAR 1.00, the InterNet Access Router

INAR is a fast, easy-to-configure freeware package that makes a dedicated IP router out of any 80x86 PC running MS-DOS. To communicate with the network interface hardware, it uses packet drivers that comply with FTP Software, Inc.'s packet driver specifications (Rev. 1.09). If you have more than one computer at your site and want to connect your LAN segment to the Internet and/or other LAN/WAN segments, this package is for you!

INAR's most prominent features include the following:

- up to eight interfaces
- router component written in assembler, so it is very fast
- propagates routing information via Routing Information Protocol (RIP) (including "poisoned reverse")
- selective default route propagation
- interfaces and static routes can be marked as hidden (to RIP) and unreachable
- transient static routes to provide boot-time default routing until RIP takes over
- supports static routes with variable subnet masks in the same IP net to ensure economic use of precious Internet IP numbers
- allows source routes to enforce local routing policies
- source IP address (reverse route) checking to enhance network security
- proxy Address Resolution Protocol (ARP) (for all known routes)
- global broadcast forwarding between subnets of the same IP net
- can send status messages to a UNIX syslog daemon
- BOOTP forwarding
- ISDN and point-to-point interfaces do not need an extra IP address
- multiple transmission protocols and dial-in/dial-out links on the same ISDN interface
- a single noncryptic, easy-to-understand configuration file for all software components
- comes with packet drivers for the most common Ethernet cards as well as with drivers for ISDN and SLIP/CSLIP
- includes sample config files for the most common cases

INAR 1.00 is available via anonymous FTP from ftp.fu-berlin.de (160.45.10.6) in a self-extracting LHA file named /pc/msdos/ network/inar/inar-100.exe.

Commercial ISDN Software

The following commercial products, in addition to Windows 95, provide ISDN support.

Microsoft TCP/IP for Windows for Workgroups

Microsoft's TCP/IP for Windows for Workgroups includes the NDIS 2 protocol, to support connecting computers running Windows for Workgroups or computers running Windows for Workgroups to Windows NT and Windows NT Advanced Server. Microsoft TCP/IP for Windows for Workgroups does not include any TCP/IP utilities; however, support for Windows Sockets is provided, which allows any Windows Sockets–compatible TCP/IP utilities (including terminal emulators and file transfer programs) to be used.

The only supported interface for Microsoft TCP/IP-32 for Windows for Workgroups version 3.11 is Windows Sockets version 1.1. Support for previous versions of the Sockets specification is not provided. In addition, there is no support provided for Raw Sockets (SOCK_RAW), DOS Sockets, or vendor-specific socket implementations.

The Windows Sockets application programming interface (API) was developed to provide a standard application interface to different vendors' protocol implementations. The official name for the dynamic-link library (DLL) used for Windows Sockets 1.1 support is WINSOCK.DLL. Previous DLL versions that were distributed with Microsoft LAN Manager (for example, WIN_SOCK.DLL and WSOCKETS.DLL) are not supported by Microsoft TCP/IP-32. For a Windows Sockets application to function with Microsoft TCP/IP-32, the application must support Windows Sockets version 1.1 (WINSOCK.DLL).

Microsoft TCP/IP-32 for Windows for Workgroups, Versions 3.11 and 3.11a

Microsoft TCP/IP-32 for Windows for Workgroups is an NDIS 3 protocol that includes the following:

- Core TCP/IP protocols, including Transmission Control Protocol (TCP), Internet Protocol (IP), User Datagram Protocol (UDP), Address Resolution Protocol (ARP), and Internet Control Message Protocol (ICMP). This suite of Internet protocols provides a set of standards for how computers communicate and how networks are interconnected.
- Support for application interfaces, including Windows Sockets for network programming and NetBIOS for establishing logical names and sessions on the network.
- Basic TCP/IP connectivity applications, including ftp and Telnet. These utilities allow Windows for Workgroups users to interact with and use resources on non-Microsoft hosts, such as UNIX workstations.
- TCP/IP diagnostic tools, including arp, ipconfig, nbtstat, netstat, PING, route, and tracert. These utilities can be used to detect and resolve TCP/IP networking problems.
- Support for DHCP automatic configuration.
- Industry standard Windows Sockets 1.1 support for third-party and public domain TCP/IP applications such as NCSA Mosaic.

This version of TCP/IP does not:

- include server-side applications for telnet and ftp
- include LPR and Gopher
- support an MS-DOS–based interface (you can use Windows Sockets instead)
- support SLIP and PPP to dial in to the Internet
- support NFS (although it will probably be provided by third-party vendors)

Microsoft TCP/IP-32 for Windows for Workgroups is available on the Windows NT Server CD and can be downloaded from ftp:// ftp.microsoft.com/peropsys/windows/public/tcpip.

> *Note: For more information on the specific bugs fixed in Microsoft TCP/IP-32 version 3.11a, query in the Microsoft Knowledge Base on the Qxxxxxx number that precedes the following titles:*
>
> *Q121317: TCP/IP-32 Version 3.11 Does Not Include Terminal Font*
> *Q120051: DNS Reverse Name Resolution Requests Are Incorrect*
> *Q120052: NBT Query Can Hang Computer or Drop Back to MS-DOS*
> *Q122293: LMHOSTS Lookup Can Cause Intermittent System Pauses*
> *Q119575: TCP/IP-32 Winsock Stops FD_READ Notification*
> *Q119918: Winsock: Accept() Sockets Are Unexpectedly Aborted*

NetManage Chameleon MS-Windows ISDN TCP/IP software

Internet Chameleon is a software package for Windows PCs that allows any user to navigate the Internet easily. The Instant Internet application in Internet Chameleon automatically signs up a user for a new Internet user account and connects the user to the Internet within five minutes. The application suite includes all the tools you need for exploring the vast resources of the Internet, including document browsing (Gopher, WebSurfer), file transfer (FTP client and server), personal communication (e-mail, NEWTNews), searching (Archie), terminal emulation (Telnet), diagnostics (PING, NEWT), and user information lookup (Finger, WhoIs). A consistent GUI makes each of these applications easy to use. Internet Chameleon is designed for mobile, home, or remote users who want dial-up access to the Internet through a modem.

Internet Chameleon is a package intended for dial-up use only, using either the SLIP, CSLIP, PPP, or ISDN protocol. NetManage's flagship product, Chameleon TCP/IP for Windows, has the additional capability of running TCP/IP over Ethernet, Token Ring, or

FDDI LANs, creating your organization's own TCP/IP network. It also includes TN3270 and TN5250 emulation, Visual Script Editor, and Visual Script Player applications, a front end to PROFS/Office Vision electronic mail, LPR/LPD support for printer sharing, and a Domain Name Server. ChameleonNFS includes all the functionality of Chameleon, plus a complete implementation of NFS client and server.

Windows Sockets is an industry standard that specifies how network applications communicate with a protocol stack, typically TCP/IP. The current revision level of Windows Sockets is 1.1. The NetManage TCP/IP protocol stack supports Windows Sockets 1.1.

ChameleonNFS 4.5's new features and applications include the following:

- over 40 applications
- six integrated networking suites
- FTP firewall support
- VT320 and Wyse emulation
- host connectivity/terminal emulation: TN3270 and TN5250
- script recorder
- auto scaling fonts
- toolbar
- WinHLLAPI interface
- Telnet
- VT320 support
- SCO ANSI
- script recorder
- Wyse 50/60 emulation
- direct serial port access
- FTP and e-mail interface
- Session Manager: manage multiple sessions from a single application
- e-mail: draft, template, sent mail folders, spell checker, return receipts on message delivery or opening, folder list integrated in main window, expanded editor, multiple address books

- new applications: Sound Player, Graphics Viewer, Calendar/Scheduler, Electronic Post It Notes
- NEWTnews: threads, offline reading
- WebSurfer WWW client
- FTP
- multiple firewall support
- macros/scripting with recorder for automated transfers
- NFS
- support for membership in multiple groups
- UNIX umask support
- NEWTScan: Scanner server
- desktop management
- name/address resolver
- NIS lookup
- PC network time: synchronizes PC clock with central network clock
- Rcommands (rcp, rsh)
- UNIX-to-Windows and Windows-to-UNIX file conversion utility
- NEWTShooter: instant data exchange between applications
- TCP/IP Protocol Stack
- NEWT-TCP/IP Stack
- dial-on-demand with automatic disconnect
- multiple default gateways
- InetD
- DHCP client
- NIS client
- OEMSETUP for ODI, NDIS, and NFS
- SNMP support for future automatic upgrades and software distribution
- WinSNMP support
- automatic installation on any Windows sockets stack
- interactive log window for manual logon and bypassing of scripting
- Windows interface for building scripts
- 100 modem setup strings

System requirements are:

- *software:*
  - Windows 3.1, running enhanced mode
  - 256 color video driver recommended for use with WebSurfer
- *hardware:*
  - 386 CPU or later
  - RAM: 4 MB
  - disk space: 7 MB
  - 1.44 MB disk drive
  - modem (14.4 KB baud or above recommended)

Combinet EVERYWARE Connection Manager

Connection Manager is a Windows-based application that provides for centralized call processing and distribution, as well as the configuration, management, authentication, and accounting for Combinet's EVERYWARE ISDN products, now sold by Cisco. With Connection Manager, an enterprise network supports more remote users per enterprise access unit, significantly reducing hardware investment. Connection Manager also provides centralized security and call logging.

Connection Manager benefits include the following:

- on-demand networking, resulting in minimal telephone charges
- compatible with standards-based ISDN BRI, Switched-56 telephone services, and Ethernet LANs
- simple installation and maintenance
- interoperable with all former Combinet (now sold by Cisco) EVERYWARE products
- computer, network operating system, and application transparency
- significant enterprise network cost savings
- centrally administered authentication and callback security
- call logging

- Combinet products include a limited one-year hardware warranty and free software updates for one year

Features include:

- Microsoft Windows user interface
- access units at enterprise are referenced by name
- enterprise unit management
- quick, transparent response time relative to ISDN/Switched-56 call setup time
- IP protocol access unit control messages can operate through routers
- selectable priorities of allocation pool access units
- online status of all access units at the enterprise
- security
- password required to access Connection Manager console
- centralized administration of call information

There are extensive options for caller information:

- call event logging
- records easily and quickly accessible through database
- call event record
- alerts
- specifications
- enterprise access units supported
- 1000 units in allocation pool
- ISDN BRI: EVERYWARE 200, 400
- Remote access units supported
- ISDN BRI: all
- Switched-56: all
- Security
- 10,000 user ID information records

Caller information options include:

- password
- remote unit Ethernet address
- ringback number

Requirements are:

- dedicated 486 33 MHz minimum (486 50 MHz recommended), 8 MB RAM, 100 MB free disk space
- Ethernet card: NDIS-compliant driver
- Microsoft Windows 3.1 or later, DOS 5.1 or later

Recommended hardware:

- remote sites: any Combinet access unit (ISDN or Switched-56) with EVERYWARE Software Release 2.3
- Enterprise: Combinet EVERYWARE 200 or 400 access unit with EVERYWARE Software Release 2.3 or later

Windows NT

Microsoft TCP/IP for Microsoft Windows NT version 4.0

Microsoft's TCP/IP for Microsoft Windows NT version 4.0 includes the following features:

- A complete set of core TCP/IP protocols, including Transmission Control Protocol (TCP), Internet Protocol (IP), User Datagram Protocol (UDP), Address Resolution Protocol (ARP), and Internet Control Message Protocol (ICMP). This suite of Internet protocols provides a set of standards for how computers communicate and how networks are interconnected.
- Support is also provided for Point-to-Point Protocol and the Point-to-Point Tunneling Protocol, both primarily Internet access (PPP usually links single machines to the Internet or another IP network; PPTP is used to connect multiple networks across the Internet, or another IP network, with encryption used to keep such traffic private).
- Support for application interfaces, including Windows Sockets for network programming, remote procedure call (RPC) for communicating between systems, and

NetBIOS for establishing logical names and sessions on the network.

- Basic TCP/IP connectivity applications, including finger, ftp, lpr, rcp (client only), rexec (client only), rsh (client only), Telnet (client only), and tftp. These utilities allow Windows NT users to interact with and use resources on non-Microsoft hosts, such as UNIX workstations.

- TCP/IP diagnostic tools, including arp, hostname, ipconfig, lpq, nbtstat, netstat, PING, route, and tracert. These utilities can be used to detect and resolve TCP/IP networking problems.

- Services and related administrative tools, including the FTP Server service for transferring files between remote computers, Windows Internet Name Service (WINS) for dynamically registering and querying computer names on an internetwork, Dynamic Host Configuration Protocol (DHCP) service for automatically configuring TCP/IP on Windows NT computers, TCP/IP printing for accessing printers connected to a UNIX workstation or connected directly to the network through TCP/IP, and the Internet Information Server (IIS, plus a host of related Web site elements like Front Page 97 and Index Server) for intranet or Internet Web services.

- Simple Network Management Protocol (SNMP) agent. This component allows a Windows NT computer to be administered remotely using management tools such as SunNet Manager or HP OpenView. SNMP can also be used to monitor and manage DHCP and WINS.

- The client software for simple network protocols, including Character Generator, Daytime, Discard, Echo, and Quote of the Day. These protocols allow a Windows NT computer to respond to requests from other systems that support these protocols.

Macintosh

PlanetPPP for Macintosh

The PlanetPPP software offers high-speed Internet and AppleTalk Connectivity over PPP for Macintosh users. PlanetPPP can be installed and configured in less than five minutes. The Installer places necessary drivers into the System's Extension folder and creates the PlanetPPP folder on your hard drive. You start the PlanetPPP application by double clicking on it, configure it for use with your Planet-ISDN board, and enter appropriate security and dialing information in the settings document. Click "Connect," and in a matter of seconds (literally) you are connected with your ISDN capable Internet service provider at 64 Kbps (56 Kbps for individuals without Clear Channel 64 Kbps access). PlanetPPP works seamlessly with MacTCP. Hence, once the PPP link is established and authorization approved, you are able to use any IP-based application (Mosaic, Eudora, Fetch, Netscape, Telnet, etc.).

PlanetPPP features:

- single B-channel synchronous HDLC PPP connections using the Planet-ISDN board
- PAP and CHAP security options
- multiple settings documents for connections to various hosts
- both IPCP (Internet) and ATCP (AppleTalk) protocols
- idle time out
- connection status window
- specification of Maximum Transmit Unit (MTU) size
- link statistics
- address and protocol compression

VMS

DEC VAX ISDN Software V1.1

The VAX ISDN software controls the ISDN signaling channel (D) and therefore controls the establishment of the two bearer channel (B) connections over the ISDN to send calls to and receive calls from separate destinations. As each channel is independently managed, two different protocols can be simultaneously run on both channels. The DIV32 driver is included in the VAX ISDN software distribution kit. Any DECnet node running ULTRIX, VMS, or MS-DOS has the ability to use the ISDN circuit once the connection has been established.

There are two software versions: VAX ISDN software V1.1 and VAX ISDN Access software (optional). The VAX ISDN software runs on the Q-bus MicroVAX hosting the DEC ISDN controller 100. DECnet VAX and VAX P.S.I. layered network software, as well as customer-developed protocols (HDLC, SDLC, DDCMP oriented), are supported.

Public ISDN networks and switches currently supported include:

United Kingdom	British Telecom ISDN 2
France	Numeris—VN2 Network
Germany	Deutsche Bundespost—1TR6 Network
Japan	INS-NET-V2 Nippon T&T Corp.
Switzerland	Tested: SwissNet1 - 1TR6 Access
United States	AT&T 5ESS-5E4 Switches

Note: Version 1.1 enables you to take advantage of the semi-permanent mode of the ISDN German network.

The following processors are supported:

MicroVAX II 3300/3400/3500/3600/3800/3900
VAXstation II 3200/3500/3620/3540
VAXserver 3300/3400/3500/3600/3602/3800/3900
VAX 4000 model 300

Distribution media, tape: nine-track/1600 bpi magtape (PE), TK50 streaming tape.

Suggested Hardware

The DEC ISDN controller 100 (DIV32) provides Digital systems with Basic Rate Access to the ISDN. It is a single-board, synchronous communication controller that can be fitted directly into a Q-bus MicroVAX system enclosure. Each module supports one ISDN Basic Rate Access line (two high-performance bearer channels and the signaling channel, 2B + D). The board has a 68000 microprocessor and 128 KB of onboard memory to downline load the level 1 software.

Prerequisite Software

Host: VMS operating system V5.2-1
VMS Tailoring optional software: VAX P.S.I. V4.3,
    DECnet VAX V5.2

VAX ISDN software order codes

Option	Order Code
Software license	QL-VZ9A*-**
Software media	QA-VZ9A*-**
Software documentation	QA-VZ9AA-GZ
Software product services	QT-VZ9A*-**

Ordering Information

Refer to the following for further information on supported processors and services: Software Product Description 31.23.01.

Summary

Although a variety of software products are available for dealing with ISDN devices and connections, most individual users will require only a TCP/IP stack or packet driver and a PPP communication program. These may be obtained separately or within a package such as NetManage's Chameleon. The most important aspect of these software packages that you need to remember is that they must be compatible with your ISDN device and your ISP's ISDN hardware and software. First check with your ISP to determine what software you will need to be compatible with theirs. Next, check the software provided with your chosen ISDN device to ensure its compatibility. If you need additional software, such as a TCP/IP stack, ask your ISP for assistance in choosing the correct package for your system.

If you are using a PC with Windows for Workgroups, the MS TCP/IP-32 stack should work with your device. Both Windows 95 and OS/2 Warp contain the appropriate drivers for use with most ISDN devices discussed here.

It's not really as complicated as it appears from the discussions here. Following the step-by-step instructions in later chapters and working closely with your ISP should make installing and configuring your ISDN software as painless as possible.

10

ISDN Telephones and Business Equipment

The primary focus of this book is to provide information about ISDN, for personal or business use by an individual. The previous chapters dealt with low- to moderately priced equipment necessary to connect your computer, any other ISDN device, and, in most cases, an analog (POTS) telephone to your ISDN line. This chapter presents a brief look at some of the other possibilities for ISDN, not only for you as an individual but also for your small office of a few people, computers, phones, faxes, and the like.

Although the idea of replacing your home phone system with ISDN phones is appealing at first thought, after you find out that you don't just attach a few $15 phones to a standard series run cable wire pair and have them work, you'll quickly change your mind. Switching your small office over to ISDN may be more appealing, since business phone rates are generally much higher than residential ones and the higher cost of the ISDN phones isn't out of line with small PBX (private branch exchange) prices. Office wiring is generally easier to change to ISDN compatible, if that's necessary. You'll be able to read more about ISDN phones later in the chapter.

Perhaps you are thinking about the more exotic realms of videoconferencing and wireless or satellite equipment. You'll even find out about this and where to go for more online information in this chapter. The appendices contain the most up-to-date sources of information we could find on these topics. Again, we suggest you jump on the Internet, visit the sites listed in the appendices, and follow their pointers to the latest and greatest products before you make your final decision to purchase any of them.

ISDN Telephones

An ISDN telephone differs only slightly from the digital phones that most businesses use with their PBX systems. However, businesses usually have a communications consultant, or access to someone from the company from which they purchase or lease the equipment, who installs, configures, and maintains their telephone system. An ISDN phone plugged into the S/T jack of your ISDN TA is going to make your system "completely digital," but is it really going to help you do your business better?

It's certainly going to cost you much more for the ISDN phone ($300 and up) than your standard telephone. Most local telephone service providers are still trying to figure out how to make their switches and software work with ISDN phones to provide the various call features that you will probably expect from any business phone or even your home phone. Count on a lot of wasted time and calls to the phone company (via your analog phone) while getting your ISDN phone up and working the way you expect it to work. In the future, when ISDN phones become the norm and their price drops accordingly, you may be more interested in checking them out again.

As if this isn't enough to dissuade you, keep in mind that to get an ISDN phone working, you must plug it into an NT1 network termination. These digital phones can't be daisy chained (serially wired) like your current analog phones. You need to run a cable directly from your NT1 or TA to each ISDN phone. Remember, too, that an ISDN phone is just an S/T device to the NT1 or TA and each S/T device is a separate entity. You can't just pick up a couple of handsets on ISDN phones in separate rooms as you can with your analog phones in your home. You have to treat them like the phone system in your office, where you must initiate a conference call to link any two phones together. This isn't because they have different phone numbers; it's because they are handled differently by their digital switching and routing equipment. Chapters 12 and 13 discuss the problems of wiring houses and office for ISDN usage.

If, after all these caveats and potential gotchas, you're still interested, here are brief descriptions of some of the ISDN phones and phonelike devices currently on the market. For the record, there are real differences between using true ISDN telephones and attaching a conventional POTS phone to an RJ-11 jack on an ISDN router, modem, or adapter. For one thing, true ISDN telephones support all kinds of advanced features (as you'll see later in this chapter) for everything from conference calling to as many as 15 levels of call waiting and all kinds of forwarding and transfer features. For another, ISDN phones offer superior signal and sound quality, just as you'd expect from a 64 KB voice channel (compared with 10 KB for conventional analog voice, including encoding and compression capabilities). Read on to learn more about these feature-laden, but expensive, devices.

AT&T 8520T ISDN Voice-Data Terminal

AT&T's 8520T voice/data terminal is an advanced speakerphone that enables the user to display a personal directory and other information on a seven-line display screen. The terminal includes 20 buttons for instant access to multiple phone lines or calling features.

In addition, 10 "soft keys" may be programmed to help manage a personal directory, to select among eight distinctive ringing patterns, or to activate other features. Dedicated feature buttons simplify such functions as call transfer and redial, and four control keys make it easy to scroll through the 144-entry personal directory.

When connected to a personal computer, the terminal handles data speeds of up to 64 Kbps and can accommodate simultaneous voice and data communications on a single ISDN telephone line. The 8520T may also be programmed to display information on the computer screen to identify incoming calls, alert the user to priority calls, and keep a log of incoming and outgoing calls. The 8520T voice/ data terminal has a manufacturer's suggested retail price of $1010.

AT&T National ISDN-2 Terminals

Two new terminals are designed to take advantage of National ISDN-2 (NI-2) technology, which adds new capabilities to the ISDN network. As NI-2 switching capabilities become available in many areas, the new terminals will equip telephone companies and Centrex administrators to download preprogrammed features to each terminal instead of programming individual telephones on site.

AT&T is offering its NI-2 terminals in 14-button and 35-button models, with such features as full speakerphone, display, menu soft keys for call management, and a message waiting light. The NI-2 terminal will work in existing NI-1 ISDN installations but will be limited to NI-1 capabilities. Likewise, NI-1 terminals will work in NI-2 installations but without the added NI-2 features.

AT&T ExpressRoute Digital Adapter 2000

The ExpressRoute Digital Adapter 2000 connects analog and digital equipment used in home offices, small businesses, and college dormitories to an ISDN line. The adapter's two data ports can connect personal computers or workstations at transmission speeds of up to 64 Kbps. Both data ports support D-channel packet services, or a single port can transmit circuit-switched data. An analog port provides access to ISDN voice services and digital conversion for telephones, group III fax machines, answering machines, and modems.

The adapter is designed to accommodate the telecommuter or home office user without modifying existing residence telephone service. Users benefit from its capability to handle high-quality voice and data communication simultaneously. The adapter's advanced voice features can accommodate multiple incoming calls and support ISDN voice features such as conference calling, call forwarding, and incoming caller identification (ICLID).

The adapter is packaged with a network terminating unit, which serves as the interface between the ISDN line and customer premises equipment. Manufacturer's suggested retail price is $850 for the package and $650 for the adapter alone.

PRI

There are three ways ISDN can be "delivered" from an ISDN-ready digital switch. In the first method, ISDN can be delivered through a direct basic rate interface (BRI) connection from an ISDN switch. Second, one or more BRIs can also be linked to ISDN Centrex service. This arrangement offers several advantages for an individual or company. Since the ISDN switch functions as their switching system, the company does not have to own or maintain a private branch exchange (PBX) or key system. It also offers a low-cost, virtually unlimited growth path. The third method is through a primary rate interface (PRI) connection.

A PRI delivers 23 B channels plus one D channel from the telephone company to a PBX, ISDN PRI router, or other control device, which then distributes the B channels as needed throughout an organization. The configuration of this setup can vary greatly. Users with heavy data traffic might configure the connection through an ISDN router, multiplexer, or controller, rather than a PBX, thereby reducing the chance of congestion through the switch.

Dynamic allocation of B channels in a PRI is possible now. However, for practical purposes, combining multiple channels in a PRI—for large videoconferences, data transfers and the like—is most often programmed into the digital switch serving the location. However, new bandwidth-on-demand controllers have begun to enable network managers to combine larger bandwidths in real time to meet specific needs. They can also monitor quality and traffic on both corporate leased-line and ISDN networks and perform dynamic allocation of B channels to relieve bottlenecks or back up error-prone or damaged lines.

Installing and configuring a PRI adapter are not things an individual usually attempts in do-it-yourself mode. A communications consultant with ISDN experience can usually save you money by letting you continue working to make money while the consultant efficiently installs and configures your ISDN system. Most consultants work closely with your local telephone company to ensure the smoothest possible transition and least downtime for you. If you insist on jumping into it yourself, here are a few PRI devices you should consider.

IBM ISDN Primary Rate Adapter

The ISDN Primary Rate Adapter provides 23 data channels of 64 Kbps, operating simultaneously, and a 64 Kbps signaling channel for communicating over an ISDN Primary Rate Service. Each channel operates full duplex. By providing digital communication over twenty-three 64 Kbps channels, many individual basic rate ISDN channels can be serviced over a single telephone company connection line. This adapter and associated software will operate with both the AT&T 5ESS and Northern Telecom DMS-100. Price: $7995.

Twenty-four 64 Kbps channels over a T-1 communication line are supported. Twenty-three of the channels are B channels for data. The 24th channel is a D channel, which provides signaling and control for the B channels. By providing digital communications on twenty-three 64 Kbps channels, many individual basic rate ISDN terminals can be serviced over a single telephone connection line into the business premises. The basic rate terminals gain access via the public switched telephone network.

A Port Connection Manager is also provided as a part of the included adapter software. The included device driver provides an

NDIS-compatible MAC layer of support. Together, these two allow this product to be used as a wide area communications adapter by the IBM LAN Distance family of products.

The IBM ISDN Primary Rate Adapter, in conjunction with IBM LAN Distance, further enhances the capability of extending the "office LAN" to remote users. Using switched Basic Rate ISDN, or switched 56 Kbps service, remote users can access the corporate LAN as though they were physically connected to the LAN with performance and response time approaching those of an office terminal connected locally to the office LAN.

The minimum system requirements and features are as follows:

- IBM PS/2 models 8595 or 9595, 750 KB random-access memory (RAM) for LAN Distance support, 1.5 MB hard disk space, VGA display monitor, 3.5 inch 1.44 diskette drive.
- Software requirements: The IBM ISDN Primary Rate Adapter support requires IBM OS/2 2.1 or greater and the IBM LAN Distance Connection Server Version 1.1 for applications that will provide remote access to the "office LAN."
- A maximum of three ISDN Adapter cards can be physically placed in the PS/2 model 8595 or 9595. The programs included with the IBM ISDN Primary Rate Adapter can support up to three Adapters.
- Warranty period: one year.

ISDN Systems, Inc.: FX-PRI ISDN/Frame Relay PC Adapter

The FX-PRI is the first adapter for the Windows NT environment with an integrated smart Tl channel service unit (CSU) and the ability to run ISDN-PRI or Frame Relay drivers. This unrivaled flexibility enables today's Frame Relay device to be upgraded to tomorrow's ISDN-PRI device simply by installing a new driver, with no change to the hardware. Or just add additional FX-PRI Adapters, and use your existing hardware platform for both ISDN-PRI and Frame Relay network connections.

With the FX-PRI Adapter, an organization can customize Windows NT–based products for the specific characteristics of their individual connectivity requirements. ISC's FX-PRI is the ideal solution for organizations requiring remote LAN access. Network service and Internet service providers will find that with the FX-PRI they can build very powerful access gateways at a fraction of the cost of devices they currently use.

The FX-PRI can be equipped with ISDN-PRI or Frame Relay drivers for Windows/NT (NDIS 3.0). By utilizing the NDIS 3.0 driver, the FX-PRI converts your NT RAS into a powerful remote LAN access server for remote ISDN and/or Frame Relay users. With the FX-PRI, Windows NT may also be used as a powerful application server.

Platform

- MS Windows NT 3.5 and higher
- ISA/EISA bus

Features

- up to three FX-PRI cards per system
- three levels of congestion control (supports committed information rate [CIR])
- T-1 and F/TI (four-wire) interfaces
- NDIS (National Device Interface Specification) 3.0 drivers
- supports maximum Private Virtual Circuits (PVCs) (1 to 1024)

Hardware

The PC Adapter is designed for the IBM PC-AT bus (ISA and EISA) with:

- onboard Smart T1 CSU (RJ-48)
- Extended Superframe Format (ESF) or Single Frequency (SF)
- B8ZS or Alternate Mark Inversion (AMI)
- FDL (ANSI or ACCUNET)

Interoperability

- Frame Relay: RFC-1490 ensures compatibility with the leading routers.
- ISDN Point-to-Point Protocol (PPP) and multilink PPP ensure compatibility with leading ISPs.

Frame Relay Standards

- Frame Relay based on ANSI T1S1
- full support of Local Management Interface (LMI) and Annex "D"
- protocol encapsulation via RFC-1490

ISDN Standards

- national ISDN-2 and CCITT
- custom AT&T
- custom Network Terminating Interface (NTI)

Protocols

- TCP/IP and IPX routing
- NetBIOS gateway
- 802.3 and 802.5

Primary Rate Incorporated
PRI-ISA48 Dual T1/ISDN Controller

If your application requires access to any T1-based service, Primary Rate Incorporated has both the hardware and software that you need. The PRI-IAS48 Dual T1/ISDN Controller is an industry standard architecture (ISA)–based T1 subsystem for data and/or digital voice communications. It contains an ISA slave interface for T1 to host computer communications with HDLC and DMA hardware to format all combinations of channelized and nonchannelized data for up to 32 full-duplex data streams. It also includes a standard Multi-Vendor Integration Protocol (MVIP) bus interface that provides a multiplexed digital telephony highway for adapter board communication within a personal computer chassis. The board comes with two T1 interfaces and complete onboard signaling and data formatting software.

The PRI-ISA48 allows your system direct access to the power and speed of T1, fractional T1, and primary rate ISDN lines. Its flexible architecture also makes it ideally suited for use in both frame and cell relay environments. The PRI-ISA48 board comes complete with the most extensive software available for any board of its kind.

The Q.931 ISDN software module provides the means to establish, maintain, and terminate network connections across an ISDN between communicating application entities. It provides generic procedures that may be used for the invocation and operation of supplementary services. PRI's Instant ISDN Software Q.931 is capable of controlling both circuit-switched and packet-switched connections. Q.931 provides its services to the upper layers via PRI's Simple Message Interface (SMI). This interface consists of two wraparound queues. One queue (L4L3) provides service requests from the higher layers to Q.931. The second queue (L3L4) provides service indications from the Q.931 to the higher layer. To perform its functions, Q.931 utilizes underlying resources such as PRI's Instant ISDN Software Q.921 to provide network connections.

Instant ISDN Software (LAPD)

The Q.921LAPD software conveys information between the Q.931 entities across the ISDN user-network interface using the D channel. PRI's LAPD includes support for multiple terminal installations at the user-network interface and multiple layer 3 entities. All data link layer messages are transmitted in frames that are delimited by flags. (A flag is a unique bit pattern.) Each frame has a CRC-16, prior to the closing flag, that may be used to detect the occurrence of one or more corrupted data bits. Both flags and CRC-16 are typically generated and interpreted by a hardware device known as an HDLC controller.

Requirements

- your existing satellite equipment
- your existing ISDN equipment
- a satellite space segment with 160 Kbps data rate for 2B + D or 64 Kbps for B + D

Interfaces

- to satellite modem via RS-449 or V.35
- to ISDN network and applications via ISDN basic rate S/T interface

ISDN Test Equipment

Unless you are going into business as an ISDN installer or systems consultant, you will probably not need any serious ISDN test equipment. Most BRI devices (adapter cards, modems, etc.) are supplied with testing software for your PC. This software tests the ISDN device and ISDN line all the way to the phone company's switch. If it finds something wrong, you generally call the ISDN service provider (phone company) and report the problem. Then let them use their expensive test equipment to find the cause of the problem. The following brief description and price of one BRI test device should let you see why you probably won't want one.

The UPA 100 BRI Protocol Analyzer

Until now, ISDN protocol analyzers have been prohibitively priced from $8000 to over $35,000. This has made it difficult to justify the purchase, especially if you just need it occasionally. However, without a protocol analyzer, it is almost impossible to resolve the "finger pointing" that commonly occurs between the service provider and the equipment vendor.

The UPA 100 is a compact unit ($9.5 \times 7.5 \times 1.5$ inches) that connects to the serial port of an IBM PC compatible or Mac computer. It captures the messages passing between the subscriber's equipment and the network, decodes them into plain English, and displays them on the screen and places them in a buffer for later analysis. Circuit-switched and packet-switched decodes of National ISDN, Northern Telecom DMS 100 Custom, and AT&T 5ESS ISDN are supported. At $2495, the UPA 100 may be the lowest cost basic rate analyzer on the market.

Summary

As you can see by this brief overview of ISDN equipment, you'll probably be well served in your home or one-person office by your PC with an ISDN TA and NT1 with an analog phone plugged into it. If you really want to use an ISDN phone with an external NT1 and uninterruptible power supply (UPS), there are several good but expensive ISDN phones available.

If you want to convert a small office with several people to ISDN, your best bet will be to hire a communications consultant to help you with it. You can probably make more money doing whatever you normally do and paying a consultant than you could save by wasting your time trying to do it yourself.

Part III

Getting Started with ISDN

Once you've made your selection of the appropriate ISDN hardware and software for your PC, only then does the real fun begin. Now it's time to get serious! You'll need to arrange to have ISDN service installed, handle the wiring from the phone company's demarcation point at your home or office, and obtain all the necessary cables and equipment. Only then can you get down and dirty and begin the installation process on your PC or network.

We begin this long, arduous, and sometimes painful process with the most basic of all questions: Should you do it yourself, or hire someone else to install ISDN for you? In Chapter 11, we debate the pros and cons of flying solo versus bringing in a professional. The remainder of Part III is devoted to stepping through the ordering and installation processes involved in bringing ISDN to your PC or your network. Even if you don't do it yourself, you'll find these chapters useful and interesting, because they'll help you understand what your expensive hired gun is up to and can point you at some things to request, some things to demand flat out, and others to avoid at all costs!

We continue the process toward working ISDN in Chapter 12, as we review the steps and requirements for a home or small-office stand-alone ISDN installation. Here, we review the elements of ordering an ISDN connection, finding an ISDN-capable service provider, installing and configuring the necessary wiring and termination equipment, and more. In Chapter 13, we cover the same ground from a different perspective, as we lead you through the mechanics of a small-business or remote LAN installation, with the added excitement of integrating ISDN with a LAN.

Chapter 14 proceeds to discuss common ISDN troubleshooting tactics, tips, techniques, and approaches that you might find helpful if and when your ISDN experience hits a snag. Chapter 15 concludes Part III (and the subject matter of the book) with an overview of the most common questions and answers on ISDN subjects, culled from the frequently asked questions (FAQs) lists from several ISDN newsgroups and mailing lists.

Our goal in Part III is to step you through the process of ordering and installing a simple ISDN setup and then cover the basics for troubleshooting your installation and answering the most common questions you're likely to have. We want you to feel comfortable with the process and to understand not just the steps involved, but the perils and pitfalls you're likely to encounter along the way. Let us close this introduction to Part III by wishing you a quick and painless installation or, at least, an all-knowing and infallible source for support when you need it!

11

Making Good ISDN Choices

When it comes to dealing with ISDN, especially configuration and installation issues, there's a fundamental decision you'll need to make: Are you going to do it yourself, or enlist the aid of a real ISDN professional? Most of the contents of this book has been created to help you take either route, by understanding requirements, costs, and equipment well enough to work intelligently with ISDN. In this chapter, we'll tackle your methods for ISDN deployment head-on and provide some input about how to find and work with a consultant, or how to go it alone with a minimum of stress and strain.

To make the correct choices regarding ISDN, you'll need a bit of a refresher on ISDN terms. Just in case you're like the rest of us and can't remember the acronyms, here's a short list of the most important ones you should know (you can also consult the Glossary at the end of this book for any other terms you might not recognize).

The "Short List" of ISDN Acronyms

- BONDing: B channel BONDing uses both B channels for data to obtain 128 Kbps transmission rates in some terminal adapters (TAs). BONDing is also referred to as multilink by Internet folks.
- BRI: Basic rate interface comprising two B channels (bearer channels at 64 Kbps) and one D channel (data channel at 16 Kbps for telephony signaling information and X.25 packet data).
- ISP: Internet service provider.
- POTS: Plain old telephone system. Your current analog telephone system.
- PRI: Primary rate interface comprising 23 B channels and one D channel with the same physical interface as a T1 circuit.
- NT1: Network termination device connected to the ISDN line's U interface and providing one or more S/T jacks for ISDN TAs and sometimes one or more POTS jacks.
- RBOC: Regional Bell Operating Company (e.g., Southwestern Bell, Pacific Bell).
- SLC: Subscriber-loop carrier (computerized substation of phone company for ISDN outside the 3.4 mile range of the central office switch; used instead of a repeater).
- SPID: Service profile identifier number(s).
- TA: Terminal adapter device between the NT1 and your computer.

Do It Yourself or Hire a Consultant?

To decide whether you want to do it yourself or hire an ISDN consultant, you need answer only these three questions:

1. Can you afford to spend a considerable amount of your time talking with your local telephone service provider, selecting and

ordering your ISDN hardware, fiddling with your telephone wiring, installing ISDN computer hardware (NT1 and TA), finding an ISDN Internet service provider, installing and reconfiguring your computer's Internet software, and troubleshooting your ISDN system over the three- to six-week time period between ordering your ISDN installation and completion and testing?

2. Are you comfortable installing hardware in your computer, setting it up, wiring your telephone lines, and installing ISDN drivers and Internet software, all by yourself?

3. Do you have more time to spend setting up your ISDN system than you have money to spend hiring a consultant?

If your answer to all of these is yes, then go for it yourself. Otherwise, find a consultant (or perhaps two or three of them) and get a bid for a turnkey system tailored to your particular circumstances.

Hiring an ISDN Consultant

For many businesses, hiring an ISDN consultant will be the most cost-effective way to acquire ISDN service. This is especially true if you have more than a couple of people and computers in your business and want to take full advantage of ISDN's capabilities.

Before you start calling consultants from the Yellow Pages, you should answer as many of the questions in the next section as you can about your own company and about your desired uses for ISDN. Any consultant worth his or her freight will ask you these questions anyway, so you can save time (and money) by having the answers ready. You will be able to better qualify consultants if you know as much as possible about your own desires and needs prior to interviewing them, anyway.

One very good method to use when searching for professional help is to prepare a written request for proposal (RFP). It should include a list of your needs, as well as the questions you want the consultant to answer prior to hiring him or her. You can use the checklist that follows in the next section to help you prepare your RFP.

Keep in mind that since ISDN is a relatively new technology, you will probably encounter a variety of ISDN consultants. Some will have come from UNIX programming backgrounds, some from tele-communications, some straight out of college, and some from who knows where. Some will try to sell you on a complete ISDN telephony and/or computerized system, whether you need it or not. Some will want you to hire them to produce custom programming for your location, whether you need it or not. Ignore these time- and money-wasting proposals.

Fortunately, some consultants will first propose to study your needs, to provide you with hardware and software alternatives that suit your needs and budget, and only then move on to the next steps. After they're sure you know what you need and how much it costs, they'll proceed to install the chosen system and to help you and your employees learn to use that system. Hire one of these consultants, but only after you check their references thoroughly and get all specifications and costs in writing. Remember, the job you save may be your own!

Checklists of Uses, Hardware, Current Phone System, Etc.

If you've made it this far into this book, you've probably already answered the questions from Chapter 5 and have looked over the information contained in Chapters 6 through 10 that is pertinent to your situation. Having decided that ISDN may be what you want or need, you are now ready for the final test. Test? Who said anything about a TEST?? Don't worry, it's open book with no time limits, and we'll even help you find the answers! In fact, it's more a test of your resolve and your ability to do business, so it's a test you'll definitely want to take!

Ask Yourself:

Which of the following cover your planned uses for your ISDN service?

_____ Home
_____ Office (nonresidence)
_____ Personal
_____ Business
_____ Single user
_____ Multiple users (how many?)
_____ Replace existing analog service
_____ Digital computer connections and additional voice line
_____ ISDN Internet connection for faster access
_____ Use current analog phone(s) with ISDN line
_____ Use ISDN phone(s)
_____ Is the telephone wiring at your location a typical analog system with a parallel circuit of the same two wires throughout the building for a single phone number?
_____ Does your location have an unused pair of telephone wires suitable for ISDN signals for each ISDN BRI you think you will need?

Ask the Phone Company:

_____ Is your location in an ISDN service area?
_____ What is the ISDN installation charge from your ISDN telephone service provider?
_____ What are the monthly charges (basic and usage) for ISDN service?
_____ What exchanges constitute the local calling area for ISDN at your location?
_____ Will your ISDN service be via a repeater?
_____ Will your ISDN service be via an SLC?
_____ Which central office ISDN switch does your service use? (e.g., Siemens, AT&T)
_____ Which protocol does the switch use? (e.g., NI-1 [National ISDN-1], AT&T 5ESS Custom, AT&T G3 PBX, Northern

Telecom DMS-100 Custom, Northern Telecom BCS-34 [PVC-1], or other)

_____ What calling features are available from your ISDN provider? (e.g., electronic key telephone system (EKTS), Call Appearance/Call Handling (CACH))

_____ Does your ISDN provider offer BRI (2B + D) with two SPIDs?

_____ Does your ISDN provider offer voice service on both B channels on the same BRI service with two SPIDs?

Ask the ISDN Software and/or Hardware Vendor:

_____ Does your chosen NT1 device work well with your chosen TA or router or bridge?

_____ Does your chosen NT1 TA, router, or bridge device have no, one, or two POTS jacks?

_____ Does your chosen NT1 TA, router, or bridge device have an internal power supply?

_____ Does your chosen NT1 device have a battery backup?

_____ Does the ISDN TA or router or bridge you are looking to purchase communicate well with the phone company's switch and protocol?

_____ Does your chosen TA or router or bridge support B-channel BONDing?

_____ Does your chosen TA or router support compression protocols? Which ones?

_____ Does your chosen TA's (or router's or bridge's) software support Point-to-Point Protocol (PPP) or the protocol your Internet service provider offers?

_____ Does your chosen TA or router or bridge have multiple S/T jacks?

_____ Does your chosen TA or router or bridge have no, one, or two POTS jacks?

_____ What types of LAN connectors does your chosen TA or router or bridge provide?

Ask the Internet Service Provider:

_____ What NT1 does your ISP suggest?

_____ What TA or router or bridge does your ISP suggest to work best with their system?

_____ What protocol does the ISP support? (e.g., asynchronous PPP, synchronous PPP, etc.)

_____ What authentication protocol does the ISP support?

_____ Does the ISP have experience with connecting your chosen TA or router or bridge to their system?

_____ Does your ISP's software support two B-channel BONDing?

_____ What are the extra charges by your ISP for two B-channel BONDing?

_____ Does your ISP's software support compression? Which kind?

_____ What are the ISDN setup charges from your ISP?

_____ What are your ISP's monthly ISDN account charges (basic and usage)?

_____ Does the ISP have an access number (called a POP) for ISDN in your local calling area?

_____ Does the ISP have an 800 number for ISDN?

Doing ISDN Yourself

In most cases, four vendors will be involved in helping you get your ISDN service completely installed and running: your local phone company, an Internet service provider (ISP), an ISDN software provider, and an ISDN hardware provider. This assumes you already have a 486 (or better) PC running Windows 3.1, Windows for Workgroups (WfW) 3.11, OS/2, Windows NT, or Windows 95. The rest of this chapter provides a brief overview of the steps you will need to follow to get ISDN up and running.

Step 1: The ISDN Phone Service

You will need to contact your ISDN dial tone provider (the local telephone company, usually RBOCs and independents) to determine whether ISDN service is available in your area and to determine the available options and prices for the service. The list of ISDN contacts in the United States in Table 11.1 should help you start your search for the perfect ISDN provider.

National ISDN HotLine	1-800-992-ISDN
Fax	201-829-2263
E-mail	isdn@cc.bellcore.com
URL	http://info.bellcore.com
System prompt:ftp	info.bellcore.com

Table 11.1   ISDN contacts in the United States.

Company	Contact	Telephone No.
Ameritech	National ISDN Hotline	1-800-TEAMDATA
		1-800-832-6328
Bell Atlantic	ISDN Sales and Tech Center	1-800-570-ISDN
In New Jersey, call your		1-800-570-4736
local telephone office.	For small businesses	1-800-843-2255
Bell South	ISDN Hotline	1-800-428-ISDN
		1-800-428-4736
Cincinnati Bell	ISDN Service Center	1-513-566-DATA
		1-513-566-3282
Nevada Bell	Small business	1-702-333-4811
	Large business	1-702-688-7100
Nynex	ISDN Sales Hotline	1-800-GET-ISDN
		1-800-438-4736
	New England states	1-617-743-2466
Pacific Bell	ISDN Service Center	1-800-4PB-ISDN
		1-800-472-4736
	24-hour automated available hotline	1-800-995-0346
Rochester	ISDN Information	1-716-777-1234

Table 11.1   Continued

Company	Contact	Telephone No.
SNET	Donovan Dillon	1-203-553-2369
Stentor (Canada)	ISDN "Facts By Fax"	1-800-578-ISDN
	Steve Finlay	1-604-654-7504
	Glen Duxbury	1-403-945-8130
Southwestern Bell	Austin, TX	1-800-SWB-ISDN
	Dallas, TX	1-214-268-1403
	North Houston, TX	1-713-537-3930
	South Houston, TX	1-713-567-4300
	San Antonio, TX	1-210-351-8050
	ISDN Availability	
	Other Locations	1-800-992-ISDN
U S West	Ron Miller	1-303-965-7153
	Ron Woldeit	1-206-447-4029
	Denver, CO	1-800-246-5226

National ISDN Long-Distance Carriers

Company	Contact	Telephone No.
AT&T	AT&T Front End Center	1-800-222-7956
GTE	Nationwide availability/pricing	1-800-888-8799
	Ron Sterreneberg	1-214-718-5608
MCI	Tony Hylton	1-214-701-6745
	ISDN availability	1-800-MCI-ISDN
US Sprint	Rick Simonson	1-913-624-4162
WILTEL	Justin Remington	1-918-588-5069

ISDN Line Configurations

With ISDN comes the ability to select from virtually thousands of configurations for setting up your phone line. Your ISDN service provider will undoubtedly give you a list of the possibilities when you contact them. They would like to sell you as many as they possibly can. Unless you're planning on using an ISDN telephone (electronic key telephone system, EKTS), you don't really need any of the "fancy" ISDN telephony features just to plug your current analog phone into the POTS jack on your NT1, TA, or router or bridge. However, you will need to be sure to get those basic features that you do need.

Depending on which regional phone company serves you, you will probably find that your choice of line configurations is an issue of economics. We recommend that you get only the features you believe you will need. You can always add more features later if you need them.

Typical ISDN line features are shown in Table 11.2.

Definitions are as follows:

- 1B: one B channel
- 2B: two B channels
- CSD: circuit-switched data on the B channel
- CSV: circuit-switched voice on the B channel
- CSVD: alternate voice OR data, on demand on the B channel
- EKTS: electronic key telephone system (a phone with intelligent keys and dialing features normally found on a business phone; most ISDN phones were designed for businesses and take advantage of EKTS features)
- POTS: plain old telephone system (there are special ISDN devices that will support your analog equipment, such as fax, modem, and analog phone; POTS in this table refers to use of those devices)

For individual personal or business use at a residence with a connection to the Internet and a POTS phone plugged into the NT1 or TA, the (2B) CSVD + CSVD 64 Kbps data per B channel line configuration, with only one voice call at a time allowed, should provide good service at a reasonable price.

Table 11.2   ISDN line features.

Number of Channels	Channel Type	Typical Use Description
(1B)	CSD	64K Internet access (data only)
(1B)	CSVD	64K Internet OR voice
(2B)	CSD + CSV	64K Internet AND voice
(2B)	CSD + CSD	64K or 128K Internet (data only)
(2B)	CSD + CSVD	64K Internet and voice, OR 128K Internet (good choice for 128K Internet and sporadic POTS)
(2B)	CSVD + CSVD	64K data and voice, OR 128K data, OR two voice lines (best choice if your ISDN provider allows two voice lines)

Step 2: ISDN Internet Service Providers

ISPs across the United States are scrambling to provide ISDN dial-up service. Some are caught between their ISDN line providers (the phone company) and their hardware and software providers (router hardware and accounting software to track connect time automatically). Many ISPs can't get the lines they need from the phone company at a price they can afford. Most can't get the ISDN hardware and software at prices that they can remarket profitably, so that you, the user, won't pay high ISDN Internet access fees to your ISP on top of high ISDN fees charged by the phone company. There's not much you can do about the phone company's fees, but ISPs' costs are coming down somewhat due to competition in the ISDN hardware and software market. So shop around before signing up for an ISDN account with an ISP.

If the catchword is to "shop around," how should you proceed to follow our advice? It's really fairly easy via the Internet. The following universal resource locators (URLs) can get you to the home pages for the majority of ISPs that offer ISDN connections. You can also ask for help finding the best ISDN ISP in your area on the *comp.dcom.isdn* USENET newsgroup on the Internet.

- Dan Kegel's ISDN Internet providers World Wide Web (WWW) site: http://alumni.caltech.edu/~dank/isdn/
- ICUS mirror of Dan Kegel's ISDN pages: http://www.icus.com/isdn_ip.html
- Internet service providers organized by services, by CyberBiz Productions: http://www.cybertoday.com/cybertoday/ISPs/Products.html#ISDN
- LAN ISDN ISPs collected by Core Competence: http://www.corecom.com/html/ISPlist.html

Make sure that you find out where the ISP is physically located. If the provider is in another town, then you may have to pay long-distance charges in addition to their standard connect fees each time you use their service. If that's the case, our advice is: "Keep shopping!"

Step 3: ISDN Internet Access Software

Usually you will need two software resources, a TCP/IP program that connects your computer's TA or router or bridge to the Internet and one or more application programs for navigating the Internet (FTP, WWW, Telnet, Archie, Gopher, News, Mail, etc.) If you're currently using Windows 95, Windows NT, or an older version of Windows with a set of programs to connect via SLIP to the Internet, you may be able to use most of them in the same manner. However, if you're using a Winsock-compliant program like Trumpet Winsock on a PC with an older version of Windows or WfW, you'll probably be better off switching to Microsoft's TCP/IP-32 software and using PPP instead of SLIP in your WWW browser, FTP program, etc. This has been discussed more fully in other chapters of this book.

Ask your ISP for help in this area. Many ISPs will provide you with the TCP/IP software, since the majority of it is either freeware or shareware. If you are using OS/2 Warp, your TCP/IP software is built into the operating system and you can use IBM's WebExplorer software directly with it. You can find out more about this package at ftp://ftp.ibm.net/pub/WebExplorer/web0331.zip.

If you're using a PC with Windows 3.1 or WfW 3.11, you can choose from the following ISDN-compatible software packages, which are all Winsock 1.1 compatible and will therefore work with most ISDN PPP applications as well as the MS TCP/IP-32 software:

Company	Web Site (URL)
AIR Mosaic	http://www.spry.com/sp_prod/airmos/airmos.html
Cello	http://www.law.cornell.edu/cello/cellotop.html
InternetWorks	http://www.booklink.com/
Microsoft Explorer	http://www.microsoft.com
NCSA Mosaic	http://www.ncsa.uiuc.edu/SDG/SDGIntro.html
Netscape	http://www.netscape.com/
WinTapestry	http://www.frontiertech.com/
WinWeb	http://galaxy.einet.net/EINet/clients.html
WebSurfer	http://www.netmanage.com/netmanage/apps/websurfer.html

Any of these packages will do the job of letting you navigate the Internet. Specifically, they are WWW browsers, but several contain additional applications such as e-mail, Gopher, and FTP clients. Most have a shareware or freeware test version for you to try. Try as many as you can stand, and use the one you like the best! (For whatever it's worth, we're most partial to Netscape today; who knows what will happen tomorrow?)

Step 4: ISDN Hardware

As we hope you've learned in the previous chapters, you will need a TA, router, or bridge with an internal or external NT1 for your ISDN system. Ask your ISP and your trusty hardware vendor about the various models they have used successfully. Refer to Chapters

6, 7, and 8 for discussions of ISDN NT1s and TAs and the methods for determining which types are best for your circumstances.

Summary

So much for the paperwork and preliminary testing. If you filled out the blanks next to the questions at the start of this chapter, you've passed the test. If you have decided to install your own ISDN system and have chosen, at least on paper, an ISDN phone service provider, ISDN ISP, an ISDN device, and a suite of Internet access and application software, you're ready to begin the process. Chapters 12 and 13 relate the gory details of a home office ISDN installation and an individual business ISDN installation respectively. So read on, McDuff!

12

Getting Your Own Home ISDN System

The time has arrived to show you a typical home, small business, or remote office installation from start to finish. We assume that, having followed the suggestions in the previous chapters, you have completed one of the checklists as follows:

1. You want to install your ISDN system yourself for your single computer with a single analog (POTS) phone plugged into your system for making calls only when your computer is running.
2. You want to install your ISDN system for several local area networked computers in your home office or small business. You expect to use ISDN primarily for Internet access.
3. You want to install your ISDN system for several local area networked computers in your home office or small business. You expect to use ISDN for access to an enterprise network.

In all cases, you want to choose cost-effective and easy-to-use ISDN hardware primarily with your computer to connect to the Internet, and other networks, via your ISDN line. You want full 128 Kbps throughput, but you want the analog phone to ring through and to have one B channel answer it, even if you're using both channels for data.

You have learned that you are inside an ISDN service area (your neighbor has it) and you know from him or her that the installation and monthly charges are within your budget. You currently have only a single telephone number at your home.

You know from looking at their home page that your ISP offers dial-up ISDN using Point-to-Point Protocol (PPP) for a price you can live with. It's now time for you to get into the game and call the first play.

Ordering ISDN Service from Your Local ISDN Dial Tone Provider

Residential ISDN is available from most local telephone companies (telcos). If you want ISDN, you can call 800 numbers for ordering and information, or if you are on the Net, you can check out the Web sites of the major carriers. Bell Atlantic has a good site we could use as an example. The smart telcos are providing questionnaires just like yours for folks to use to determine what they want and need before they try to order.

Call your local telephone company's information line and get connected to their ISDN order line, if they have one. Most likely it will be in the "business" rather than "residential" department, but don't let that bother you. Tell the nice person that you want to order an "ISDN BRI 2B + D" line installed at your house . . . then wait for the inevitable pause from the phone company person. If he or she doesn't pause but says, "Certainly, may I have your present phone number?" you've landed a winner who knows what's going on.

After you two determine that you do indeed live in an ISDN service area, get answers for these questions (for the purpose of this discussion, we'll assume you got the following answers):

$150	What is the ISDN installation charge?
	What calling plans do you offer?
$70 flat	What are the monthly charges (basic and usage) for ISDN service?
list of exchanges	What exchanges constitute the local calling area for ISDN at your location?
no	Will your ISDN service be via a repeater?
yes	Will your ISDN service be via an SLC (subscriber-loop carrier)?
Siemens	Which central office ISDN switch do they have? (e.g., Siemens, AT&T)
NI-1	Which protocol does the switch use? (e.g., NI-1 [National ISDN-1], AT&T 5ESS Custom, AT&T G3 PBX, Northern Telecom DMS-100 Custom, Northern Telecom BCS-34 [PVC-1], or other)
NA	What calling features are available (e.g., EKTS, CACH)? At what price?
yes	Does your ISDN provider offer BRI (basic rate interface, 2B + D) with two SPIDs (service profile IDs)?
yes	Does your ISDN provider offer voice service on both B channels on the same BRI service with two SPIDs?
same price	What are the prices of 2B (data) versus 2B (one data/one voice) versus 2b (both voice or data)?

Write these answers down so you can refer to them later. If you like what you hear, ask when the service could be installed. There will be a wait while the person checks the installation database and gets back to you. No matter what you are told, you can't do much about it, so either you order the installation or you don't.

When you place your order, have the phone company representative confirm the installation price and monthly service for the features you have ordered. You will probably be given an order confirmation number and a phone number to dial to check on the progress of your order. Write these down also. You will probably need them. (We're not pessimistic, just realistic.)

While TPC (the phone company) is getting ready to install your line, or turn it on, you can get ready for the big day by purchasing your equipment and software and signing up for an ISDN account at your Internet service provider (ISP).

Purchasing Your ISDN Equipment

Today, terminal adapters (TAs) are available by mail order, from computer stores, and by direct order from vendors from the Web or Web storefronts. Same is true for industry standard architecture (ISA), PCMCIA, and routers/bridges. Data Comm WAREHOUSE ships overnight, so instant gratification is a reality.

When choosing equipment, look beyond price and compare features. If you expect to use idle ISDN B channels for fax or an additional voice line, be sure the unit you consider has an analog port. If you are a Windows 95 user, determine whether the ISA or PC card you consider supports Microsoft's Plug and Play. If you are a Mac user, be sure to confirm that the card or terminal adapter is available with Mac software and cables.

For routers and bridges, feature sets can seem very intimidating. For Internet use, and for connecting a single local area network (LAN) segment, all of the routers in Table 12.1 will meet the following minimum criteria:

- one ISDN BRI with integrated S/T/U interfaces (integral TA and network termination [NT1])
- one Ethernet interface (10BaseT)
- for routers, Internet protocol (IP) routing software able to support:
  - variable-length subnet mask (VLSM, i.e., ability to assign and process classless IP addresses)

Table 12.1 Hardware features and pricing.

Product	# ISDN BRIs	ISDN interface	# LANs	LAN RJ-45 Connector	LAN AUI Connector	LAN BNC Connector	# Serial (WAN) Ports	Serial RJ-45 Connector	Serial 25-Pin Connector	Serial 9-Pin Connector	Analog (Voice) Port	Console Port	Console 9-Pin Connector	Console 8-Pin DIN Connector	Console RJ-45 Connector	On/Off Switch	Front-panel LED/LCDs	Rear-Panel LCDs/LEDs	Power Supply	Unit Price
3 Com Access Builder 500	1	S/T	1	•	•		1		•		1	1					•	•	I	$1595
3Com Office Connect 530	1	S/T	1	•		•	1		•		1	1	•					•	E	$1495
ADC/Kentrox PACESETTER	1	U	1	•			1	•				1				•		•	E	$1195
ACC Congo Voice Router	1	U	1	•							2	1	•				•	•	E	$899
Cisco 1004	1	U	1	•								1				•		•	E	$1595
Cisco CPA766	1	S/T,U	1	•	•						2	1	•				•	•	E	$949
Gandalf XpressConnect 5242i Edge Router	1	U	1	•							1	1	•					•	E	$1450
Livingston Office Router	1	U	1	•	•							1				•	•	•	I	$1195
Proteon GlobeTrotter 70	1	U	1	•								1	•				•	•	E	$995
Shiva AccessPort	1	U	1	•							2	1	•				•	•	E	$995
Xylogics CLAM Bridge	1	S/T	1	•														•	E	$1195
Xylogics CLAM Router	1	S/T	1	•								1				•		•	E	$1195
Xylogics Marlin Bridge	1	S/T	1	•	•		1			•		1	•					•	I	$2695
Xylogics Marlin Router	1	S/T	1	•	•		1			•		1	•					•	I	$2695

Copyright, 1996, Strategic Networks, Inc. Reproduced by permission from "1996 ISDN Router and Bridge Evaluation Report."
Key: •, feature present.
Note: CLAM's RJ-45 LAN port doubles as console port using special connector or "Y" cable (provided).

- static route configuration support (for multisegment LAN environments)
- PPP encapsulation for serial interface

- IP packet filtering capabilities, nominally input and output filters on source and destination IP addresses and UDP/TCP port numbers
- diagnostic capabilities (e.g., PING and test commands such as "dial ISDN number")
- local console management through terminal emulation
- Telnet remote management (Telnet server on router required, Telnet client on router is considered an added feature)
- Simple Network Management Protocol (SNMP) agent support

If this already seems too overwhelming, hire a consultant, contact your enterprise network administrator, or contact your ISP for assistance. You may want to consult online sources (newsgroups, Web sites, users groups) to see if any of these sources can answer questions you may have. But much of the information we provide in this book is intended to help you make these decisions, so perhaps you ought to simply read on!

Ordering Your ISDN Internet Service

You did your homework and they are supposed to have the service available at a price that seemed OK at the time. Check the price again and be sure to ask about setup charges and monthly charges and/or connect time charges. Also ask if they offer two B channel BONDing and what it costs. Be sure to confirm that the ISDN telephone number of the ISP's ISDN access server is in the same serving area as your ISDN telephone number. (In some cases, we discovered that ISDN users and ISPs in the same town may be foreign exchanged to different central offices.) Write everything down immediately. If everything still looks good, place your order and see when they can have their end ready.

Bear in mind that few ISPs have automated the ISDN setup on their end as they have for PPP accounts. It may take as much as 30 minutes for their network person to configure an account for you, when they get the magical "round-tuit."

They will probably want to know what NT1, digital modem ISA card, or PCMCIA card you are using in addition to what software you will use to dial up and connect your PPP link. You tell them what you're using, and they should be happy.

If, for some reason, they say their Internet server (hardware or software) doesn't work well with your planned system, ask if they have a better suggestion. In many cases, ISPs provide a list of equipment they have tested (as an example, many of the products described in this book have been tested and certified by Core Competence for use with MCI's Internet service). In some cases, Internet service providers may package, or bundle, an ISDN modem or card with service. Most of the time, this is a good deal, if not for the price, for the ease of mind that comes with the fact that the ISP has tested the product with its equipment and is prepared and obligated to help you get it on line. Then listen, write it down, and ask if they will help you install and configure it for free.

They will probably tell you that they can be ready for you in a couple of days, which is sooner than you need them to be. Tell them the installation date for your ISDN service, and ask if you can call them back when it is installed and you have your card installed in your computer. They will say, "Sure."

If you are preparing to use a router or bridge, it is again a good idea to ask your ISP if they have a list of certified ISDN equipment and if they are offering a router or bridge as part of the ISDN subscription. Ask the same questions regarding costs and multilink availability. You may also want to ask what kind of access server equipment the ISP uses. If you want to take advantage of compression (and you do want to use compression because of how improved your performance will be), your router/bridge purchasing decision will probably be governed by the ISP's choice of access servers. This is because most vendors have proprietary methods of negotiating and performing compression. The good news is that Internet standards are finally in place for compression negotiation and compression protocols, so although this may be an issue today, it will probably disappear over time (within a year).

Be prepared to discuss your IP addressing needs with the ISP. IP addressing is a scarce commodity these days, so don't be surprised if you are given exactly what you need and no more. Most ISPs will allow you only a 4-, 8-, or (wow!) 16-address "splinter" of a class C address. If you want more, you may have to enumerate the equipment you'll be addressing.

Some routers now have "network address translation" features that allow you to forego the worry over IP addressing. The ACC Congo, Cisco CPA 766, and ADC Kendrox Pace Setter are examples of routers that use a single address assigned by your ISP for all traffic your private LAN-connected PCs send to the Internet. Ask your vendor when you shop!

Discuss domain naming registration with your ISP. A domain name uniquely identifies your organization or company. Most ISPs will sponsor your domain name registration with an organization called the InterNIC. Be prepared to pay a registration fee for the name or names you choose to register, and be prepared to wait a while for the registration process to be completed. Unless you have the punch of the Dole '96 campaign and can circumvent the queue to register www.dinosaur.com, you should expect anywhere from a 10-day to six-week delay. Once the domain name is registered, the ISP will normally act as your primary domain name server (DNS), and will also undertake the responsibility of establishing a secondary DNS with another ISP as well.

You will also want to discuss what Internet services the ISP will provide for you: POP mail accounts (ask how many), FTP server (ask how much storage you get and whether the server will be configured for anonymous FTP), and Web server (ask whether you get basic Web server applications), CGI (Common Gateway Interface)/Java, etc., how much storage you get, and how much additional storage costs). You should also get Telnet access to the computer system on which your FTP and Web files will be stored. If you are going to do your own Web development, it's a good idea to learn what operating system and what servers and Web applications your ISP is using as well.

A Primer on IP Addressing

Class-full IP addressing adheres to the strict 8-bit (byte) boundaries defined in the original IP addressing scheme, even in the presence of subnet masking, whereas classless IP addressing accommodates variable-length subnet masking at the bit level. Organizations with class B addresses, for example, are assigned a globally unique 14-bit network number and a 16-bit field for host assignment within the unique network number. Within a class-full environment, such organizations may subdivide the 16-bit host field into a 1-byte extension to the network field and a 1-byte host field; the resulting 24-bit network number may be advertised using a routing protocol such as RIP version one through the use of a *fixed-length,* 24-bit subnet mask (where the number of 1 bits in the mask represent the total length of the network part of the address).

In today's more common *classless* IP addressing environment, organizations are more apt to be assigned one or a contiguous block of class C addresses (each having a 22-bit network number and an 8-bit host number). Individual class C IP numbers are typically subdivided using a *variable-length* subnet mask of between 25 and 29 bits, whereas organizations assigned a block of class C addresses use shorter VLSMs (sufficiently long to guarantee uniqueness of the block) (Table 12.2).

Table 12.2   Variable-length subnet masks (VLSMs).

Mask Bits	Host Bits	Subnets	Hosts/Subnet
25	7	2	126
26	6	4	62
27	5	8	30
28	4	16	14
29	3	32	6

The Benefits of Using Data Compression

Data compression reduces the amount of information that must be transmitted from one computer to another over ISDN. Most ISDN routers and bridges support some form of data compression. An algorithm is applied to the data portion of each packet processed by the router or bridge to determine whether there are patterns of repeated data in the packet, for example, blank characters in a text file. Instead of transmitting a full-sized packet containing lots of blank characters, the sending router will compose a packet with special tags that says to the receiving router, "at this point in this packet, you should insert 50 ASCII blank characters." The receiving router expands the compressed data in the packet and restores the data portion to the exact contents sent by the host computer that generated the packet. If, for example, a sending router were to find 10 instances in which 50 ASCII blank characters could be compressed into special tags, and the tags were a few bytes each, a packet that started out carrying 1500 bytes of data could be shrunk into one slightly over 1000 bytes, representing a better than 30 percent savings on transmission time. (Think about it: Fewer bits to transmit at the same bit rate per second mean a shorter time to transmit.)

The use of data compression in most cases results in substantial performance gains and cost savings. Using data compression, it is possible to realize 128 kilobits per second or higher throughput using a single B channel rather than two. This is significant, because service providers often impose usage charges per "B-channel minute" or per "B-channel hour." The best performing remote access products typically demonstrate higher effective throughput in configurations where compression is applied to single B-channel data transfers than in those where two B channels are operated in a multilink configuration without data compression.

Of course, if you use two B channels and run compression, you can get some really, really impressive throughput, especially when your TCP/IP hosts are properly tuned. Figure 12.1 illustrates some performance gains using 1- and 2-B channels with and without compression.

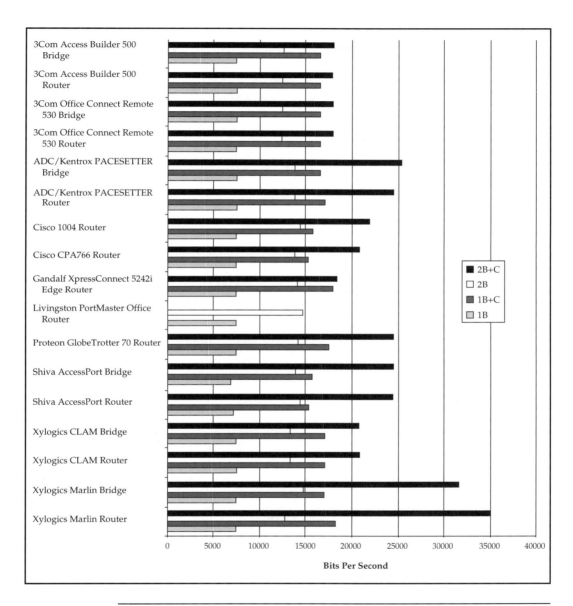

Figure 12.1 Compression Results with Window Size 4K Postscript File Throughput. Copyright, 1996, Strategic Networks, Inc. Reproduced by permission from "1996 ISDN Router and Bridge Evaluation Report."

Also, tuning of TCP/IP host software can measurably affect performance. In our tests, we varied the receive window offered by TCP. This parameter governs the amount of data that can be received before the sending host must wait for an acknowledgment. The best-performing remote access products participating in this evaluation performed best with large receive windows. Using the best-performing products tested, an increase in offered TCP receive window size from 4 to 24 kilobytes on a host receiving a file can result in a twofold or better increase in throughput during file transfers. Even a more modest increase in TCP receive window size (from 4 to 8 Kb) produces better results.

Establishing Your ISDN Service with Your Enterprise Network Administrator

The process of establishing your ISDN service with your enterprise network administrator will likely be governed by the ISDN, dial, and secure access policies adopted by your company. Still, many of the same questions you would ask an ISP for LAN-ISDN access apply. In many cases, your company may dictate the equipment and connectivity arrangements to you. If you are extremely fortunate, the company may have a process in place so that your equipment will be purchased and preconfigured by company network operations staff.

ISDN Dial Tone Service: Wiring, Installation, Configuration, and Testing

Wiring Your Home for ISDN

In the scenario for this installation, the house has only one POTS telephone currently installed. This leaves a second pair of wires in the normal four-wire cable to use for your ISDN service. Now everything you read will tell you that you should use only a twisted-pair wire for ISDN. Although this is true, many if not most standard house wires will support ISDN and POTS with no crossover at all. It doesn't hurt to give it a try. Of course, you can always buy a few meters of four-wire twisted-pair phone cable at your local Radio Shack or hardware store and run it from your demarc (demarcation point: the telephone box on the outside of your house where the lines come in) to the room where your computer is located.

You may be a little worried about getting shocked when dealing with your telephone wiring. It's possible, but only when the telephone rings. The current is approximately 110 volts but the amperage is low, so unless you're wearing a pacemaker, it should just tingle a lot and scare you. So don't do the wiring standing on a ladder unless you don't touch the metal of the wires or the screw posts with your bare skin or unshielded metal tools. Use common sense, and you should be just fine.

Whether you use existing wiring or new cable, you'll need to have two wires at the demarc to connect to the ISDN line the phone company installs. You need to put either an RJ-11 or an RJ-45 jack on the other end of the cable next to your computer. If you are using your existing house phone wiring, you can purchase a double RJ-11 wall jack plate to replace your existing single jack plate. Simply wire the existing two POTS wires (usually red and green) to one of the jacks and the other two wires (usually black and yellow) to the other jack, making sure you use the inside (middle) two terminals on the jack. Test the POTS phone to make sure it "breaks" the dial tone and will call out on your existing POTS line.

If you're using a new cable, you can purchase an RJ-11 or RJ-45 jack that attaches to the wall or one that looks like the female equivalent of the plug that fits on the end of the cable itself. Most good electronics stores carry at least one of these, if not both. Be sure to match jacks against the type of termination (RJ-11 or 45) your NT1, TA, or router offers.

To test the integrity of the second pair of wires (that you are going to use for your ISDN line), plug your POTS phone into the jack with the second pair. Go out to the demarc and take your current POTS wires (red and green) off of their connectors and replace them with the other pair (black and yellow). Go back inside and try dialing out on the phone. If it doesn't break the dial tone, go back outside and reverse the black and yellow wires and try again. If this still doesn't work, you may have a short in the black and yellow wire pair.

You can test this directly with a volt/ohmmeter by twisting the black and yellow wires together at the demarc, after removing them from the screw posts, and using the ohmmeter on the other ends (at the RJ-11 jack inside) to see if you get any resistance. It's really quite straightforward.

After your wiring passes these tests, you're ready for the telephone company to connect the ISDN line. For a comprehensive look at ISDN wiring, call the North American ISDN Users Forum (NIUF) at 301-975-2937 or e-mail *dawn@isdn.ncsl.nist.gov* and request the "ISDN Wiring Guide for Residential and Small Businesses." It will tell you much more than you probably care to know, but who knows, it may make for interesting conversation at your next ISDN user group meeting.

ISDN Installation by the Phone Company

The simplest case for ISDN installation will occur if you live within 18,000 feet of one of the phone company's ISDN switches, if you have only a single POTS number at your house, and if your local cable bundle has an unused cable pair suitable for ISDN. Just about all the phone company has to do in that case is to get on their computer and digitally "flip a few switches" to connect everything and test it up to your demarc. They will then send an installation person to your house to connect the two wires of your existing cable to the proper screw posts in your demarc and test the ISDN line with their really cool ISDN line tester. This is all they are really required to do to "install" your ISDN line.

However, if you have your wiring ready, the installer will usually connect it at the demarc and may even go inside and test it for you for FREE. Don't assume anything, though, since many of the RBOCs charge $35 or more just to walk into your house to do anything and then charge $15 every quarter of an hour ($1 per minute) thereafter.

If you have your wiring ready, your computer running, and your ISDN equipment set up, you can try using your POTS phone plugged into the analog port of your ISDN TA to see if the ISDN line works. Before trying this, you should start your computer or external ISDN device by turning it completely off and then back on after all of the wiring is completed and plugged in. This ensures that the ISDN device looks at your ISDN line and properly runs the drivers. If all of them load without error messages, your POTS line should work and you should be able to use your ISDN line for Internet calls after you configure your Internet software with your ISP's help.

Just a word or two about your friendly phone company ISDN installer. Since ISDN is quite new and used predominantly by businesses, most of the ISDN installers are from the business department rather than the residential department. They are generally knowledgeable and well educated in dealing with ISDN systems. You'll probably find them extremely polite and quite accommodating if you treat them with respect and in a businesslike manner. They are used to installing larger systems for businesses rather than dealing with hundreds of irate home owners' noisy phone line problems every time it rains. They really want your ISDN line to work well and will do everything they can to see that it does.

Installing Your Home or Business LAN

If you are connecting several computers in a LAN arrangement, your best bet is to use unshielded twisted-pair (UTP) cables and a multiport repeater or "hub" that supports 10BaseT Ethernet. Hubs are pretty much a commodity these days, and a five-port hub can be had for as little as $80. We recommend Ethernet 10BaseT because most routers and bridges come with the RJ-45 termination for 10BaseT Ethernet. Many do come with a BNC connector for ThinNet (10Base2), so you can choose this alternative as well. We'd observe that 10BaseT won't save you big bucks if you end up connecting lots of equipment and it may turn out to be a wiring headache, so we'd recommend you imitate the serious LAN builders and use hubs. Who knows? You may eventually install a wiring closet in your basement!

Constructing your physical LAN is pretty easy. Connect a 10BaseT Ethernet cable from the RJ-45 termination on your PC to any port on the hub. Do this for all your PCs. Connect your router in the same manner.

Your local telephone company may use RJ-45 terminations for your ISDN service. Your router vendor may include both ISDN and a courtesy Ethernet cable for you, and these are not always clearly distinguished. The good news is that a correctly terminated Ethernet cable will work if you happen to use this to connect your router to your ISDN line. Since the opposite is not true, we recommend you buy an extra properly terminated Ethernet cable and use common cabling throughout. We throw the ISDN cables out, but you can use them to hang plants.

By the way, never connect an Ethernet cable from your hub to the ISDN port on your router or to the ISDN termination the telephone company provides. For that matter, don't connect a cable from any PC Ethernet NIC to the ISDN port on your router or to the ISDN termination, either. Bad things will happen.

ISDN Equipment Installation and Testing

OK, so your new ISDN interface device arrived today. You probably can't wait to plug it into your computer, flip the power switch, and start communicating at 128 Kbps over the Internet. Sorry, but you'll have to wait just a little while longer, because installation and configuration require advanced planning and a bit of work.

Whether you wait for your ISDN line to be installed before you install your ISDN device is sort of a catch-22 situation. You can't completely test the ISDN line inside your house without a working interface, and you can't completely test the interface without a working ISDN line. You can, however, partially test the ISDN device without a working ISDN line, so you should get as far as you can before the phone company installer arrives.

If all goes well, installation, setup, and checkout of your ISDN device will take you anywhere from a few minutes to half an hour; if not, it can take anywhere from a few hours to a few days. This doesn't necessarily mean that something is wrong with the interface; rather, installing interfaces can be complicated by hardware conflicts, driver conflicts, and outdated software (either from the vendor or on your desktop machine). Working through each of these elements takes considerable effort, especially when you're a novice.

Any well-written installation manual will take you step by step through its installation and configuration process; most manuals will also contain examples of configuration steps and related configuration files or registry entries for the most common desktop operating systems. Here, we'll quickly take you through the main steps, along with our comments on what some vendors' manuals may overlook.

Step 1

This doesn't appear in too many vendor manuals but is an essential step nonetheless. For maximum protection, most experts recommend that you make a full backup of your system before installing new hardware or software components. At a bare minimum, you'll want to make a backup of your configuration and related system files (for Windows 95 or Windows NT, this would require a Registry backup; for Windows 3.X, this should include the following files: AUTOEXEC.BAT, CONFIG.SYS, WIN.INI, SYSTEM.INI, and PROTOCOL.INI on another directory of your hard disk as well as on a floppy disk). Several changes will be made to these critical configuration elements during installation and setup, and you want to make sure you can get back to square one if things get too fouled up.

Step 2

If you're not using Windows 95, build a map of your PC's interrupt settings, memory base (MEMBASE settings), DMA (Direct Memory Access) settings, and the like (you can use a program like Microsoft Diagnostics or any of the reputable third-party diagnostic tools like System Sleuth to figure out what new configuration settings are possible on your machine). Check the vendor's manual to make sure what you have available matches a legal configuration for the device. If you're running Windows 95, and the ISDN interface supports plug and play, you can simply insert the device and let the Hardware Wizard discover the interface when you next boot the machine. If all goes well, you'll be up and running immediately thereafter. Otherwise, you'll have to get the device installed and working through a process of elimination and repeated testing. Although this may sometimes require reconfiguring other system elements that already occupy all of the legal configurations for your ISDN interface, such problems can invariably be solved by working through possible configurations one at a time, until a set that works for all system elements is found.

Step 3

If your ISDN line hasn't been installed, skip the section on plugging the RJ-45 plug of the cable into the U interface on the device. By the way, a standard RJ-11 plug will plug into an RJ-45 jack just fine. Since the ISDN line uses only the middle two wires, in any order it seems, just about any phone wire with RJ-11 plugs on both ends will work with ISDN. To be on the safe side, though, you should keep the wire colors the same throughout your wiring. That is, red to red, green to green, etc.

Step 4

Plug your POTS phone into the RJ-11 jack on the device. Of course, it won't work unless you have the ISDN line installed.

Step 5

Turn your computer on.

Step 6

After you have successfully loaded the necessary ISDN and TA drivers, you'll need to configure the ISDN connection itself. Here's where you'll typically have to provide the following information about your ISDN service, which you should be able to get from your phone company order line person when confirming your installation date:

Item	Quantity	Example 1	Example 2
ISDN telephone numbers	2	512-111-0000	512-111-0001
ISDN SPIDs	2	512-111-0000-01	512-111-0001-01
Telco switch type	1	National ISDN (NI-1)	
Device names	2	PCname	ISPname
ISP ISDN access	1	512-111-1234	

SPIDs vary for different switch types, so don't worry if yours look different from these!

It will be obvious when you run other programs if there is a conflict. If that happens, run the setup program again and try another setting. This is where it becomes time consuming if things don't work the first time and you don't know where to start changing settings. There is no great way to tell, either.

For Windows 95, use the System Control Panel to diagnose the problem, or the Modem Control Panel. For other systems, your first choice is to use one of the Windows diagnostic programs like Win-Probe. The second is to use the Microsoft System Diagnostics (MSD) program in DOS and to look for potential conflicts. This won't tell you about Windows conflicts, but most conflicts occur at the DOS level anyway. If you need to make changes, write them down and change only one setting at a time, then rerun your system to see if it works properly. Keep trying until you get things working or until you run out of alternatives.

Step 7

This step tests the ISDN line itself and can't be taken until you have your ISDN line installed and the phone company says it is working properly. These diagnostics actually test the line all the way to the phone company's switch and back. If you try to run this test without a working ISDN line, you will get a "layer 1 link failure" or "line failure" error message, which usually means the ISDN device isn't finding or recognizing a working line. Layer 1 is the first ISDN layer from your NT1. If the phone company's switch isn't properly configured or your card isn't configured for the switch, you will probably get a "layer 2 link failure."

If your ISDN line is installed and properly configured and the line diagnostics find no errors, you should be able to use your POTS phone to make calls at this point. Try it, and see if it works.

Step 8 ... and More

At this point, you'll be ready to run the vendor's diagnostic software, to check out your connection, addressing, and the ability to place an "ISDN call." These are necessary preambles to establishing a working ISDN data connection, because they test your device's ability to establish a working ISDN session of any kind.

Step 9

Now that you have your ISDN line installed and configured and your NT1 and TA running smoothly with your computer system, you're ready to complete your Internet connection. Call your ISP and get them to activate the ISDN account that you ordered a few days/weeks ago. You'll need several pieces of information from them to enter into your system:

Their ISDN phone number	###-####
Your ISDN account number	###
Your IP address	123.12.1.###

Your default gateway	123.12.1.###
Your subnet mask	255.255.255.###
Their DNS (domain name server) address	198.3.118.11
Your username	yourusername
Your password	********

You will need to put these pieces of information into your TCP/IP or other similar program's configuration so it can perform the "dial-up" function that perhaps you were having Trumpet Winsock perform with your SLIP account.

Establish a working connection to your ISP through the interface. This will involve dialing their ISDN access number and working your way through any authentication hurdles, which may be followed by some scripting work to get yourself logged in and to establish a PPP session. Normally, if your ISP supports the kind of ISDN device you're using, they'll be able to provide any necessary scripting details or instructions. Otherwise, you'll end up working with them, their ISDN hardware vendor, and your own ISDN hardware vendor to work out the details. If this happens, be prepared to spend some time hashing out the details (this is one of the reasons why we strongly recommend that you inquire about—and purchase—ISDN hardware that's recommended by your ISP!).

Whenever you activate your WWW browser, e-mail application, news reader, or FTP program, your ISDN connection should be established automatically within less than one second. If you have properly configured all of the necessary components previously discussed, you should be able to run all of your existing Internet applications via your new ISDN service and PPP accounts just as you previously did using your POTS line and SLIP account, at a much faster rate. If something doesn't work properly and you can't use your Internet account, refer to Chapter 14 for troubleshooting assistance and call your ISP's customer support line.

Step 10

You are now finished configuring your ISDN device. You may want to create a shortcut on your desktop from the Dial-Up Networking service (if you're running Windows 95 or Windows NT) for this connection, to make it easy to establish an ISDN session by double-clicking the shortcut icon thereafter. For earlier versions of Windows (or other operating systems and stand-alone devices), you'll need to figure out how to launch and use the communications software that establishes an ongoing ISDN session.

Installing Your ISDN Router or Bridge

Here, the steps will not differ that much from the overall activities you might perform to install a PC-attached ISDN device, but the details differ considerably. In general, the following sequence of activities must be performed:

1. Obtain the necessary protocol configuration information from your ISP or connectivity provider.
2. Make sure you have a working ISDN line.
3. Connect the device to the ISDN line, and follow the vendor's instructions to determine that the device can recognize and communicate with the ISDN line.
4. Run the vendor's supplied configuration utility, and insert all necessary protocol and device settings. Here, again, working with equipment that your ISP or connectivity provider knows and understands furthers your chances of success: If they already know the device, they should be able to tell you exactly what to do and to provide all necessary data to be entered.
5. Run the vendor's diagnostic software, and ensure that the device can communicate with your ISP.
6. Supply necessary IP address information. Note: Some ISDN routers can provide Dynamic Host Configuration Protocol (DHCP) support, so you may be able to supply an address range and related exclusions, and let the router manage IP addresses for your workstation. Some such devices even support address translation, so that manual IP address configuration and man-

agement for workstations is no longer necessary. For small networks, it doesn't get any easier than this!

7. Test a connection from a workstation through the router or bridge to your ISP. If it works, you're through; if not, it's time to put on your troubleshooting hat.

Given that ISDN routers and bridges cost from $500 to $1500, their vendors are usually quite good about including adequate installation manuals and step-by-step instructions. Nevertheless, it's wise to stick with equipment that's familiar to your ISP or communications provider, because that doubles your chances of satisfactory installation support (one chance from the vendor and another from your ISP).

Modem Installation

The following paragraphs provide example installation and configuration instructions for some of the ISDN adapter cards we've tested.

USR Sportster 128K

Power off and unplug the PC. Install the ISA card in an available 16-bit expansion slot, taking care to ground yourself before touching or installing the ISA card. Connect power to the PC and boot the system.

Install the Configuration Manager from the diskette provided (typical setup procedure), then launch the application. Following a single click on the Configuration Settings button of the Manager Utility, the user accesses four menus. The General settings menu is used to configure ring patterns, voice-call preemption of data calls, and to select TurboPPP, an enhanced data driver. This menu is also used to secure the settings. We recommend the use of the TurboPPP, but all other settings can be left to defaults. Use the Telephone Company menu to set the ISDN switch type, SPIDs, and directory numbers according to the information provided by your ISDN service provider. The

Adapter Card menu can be used to modify the I/O Base Address and IRQ for the card, but if the card is installed with jumpers set to allow the installation software to determine the appropriate settings, these should not be changed. The Installed Components menu identifies the Windows components that will use the adapter card. WinISDN must be identified here.

Windows 3.11 and OnNet 2.0 Configuration:
USR Sportster 128K

Click on the Dialer icon to bring up the main menu, and select New Connection. Name the connection. Fill in the configuration parameters presented by the connection profile menu (select the WinISDN driver, select PPP, set the assigned host and domain name server (DNS) IP addresses, enter the ISP-provided username and password, and indicate that the user will not be prompted for input). Save the changes and close the window, returning to the Dialer main menu. Select Connect To Network to start the dialer.

Windows 95 and MS TCP/IP Configuration:
USR Sportster 128K

At the time we evaluated this card, product documentation indicated that this card was not yet supported by Microsoft's Windows 95 Dial-Up Networking. (Support should now be available.) Documentation indicates that this card can be used with the OnNet 2.0 dialer under Windows 95 as well.

USR Sportster 128K Manager Log

The Sportster 128K Manager provides a diagnostic logging capability to assist in error resolution. The following is a sample of that log, illustrating a successful call:

```
02/19/96 10:31:51 AM Driver is ready and waiting for the reset
command. 02/19/96
   10:31:51 AM Starting TAPI services for Telephony (1). 02/19/96
```

10:31:51 AM Sportster ISDN 128K, v4.04.1. Built Dec 8 1995 02/19/96
10:31:51 AM Running diagnos
    02/19/96 10:31:51 AM FIFO access test failed.
    02/19/96 10:31:51 AM Reset received: Re-configure and start the
card.
    02/19/96 10:31:51 AM IRQ = 15 IObase = 200 Switch Type = Na-
tional ISDN
    02/19/96 10:31:51 AM PhoneNumber 1 = 8308392 SPID 1 =
018308392000.
    02/19/96 10:31:51 AM PhoneNumber 2 = 8308907 SPID 2 =
018308907000.
    02/19/96 10:31:51 AM Installed IRQ 15.
    02/19/96 10:31:51 AM MAC address is 0.20.69.d0.10.ef
    02/19/96 10:31:51 AM The boards eeprom
settings are: 02/19/96 10:31:51 AM   Board
Type: U
    02/19/96 10:31:51 AM   Data
Only: No
    02/19/96 10:31:51 AM   External
Ring: Yes
    02/19/96 10:31:51 AM Voice override enabled.
    02/19/96 10:31:51 AM Accept voice calls as data is
disabled. 02/19/96 10:31:51 AM Beep on data call connect enabled.
02/19/96 10:31:51 AM Turbo PPP enabled.
    02/19/96 10:31:51 AM Terminating TAPI services for
Telephony.
    02/19/96 10:31:51 AM Physical wire connection to Switch estab-
lished. 02/19/96 10:31:51 AM Starting TAPI services for Telephony
(1). 02/19/96 10:31:51 AM Sportster ISDN 128K, v4.04.1. Built Dec
8 1995 02/19/96 10:31:51 AM ISDN connection to the switch has
been lost.
    02/19/96 10:31:51 AM ISDN connection to the switch has been
established. 02/19/96 10:31:51 AM ISDN connection to the switch
has been established. 02/19/96 10:31:51 AM Dialing a digital data
call to 18008331234. 02/19/96 10:31:51 AM Will dial second data
call to 18008331234. 02/19/96 10:31:51 AM The destination is
ringing.
    02/19/96 10:31:51 AM Tones are being turned off.
    02/19/96 10:31:51 AM Establishing PPP connection to
18008331234.
    02/19/96 10:31:51 AM Connected digital data call at 64000 bps
to 18008331234. 02/19/96 10:31:51 AM Protocol in use is Point To
Point Multi-Link Emulation (TurboPPP).

Windows 95 and MS TCP/IP Configuration: Diamond Multimedia NetCommander ISDN

When the system is booted, Windows 95 recognizes the new hardware and asks where to find drivers. Select "Drivers from disk provided by manufacturer" if not already selected. Insert the diskette titled Supra NetCommander ISDN Setup disk and click OK. The Install from Disk window appears, and should point to the disk drive in which the Supra NetCommander ISDN Setup disk resides. Click OK. The Select Device window should locate the correct Manufacturer/Model. Click OK. Windows 95 automatically installs all necessary drivers, then asks for a diskette titled Microsoft ISDN Accelerator Pack for Windows 95. Install this disk and click OK. Windows 95 installs software from both the accelerator disk and the ISDN Setup disk (considerable swapping of disks). When the Setup application is finished, it will reboot the PC and run the NetCommander ISDN configuration utility.

The first configuration window suggests a location for the program files. Accept the defaults if appropriate for your system, then click Next. At this point, if an IRQ conflict exists between this ISDN card and any other installed hardware, the user is prompted to correct the conflict before continuing. If this occurs, use the Start button to launch Settings/Control Panel and click System. Select the Device Manager tab and click My Computer to view current IRQ settings. Click the ISDN card (a multipurpose adapter) and select the Resources tab if necessary to change the default IRQ assigned to the ISDN card. Reboot the PC to rerun the NetCommander ISDN configuration utility. If the problem has been resolved, the Configure ISDN Service window will now appear.

The Configure ISDN Service window offers a choice of viewing an ISDN order form (useful if the subscriber has not yet ordered service). We assume the subscriber has ISDN service and click OK. At the Switch Type window, select/highlight the switch identified by your service provider, then click Next.

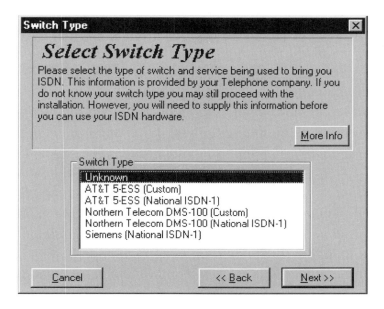

At the SPID window, enter service profile identifiers (if appropriate for your switch type), then click Next.

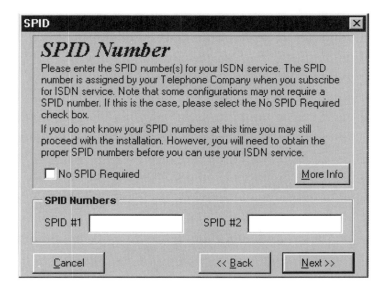

At the Phone Numbers window, enter the seven-digit phone number (no area code), then click Next.

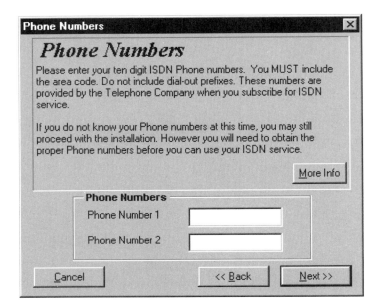

Click Next at the Save Configuration window to load the configuration into the modem. The final Congratulations! window provides a ReadMe button which conveniently displays changes to software or the product that might not be in the documentation.

Exit Setup and reboot the PC. Use Make New Connection in Dial-Up Networking to create a new connection profile for access to your ISP. Enter a connection name and select Supra NetCommander ISDN from the modem list. Click Next. Enter the phone number for your ISP's access server. Click Next. Click Finish. From the Dial-Up Networking window, click the dialer icon for your ISP using the right mouse button, and choose Properties. Click Connection, confirm that the speed preference matches your ISDN service (e.g., 64K data or 56K data), then click OK. Click Server Type. Choose PPP: Windows 95, Windows NT 3.5, Internal from the list of dial-up servers. Check that only TCP/IP is selected from the Allowed Network Protocols, then click TCP/IP settings. If your ISP has provided a static IP address, choose Specify an IP address and enter the assigned address in the corresponding fields; otherwise, if the ISP's server will dynamically assign an address, choose Server Assigned Address. If your ISP has provided a IP addresses for DNS name servers, choose Specify name server addresses and enter the assigned addresses in the corresponding fields; otherwise, if the ISP's server will provide a name server address, choose Server Assigned Name Server Address. Confirm that Use IP compression and Use default gateway on remote network are selected, then click OK in each succeeding window until the connection is closed.

Click the dialer icon for your ISP using the right mouse button, and choose Connect. Enter the username and CHAP secret assigned to you by your ISP. A progress window appears; if the system fails to connect, use the AutoISDN utility installed during Setup to diagnose the problem (see earlier note).

Diamond Multimedia AutoISDN Diagnostic Log

The AutoISDN application provides additional configuration, connection status monitor, problem diagnosis, and logging capabilities, as shown in the following figures.

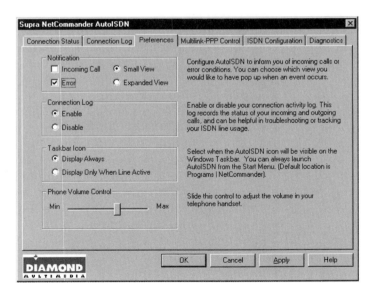

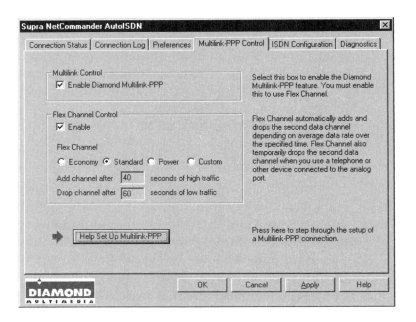

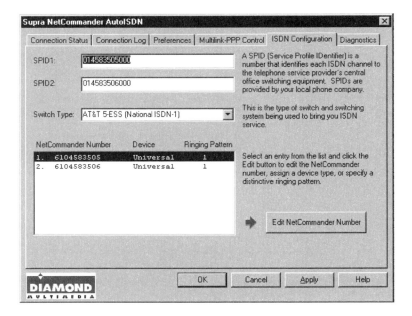

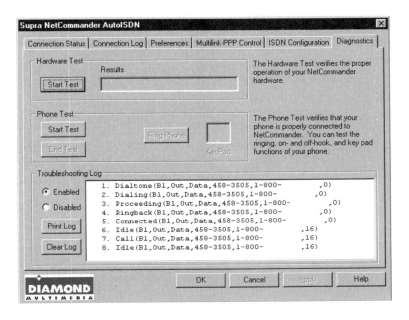

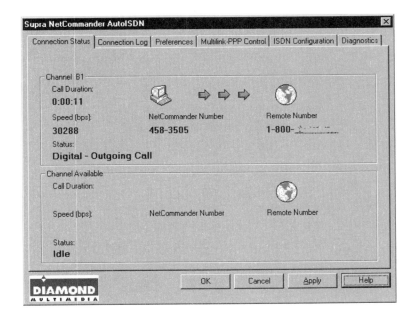

Windows 95 and MS TCP/IP Configuration: Eicon Diva ISDN for Windows 95

Insert the Diva for Windows 95 drivers diskette. From the Control Panel, start the Network applet. Click the Add button, select Adapter, then click the Add button. From the Select Network Adapters window, select Have Disk. Select the drive that holds the Diva diskette, then select the ISA version of the Windows 95 driver. Click OK to install the driver software. Once the driver software is installed, click OK to exit the Network applet. A Diva adapter driver Properties window will appear. Set the ISDN switch type and SPIDs. Click on the Resources tab and select an IRQ for the adapter (the software uses an asterisk [*] to identify IRQs that would result in a conflict). Close the Properties window. Shut down and restart the PC.

Use Make New Connection in Dial-Up Networking to create a new connection profile for access to your ISP. Enter a connection name, and select G. Diehl RNA Modem from the modem choices list. Click on Configure. The maximum speed should be set to 115200. Click on the Connections tab, then click on the Advanced button. Enter the AT command string "AT&F9" (HDLC framing to a remote access server). Configure a virtual ISDN COM port to allow WinCIM to connect to the Diva Card, again using the Network applet Control Panel. Select the G. Diehl (Eicon) Interface... from the installed network components list and click Properties. Click Advanced and identify a COM port for the Diva. Click OK and restart the PC. To connect, open Dial-Up Networking in Control Panel, and click the connection icon using the right button. Choose Connect from the drop-down menu. The Connect to: window appears. Enter the username and CHAP secret provided, confirm that the number your ISP has provided for dial-up ISDN is correct, then click on the Connect button. When the progress window indicates that the PC is connected, open Internet applications to access Internet services.

Eicon DILOG Logging Utility

The Diva comes with a utility called DILOG that runs under DOS. The utility records all the events that occur at the digital modem in an ASCII text file. The following is sample of this log:

```
ISDN Log Facility for DOS, Version 5.03, Rev. 95-43-INTERN

0:0280:700 - L1_UP
0:0280:702 - SYNC_LOST
0:0372:570 - ACTIVATION_REQ
0:0372:571 - EVENT: Layer-2 failed, resend SPID '018308392000'
0:0376:809 - SYNC_GAINED
0:0376:819 - D-X(008) FC FF 03 0F F3 BF 01 FF
0:0376:819 - L1_UP
0:0376:826 - D-X(008) FC FF 03 0F FA BF 01 FF
0:0378:851 - D-X(008) FC FF 03 0F E3 C7 01 FF
0:0378:853 - D-X(008) FC FF 03 0F E5 C7 01 FF
0:0379:473 - SYNC_LOST
0:0380:293 - L1_DOWN
0:0380:495 - SYNC_GAINED
0:0380:578 - L1_UP
0:0380:870 - D-X(008) FC FF 03 0F C6 CF 01 FF
0:0380:884 - D-X(008) FC FF 03 0F D3 CF 01 FF
0:0382:892 - EVENT: Layer-2 failed, resend SPID '018308907000'
0:0382:905 - EVENT: Layer-2 failed, resend SPID '018308392000'
0:0383:891 - D-X(008) FC FF 03 0F 93 DB 01 FF
0:0383:906 - D-X(008) FC FF 03 0F A2 DB 01 FF
0:0385:911 - D-X(008) FC FF 03 0F 77 E3 01 FF
0:0385:934 - D-R(008) FE FF 03 0F 77 E3 02 C1
0:0385:935 - D-X(003) 00 C1 7F
0:0385:936 - D-X(008) FC FF 03 0F 90 E3 01 FF
0:0385:959 - D-R(008) FE FF 03 0F 90 E3 02 D3
0:0385:960 - D-X(003) 00 D3 7F
0:0385:977 - D-R(003) 00 D3 73
0:0385:978 - SIG-x(017) 08 00 7B 3A 0C 30 31 38 33 30 38 33 39
32 30 30 30
          Q.931 CR0000 INFO
               SPID 30 31 38 33 30 38 33 39 32 30 30 30
0:0385:979 - D-X(021) 00 D3 00 00 08 00 7B 3A 0C 30 31 38 33
30 38 33 39 32 30 30 30
0:0386:005 - D-R(004) 00 D3 01 02
```

```
0:0386:084 - D-R(011) 02 D3 00 02 08 00 7B 3B 02 80 80
0:0386:084 - D-X(004) 02 D3 01 02
0:0386:085 - EVENT: SPID accepted '018308392000'
0:0386:206 - D-R(014) 02 D3 02 02 08 00 7B 95 2A 04 80 80 01 50
0:0386:206 - D-X(004) 02 D3 01 04
0:0386:935 - D-X(003) 00 C1 7F
0:0386:951 - D-R(003) 00 C1 73
0:0386:952 - SIG-x(017) 08 00 7B 3A 0C 30 31 38 33 30 38 39 30
37 30 30 30
          Q.931 CR0000 INFO
                   SPID 30 31 38 33 30 38 39 30 37 30 30 30
0:0386:954 - D-X(021) 00 C1 00 00 08 00 7B 3A 0C 30 31 38 33
30 38 39 30 37 30 30 30
0:0386:980 - D-R(004) 00 C1 01 02
0:0387:022 - D-R(011) 02 C1 00 02 08 00 7B 3B 02 81 80
0:0387:023 - D-X(004) 02 C1 01 02
0:0387:024 - EVENT: SPID accepted '018308907000'
0:0387:085 - D-R(014) 02 C1 02 02 08 00 7B 95 2A 04 80 80 01 50
0:0387:086 - D-X(004) 02 C1 01 04
0:0396:207 - D-X(004) 00 D3 01 05
0:0396:223 - D-R(004) 00 D3 01 03
0:0397:085 - D-X(004) 00 C1 01 05
0:0397:101 - D-R(004) 00 C1 01 03
0:0406:224 - D-X(004) 00 D3 01 05
0:0406:241 - D-R(004) 00 D3 01 03
0:0407:102 - D-X(004) 00 C1 01 05
```

This log is useful for an advanced user but would be useful to a
novice user only when speaking to the manufacturer's technical
support or to help desk staff.

Windows 95 and MS TCP/IP Configuration:
Digi International DataFire-U

Open the Add New Hardware Wizard. Click Next to begin installing
new hardware. Set the No radio button to install the card manually,
then click Next. Choose Network Adapter from the list of hardware
types to install, then click Next. Select Drivers from the disk provided by the manufacturer if not already selected. Enter the directory name where the Digi International drivers were expanded and
click OK. The Select Device window should locate the correct Man-
ufacturer/Model; select Digi DataFire-U and click OK. Windows 95

automatically installs all necessary drivers, then asks for a diskette entitled Microsoft ISDN Accelerator Pack for Windows 95. Enter the directory name where the pack was expanded (e.g., C:\MSIDN) and click OK. Windows 95 installs software from both the accelerator directory and the Digi International directory (considerable swapping of directories). When the Setup application is finished, it will reboot the PC and run the ISDN Configuration Wizard.

The ISDN Configuration Wizard will prompt you to enter your switch type, service profile identifiers, and telephone numbers. Enter these values and click Next. The Wizard requests the accelerator directory and the Digi International directory locations, indicates when installation is complete, and suggests rebooting the PC.

After rebooting, use Make New Connection in Dial-Up Networking to create a new connection profile for access to your ISP. Enter a connection name, select DATAFIRE ISA1 U-Line 0 from the modem list, and click Next. Enter the phone number for the access server and click Next. Click Finish.

From the Dial-Up Networking window, click the icon using the right mouse button, and choose Properties. Click Configure, confirm that the speed preference matches your ISDN service (e.g., 64K data or 128K bonded), then click OK. (If desired, SPIDs and telephone numbers may also be modified by clicking on the Configure window Advanced button.) Click on Server Type. Choose PPP: Windows 95, Windows NT 3.5, Internal from the list of dial-up servers. Check that only TCP/IP is selected from the Allowed Network Protocols, then click TCP/IP settings. If your ISP has provided a static IP address, choose Specify an IP address and enter the assigned address in the corresponding fields; otherwise, if an access server will dynamically assign an address, choose Server Assigned Address. If your ISP has provided IP addresses for DNS name servers, choose Specify name server addresses and enter the assigned addresses in the corresponding fields; otherwise, if an access server will provide a name server address, choose Server Assigned Name Server Address. Confirm that Use IP compression and Use default gateway on remote network are selected, then click OK in each succeeding window until the connection is closed.

Click the icon using the right mouse button, and choose Connect. Enter the username and CHAP secret assigned by your ISP. A progress window appears indicating connection status.

DataFire-U Diagnostic Utilities

Two diagnostic utilities were provided with the Digi International Windows 95 software downloaded from Microsoft's Web site. Both are DOS programs that can be executed through Windows 95 DOS emulation by clicking on the files in Explorer or launching them from the Start/Run menu. However, the programs run and exit the DOS window too quickly to see the program output. To correct this, create a batch file using Notepad or any other text editor, include a PAUSE command at the end of the batch file, and run the batch file instead.

The line status utility produces the following output when the ISDN line is improperly installed (e.g., bad cable, not plugged into the RJ-45 jack correctly).

```
lineinf -v
Lineinf - Version 2.00
Copyright 1992-1996, Digi International Inc. All rights
reserved

Line: DATAFIRE - ISA1U-Line0
Layer 1 Tx State: Stop! (0)
Layer 1 State: INFO 0
Layer 1 Rx State: Stop! (0)
Layer 1 Rx State: INFO 0
Layer 2 State: Stop! (0)
Layer 2 State: Initialized
Layer 3 State: Stop! (0)
Layer 3 State: Awaiting Layer 2 Establishment
Layer 3 State: Stop! (0)
Layer 3 Service: Not Determined
```

A correctly connected ISDN line produces the following output.

```
lineinf -v
Lineinf - Version 2.00
```

```
    Copyright 1992-1996, Digi International Inc. All rights
reserved

    Line: DATAFIRE - ISA1U-Line0
    Layer 1 Tx State: Go! (2)
    Layer 1 State: INFO 3
    Layer 1 Rx State: Go! (2)
    Layer 1 Rx State: INFO 4
    Layer 2 State: Go! (2)
    Layer 2 State: Multiframe Established
    Layer 3 State: Go! (4)
    Layer 3 State: Active
    Layer 3 State: Go! (2)
    Layer 3 Service: Full
```

The trace utility can be used to generate a variety of ISDN protocol debug message logs, as illustrated by the following option output.

```
    trace
    Digi ISDN BRI Trace - Version 2.00
    Copyright 1992-1995, Digi International Inc. All rights
reserved

    Usage - trace -a -p -l2 -l3 -raw -?
    -a- trace all lines
    -p- show decode for all ISDN Protocols
    -l2- show decode for ISDN Layer 2 (Q.921)
    -l3- show decode for ISDN Layer 3 (Q.931)
    -raw- show raw hex dump of all ISDN Protocols
    -?- show this screen
```

Summary

With all of the complexities of installing and configuring the various ISDN components, don't be surprised if everything doesn't work perfectly the first time you try it. Try to be patient and check your setup parameters carefully when you enter them. Proceed deliberately, step by step. Test after each step. Write everything down as if you were the one writing this book for someone else to follow for a first-time installation.

To help keep your blood pressure down, don't expect your ISDN service to be up and running as continually and reliably as your tried and true POTS line. Accept it as a fact of life that ISDN service is new to everyone, TPC and you included, and that everyone wants it to be as reliable as possible. But it is newly developed, highly technical, completely computerized, digital transmission that is going to be more susceptible to weather-related problems and other perturbations than POTS lines until all of the "kinks" are worked out of the system. Keep the phone company's repair number handy and give them a call any time you can't call out on your POTS phone that's plugged into the NT1 or TA's POTS jack when your computer is running and the ISDN software is all properly loaded and apparently functioning properly.

Check out Chapter 15 for helpful tips and ideas on making your ISDN service more useful and more reliable once you get it up and running.

13

Individual Office ISDN Systems

An individual office ISDN system is quite similar to the home system described in Chapter 12. For the purposes of this chapter, a "small office ISDN system" is defined by these specifications:

1. You want to install the ISDN system yourself.
2. You have a single PC running DOS 6.x and Windows 3.1, WfW 3.11, Win95, or OS/2 Warp.
3. 24-hour use of POTS line via ISDN.
4. Attach multiple POTS phones to the same line (same phone number).
5. Full 128 Kbps throughput with analog phone to ring through one B channel.
6. Internet connection at full 128 Kbps.
7. Capability of using ISDN phones and other ISDN devices (fax, etc.).
8. Use existing analog modem via ISDN (POTS) line.

Given these specifications and the same basic affirmative answers to the questions in Chapter 11 regarding installing the system yourself, you should proceed in the manner discussed in the previous chapter. This chapter will not reiterate all of those details but rather will note differences and provide additional instructions regarding both home and nonresidential installations. If you desire more complex ISDN services, we strongly suggest you contract with an ISDN consultant. This should help to ensure that you get the best system for your particular needs, in the optimal time frame, at a reasonable price (we hope, anyway).

Ordering the ISDN Service from Your Local ISDN Dial Tone Provider

Call your local telephone company's business order number and get connected to their ISDN order person, if they have one. Tell the operator that you want to order an ISDN basic rate interface (BRI) 2B + D line installed at your place of business (residence or office); then wait for the inevitable pause from the phone company person. If he or she doesn't pause but says, "Certainly, sir, may I have your present phone number?" you've landed a winner who knows what's going on.

After you two determine that you are located in an ISDN service area, get answers for these questions (assume you got the following answers):

$150	What is the ISDN installation charge?
$70 flat	What are the monthly charges (basic and usage) for ISDN service?
	What exchanges compose your local ISDN calling area?
no	Will your ISDN service be via a repeater?
yes	Will your ISDN service be via an SLC (subscriber-loop carrier)?
AT&T	Which central office ISDN switch do they have? (e.g., Siemens, AT&T)

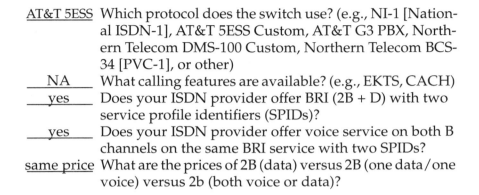

AT&T 5ESS — Which protocol does the switch use? (e.g., NI-1 [National ISDN-1], AT&T 5ESS Custom, AT&T G3 PBX, Northern Telecom DMS-100 Custom, Northern Telecom BCS-34 [PVC-1], or other)

NA — What calling features are available? (e.g., EKTS, CACH)

yes — Does your ISDN provider offer BRI (2B + D) with two service profile identifiers (SPIDs)?

yes — Does your ISDN provider offer voice service on both B channels on the same BRI service with two SPIDs?

same price — What are the prices of 2B (data) versus 2B (one data/one voice) versus 2b (both voice or data)?

Write the answers down so you can refer to them later. To meet your requirements for 128 Kbps with automatic switch-over for an incoming voice call, you will need your service to have both B channels provisioned with data capabilities and at least one of them with voice capabilities. Go for both voice, if the cost isn't prohibitive, especially if you want to use an ISDN phone or two on your system.

If you want special telephone features similar to those on business Centrex systems and you plan to use an ISDN phone, discuss this with the phone service representative and order those you desire. The features available depend on the Regional Bell Operating Company (RBOC) and the type of switch they are using in your vicinity. Some switches have capabilities very similar to those of Centrex business lines, but some are quite limited in their functionality.

If you like what you hear, ask when the service can be installed. No matter what you are told, you can't do much about it, so either you order the installation or you don't. When you place your order, have the phone company representative confirm the installation price and monthly service for the features you have ordered. You will probably be given an order confirmation number and a phone number to dial to check on the progress of your order. Write these down also. You will probably need them. (We're not pessimistic, just realistic.)

While TPC (the phone company) is getting ready to install your line, or turn it on, you can get ready for the big day by purchasing your equipment and software and signing up for an ISDN account at your Internet service provider (ISP).

Purchasing Your ISDN TA/NT1 Interface Card

To meet your specifications for 128 Kbps for Internet and 24-hour POTS usage via ISDN, you will need to make sure that the type 1 network termination (NT1) and terminal adapter (TA), or the combined TA/NT1, that you purchase meet the following criteria:

- NT1 with separate power supply or combined TA/NT1 with an external power cable, or you are willing to leave your computer turned on 24 hours a day.
- The TA is capable of two B channel BONDing with automatic switch to voice for an incoming POTS call.
- The TA has at least one S/T jack if the NT1 is external or U jack if the NT1 is internal.
- Either the NT1 or the combined TA/NT1 has at least one POTS jack.

Several of the NT1s and TAs described in earlier chapters meet these criteria. Talk with your local hardware vendor and your ISP concerning the best combination for your specific needs. You may be able to get the hardware from a mail order company such as the ISDN Warehouse or another one you may find via the Internet or in your local area.

Ask around, but remember that it will probably take TPC upward of three weeks to install your line. If you have to wait for delivery, go on to the next step. If you're lucky and find the card locally, buy it, take it home, take it out of the box, look at it, put it back in the box, then give your ISP a ring to make sure you can get an ISDN dial-up account using Point-to-Point Protocol (PPP) (as the information on their World Wide Web [WWW] site promises).

Ordering Your ISDN Internet Service

When you call your ISP, confirm that they offer two B channel BONDing so you can get the 128 Kbps transmission that you specified. Check the cost. Most ISPs will charge you for each 64 Kbps channel you use. The charges may include a monthly service fee in addition to actual per-second usage on each channel. As you undoubtedly do with all of your business relationships, get all prices, terms, and conditions in writing from your ISP.

Bear in mind that few ISPs have automated the ISDN setup on their end as they have for analog dial accounts. It may take as much as 30 minutes for their network person to configure an account for you. They will want to know what TA and NT1 you are using, in addition to what software you will use to dial up and connect your PPP link. They will probably tell you that they can be ready for you in a couple of days, which is sooner than you need them to be. Tell them your installation date for your ISDN service, and tell them you will call them back when it is installed and you have your card installed in your computer.

Wiring Your Office for ISDN

If you're installing the ISDN in your home office, follow the instructions in Chapter 12. If your location is a separate business office, you may need to contact the owner or property manager before doing any wiring inside your office. Since most office buildings have telephone wiring panels inside closets on each floor or sometimes in each office suite, wiring shouldn't be a problem. The phone company ISDN installation person will bring the ISDN line at least to the nearest wiring panel and perhaps all the way to your office. Most offices are wired with at least eight wire twisted-pair cable, which should give you plenty of unused pairs, only one of which is needed for your ISDN service.

Since this is a business installation, you may need to call in a phone wiring company if your office property manager or owner requires it.

If they do not require it, and if you are handy with a screwdriver, you can easily plug the wires into the proper spots on the wiring panel, IF you can get to it, and IF you know which wires are yours. It may be most cost effective to have the phone company installation person go ahead and plug in the wires all the way to your office and test them at that location. The installation person can also put an RJ-45 jack on the end of the cable if you don't already have one in the wall of your office. Most multiline business telephones use RJ-45 plugs and jacks, so many offices already have the proper jacks in the wall.

For a comprehensive look at ISDN wiring, contact the North American ISDN Users Forum (NIUF) at 301-975-2937 or e-mail *dawn@isdn.ncsl.nist.gov* and request the "ISDN Wiring Guide for Residential and Small Businesses." It will tell you much more than you probably care to know, but who knows, it may make for interesting conversation at your next ISDN users group meeting.

ISDN Installation by the Phone Company

The simplest case for ISDN installation occurs if your business location is within 18,000 feet of one of the phone company's ISDN switches. Just about all the phone company has to do in this case is get on their computer and digitally "flip a few switches" to connect everything and test it up to your office. They will then send an installation person to your location to connect two wires of your existing cable to the proper punch-down tabs in your wiring panel and test the ISDN line with their really cool ISDN line tester. This is all they are really required to do to "install" your ISDN line.

If your computer is running and your NT1 and bridge or router are all set up, you can try using your POTS phone plugged into the bridge or router or NT1 to see if the ISDN line works. Before trying this, you should start your ISDN bridge or router by turning it completely off and then back on after all of the wiring is completed and plugged in. This ensures that the bridge or router looks at your ISDN line and properly loads its line interface software. If the unit initializes, load without error messages, your POTS line should work and you should be able to use your ISDN line for Internet calls after you configure your Internet software with your ISP's help.

Configurations

The remainder of this chapter is dedicated to the configuration of several of the leading routers. The purpose here is to give you a sense of the configuration process. Equipment changes with time, so yours may be significantly different from the equipment shown here.

Sample Configuration: Cisco 1004

The Cisco 1004 supports the same command-line interface as all Cisco Internetworking Operating System (IOS) routers. The examples provided here were created using IOS release 10.3.3. Be aware that commands may be deprecated or modified, or new commands may be introduced in subsequent releases.

SETUP (Cisco IOS)

The following sample SETUP dialog illustrates first-time configuration of a c1004 ISDN router. The SETUP program is initiated automatically the first time the c1004 is powered on, or it can be initiated manually any time thereafter by entering enable mode and executing the setup command. The router reboots once the setup program is complete, and the new startup-config takes effect.

```
--- System Configuration Dialog ---

At any point you may enter a question mark '?' for help.
Refer to the 'Getting Started' Guide for additional help.
Use ctrl-c to abort configuration dialog at any prompt.
Default settings are in square brackets '[]'.
Would you like to enter the initial configuration dialog? [yes]:

First, would you like to see the current interface summary? [yes]:

Any interface listed with OK? value "NO" does not have a valid configuration

Interface     IP-Address     OK?     Method     Status     Protocol
Ethernet0     unassigned     NO      not set    up         up
BRI0          unassigned     NO      not set    up         up

Configuring global parameters:
```

```
    Enter host name [Router]: myhost

The enable secret is a one-way cryptographic secret used
instead of the enable password when it exists.

    Enter enable secret: ourEnablesecret

The enable password is used when there is no enable secret
and when using older software and some boot images.

    Enter enable password: ourEnablePW
    Enter virtual terminal password: ourTelnetPW
    Configure SNMP Network Management? [yes]:
      Community string [public]: ourcommunity
    Configure IP? [yes]:
      Configure IGRP routing? [yes]:
        Your IGRP autonomous system number [1]: 5
    Configure AppleTalk? [no]:
    Configure IPX? [no]:
Enter ISDN BRI Switch Type [none]: basic-ni1

Configuring interface parameters:

Configuring interface Ethernet0:
  Is this interface in use? [yes]:
    IP address for this interface: 206.128.230.38
    Number of bits in subnet field [0]: 4
    Class C network is 206.128.230.0, 4 subnet bits; mask is 255.255.255.240

Configuring interface BRI0:
  Is this interface in use? [yes]:
  Configure IP on this interface? [yes]:
  Configure IP unnumbered on this interface? [no]: yes
    Assign to which interface [Ethernet0]:
```

The following configuration command script was created:

```
hostname myhost
enable secret 5 $2$W3nz$Yopzn1ov0UxAiq.
enable password ourEnablePW
line vty 0 4
password ourTelnetPW
snmp-server community ourcommunity
ip routing
no appletalk routing
no ipx routing
```

```
isdn switch-type basic-ni1
interface Ethernet0
ip address 206.128.230.38 255.255.255.240
interface BRI0
no ip address
ip unnumbered Ethernet0
router igrp 5
network 206.128.230.0
end

Building configuration...[yes/no]: yes
Use the enabled mode 'configure' command to modify this configuration.

Press RETURN to get started!

%LINEPROTO-5-UPDOWN: Line protocol on Interface Ethernet0, changed state to up
%LINK-3-UPDOWN: Interface BRI0, changed state to up
%LINK-3-UPDOWN: Interface Ethernet0, changed state to up
%SYS-5-RESTART: System restarted --
```

At this point, the configuration file can be expanded and modified by executing the configure terminal command. Our sample configuration file, which follows, is listed by executing the show config command.

```
myhost#show conf
Using 815 out of 7506 bytes
version 10.3
no service pad
hostname myhost
enable secret 5 $2$W3nz$Yopzn1ov0UxAiq.
enable password ourEnablePW
username isp-svr password 7 131B172E060D1F12345222C
isdn switch-type basic-ni1
interface Ethernet0
 ip address 206.128.230.38 255.255.255.240
 ip irdp
 ip hello-interval eigrp 5 20
 ip hold-time eigrp 5 60
interface BRI0
 ip unnumbered Ethernet0
 encapsulation ppp
 dialer map ip 204.70.100.1 name isp-svr 18008331234
 dialer-group 1
 isdn spid1 018301234000
 isdn spid2 018301235000
```

```
router eigrp 5
 passive-interface BRI0
 network 206.128.230.0
ip classless
ip route 0.0.0.0 0.0.0.0 204.70.100.1
ip route 204.70.100.0 255.255.255.0 BRI0
access-list 1 permit any
snmp-server community ourcommunity RO
dialer-list 1 list 1
line con 0
line vty 0 4
 password ourTelnetPW
 login
end
```

Beware of CHAP passwords (secrets) longer than 11 ASCII characters. When we entered a longer CHAP password, CHAP negotiation succeeded for all calls made until the next reload. Following reload, CHAP negotiation consistently failed with error messages as shown. If you have been given a password longer than 11 characters, request a new password. As a temporary work-around, remove and then reenter the longer CHAP password after each reload:

```
no username isp-svr
username isp-svr password 7 131B172E060D1F12345222C
```

As noted in the documentation, (at least) one static route is always needed to point to the next hop to enable ISDN calls through BRI. When connecting to some ISPs, you may be required to use an unnumbered BRI interface that inherits the address assigned to the Ethernet interface (`ip unnumbered  Ethernet0` under `interface bri  0`). We entered the following static routes, which configure the ISP's access server as our default gateway, accessed via BRI0:

```
ip route 0.0.0.0 0.0.0.0 204.70.100.1
ip route 204.70.100.0 255.255.255.0 BRI0
```

To support our multisegment LAN with classless addressing, we configured the c1004 to use Enhanced Interior Gateway Routing Protocol (EIGRP) rather than IGRP (the default). This involved entering the following commands:

```
ip classless
no router igrp 5
router eigrp 5
```

Cisco routers offer a wide range of debug and monitor commands, including show, PING, traceroute, and debugging at the event and packet levels for all interfaces, PPP, IP, TCP, User Datagram Protocol (UDP), and router protocols. The context-sensitive help is sufficient in many cases to assist you in using these features for diagnostic purposes as well as education.

Show commands display configuration information; for example, sho arp displays the arp table:

```
sho arp
Protocol   Address          Age (min)   Hardware Addr    Type    Interface
Internet   206.128.230.34      -         0000.0c31.ae23   ARPA    Ethernet1
Internet   206.128.230.38      42        0800.0377.0405   ARPA    Ethernet1
Internet   206.128.230.37      3         0000.0c31.ae22   ARPA    Ethernet1
```

Debug commands can be used to perform real-time event or packet monitoring. When debug ppp negotiation is set on, the entire PPP negotiation process is displayed in real time on the console (or at a Telnet window if the command terminal monitor is entered).

Sample Configuration: Farallon Netopia

The Netopia configuration interface is menu driven. The Main Menu offers the user an Easy Setup process, which is sufficient to configure the router for use in a single LAN segment configuration at the remote site. Other menu choices provide access to more advanced configuration features; access to statistics, tests, and utilities; and access to system security configuration features:

```
            Main Menu
      Netopia PN440  v1.01
      Easy Setup...
      Advanced Configuration...
      Statistics, Tests, Utilities...
      Quick Menus...
      Quick View...
      Security...
```

```
Return/Enter for an overview of the most important statistics.
You always start from this main screen.
```

Use the arrow keys to select among choices within a menu. Jump to a highlighted selection by depressing the Return or Enter key. The ESCape key allows you to return to a previous menu (note that previous menu and next menu are choices within most menus). The Return key completes (confirms) a change/selection to a configuration parameter.

Quick Menu provides an overview of all configuration menus; the user can jump directly to any submenu by moving arrow keys to the desired menu (current selection is highlighted), then pressing the Return/Enter key:

```
Quick Menu

  Connection Profiles          ISDN Setup            SNMP Setup
  Add Connection Profile                             Add IP Trap Receiver
  Change Connection Profile    General IP Options     Change IP Trap Receiver
  Delete Connection Profile                          Delete IP Trap Receiver
                                                     Add DDP Trap Receiver
  Filter Sets                  EtherTalk II Setup    Change DDP Trap Receiver
  Add Filter Set               LocalTalk Setup       Delete DDP Trap Receiver
  Change Filter Set            EtherTalk I Setup
  Delete Filter Set            AURP Setup

  Scheduled Connections        DHCP Setup            Console Configuration
  Add Scheduled Connection     MacIP Setup
  Change Scheduled Connection
  Delete Scheduled Connection  TFTP
                               PC Card Config/Xfer
  Security
```

```
This Menu allows you to visit most configuration screens.
```

Return from Quick Menus to the Main Menu by pressing the ESCape key. Navigate through the menu choices using arrow keys, select Easy Setup, then press ENTER. You are presented with the WAN Configuration menu:

```
WAN Configuration
```

```
        Switch Type...      National ISDN-1 (NI-1)
            SPID 1:         018301235000
            SPID 2:         018301234000
        Directory ID 1:     8301235
        Directory ID 2:     8301234

        NEXT SCREEN                 PREVIOUS SCREEN
```

Return/Enter to select <among/between> ...
Here you enter information supplied to you by your ISDN phone company.

> Use this menu to configure the ISDN switch type and, if relevant, service profile identifiers (SPIDs) and directory numbers (illustrated). Use arrow keys to navigate to the NEXT SCREEN selection and press ENTER. You are presented with the Minimal Connection Profile menu:

```
Minimal Connection Profile (Easy Setup)

        Connection Profile Name:        Easy Setup Profile

        Telephone Number to Dial:       18008331234

        Remote IP Address:              204.70.100.1
        Remote IP Subnet:               255.255.255.0
        Authentication (Security)...    CHAP
        Send User/Host Name:            myhost
        Send Password/Secret:           ****************
        Receive User/Host Name:         isp-svr
        Receive Password/Secret:

                NEXT SCREEN             PREVIOUS SCREEN
```

Return accepts * ESC cancels * Left/Right moves insertion point * Del deletes.
Enter basic information about your WAN connection with this screen.

> Use this menu to specify the ISDN number, IP address, and IP subnet mask for the ISP's access server. Navigate to Authentication (Security). Press the return key to see/select CHAP from the menu choices (none, PAP, CHAP). Enter the User name and CHAP secret provided by your ISP in the Send User/Host Name and Send Password/Secret fields (you will be required to enter the secret twice, for confirmation). Enter the name of the ISP's access server (optional) in

the Receive User/Host Name field. Advance to the next screen for IP Setup:

```
IP Setup (Easy Setup)

            Ethernet IP Address:                 206.128.230.38
            Ethernet IP Subnet Mask:             255.255.255.0
            Default Gateway IP Address:          204.70.100.1
            Domain Name Server IP Address:       204.70.57.242


NEXT SCREEN                    PREVIOUS SCREEN

Enter IP Address in this decimal and dot form: xxx.xxx.xxx.xxx
Set up the basic IP attributes of your Netopia in this screen.
```

Enter the IP address and subnet mask that are to be assigned to the Netopia's Ethernet interface. The gateway IP address should be provided automatically (if the minimum configuration profile has been configured); the domain name server address is optional.

Advance to the next screen (note: The Netopia PN440 will have an additional menu for MacIP options; we omit this here).

```
DHCP Dynamic IP Address Serving (Easy Setup)

            Enable DHCP:                         On
            Number of addresses to allocate:     4
            First Address:                       206.128.230.41

     RESET DEVICE        TO MAIN MENU       PREVIOUS SCREEN


Return accepts * Tab toggles * ESC cancels.
Configure DHCP Dynamic IP Address allocation with this Screen.
```

The Dynamic IP Address Serving menu can be used to provide the Netopia with a range of client addresses that it may use in response to DHCP (Dynamic Host Configuration Protocol) configuration requests from host systems on the local Ethernet. In this example, we tell the Netopia to assign up to four IP addresses to hosts, beginning with address 206.128.230.41. (Farallon supplies PC or MAC client software that supports DHCP.) Upon completing the entries for this menu, select Reset Device to install the new configuration and re-start the unit, or return to the Main Menu for additional configuration options:

```
Advanced Configuration


            WAN (Wide Area Network) Setup...


            General IP (Internet Protocol) Options...
            AppleTalk Setup...


            Dynamic IP Address Serving (DHCP/MacIP)...


            Scheduled Connections...
            Filter Sets (Firewalls)...


            SNMP (Simple Network Management Protocol)...


            Trivial File Transfer Protocol (TFTP)...
            PC Card Config/Firmware Transfer...


            Console Configuration...



Return/Enter for ISDN, PPP/MPP, and Connection Profiles modification.
Use this screen if you want options beyond Easy Setup.
```

The ISDN Setup selection of the WAN Setup menu can be used to modify ISDN SPID, directory number, and switch information.

The Connection Profiles selection can be used to display, add, change, and delete connection profiles, including the Easy Setup Profile configuration already created. Subscribers with multilink service would configure this feature by first selecting the Easy Setup Profile, next selecting MPP/PPP Options, and then selecting from the choices offered for the parameter B-Channel Usage (1 B Channel, Dynamic, 2 B Channels).

```
            Change Connection Profile

      Profile Name:              Easy Setup Profile

      Profile Enabled:           Yes
```

```
              Remote IP Address:              204.70.100.1
              Remote IP Mask:                 255.255.255.0

              Number To Dial:                 18008331234
              Optional 2nd Number:

                              MPP/PPP Options...
                              Telco Options...
                              Additional Options...
```

```
Type to enter name, Left/Right/Delete to edit and move cursor.
Modify Connection Profile here. Changes are immediate.
```

To place a test call manually, choose Establish Connection from this menu, select the Easy Setup Profile, and press RETURN. The Call Status menu will report on the success or failure of the call as it progresses.

The General IP (Internet Protocol) Options menu can be used to change IP parameters configured during Easy Setup and to enable routing. In this example, we change the domain name server we configured initially to be our secondary, make a local host our primary name server, and add a default domain name:

```
General IP (Internet Protocol) Options


              IP Address:              206.128.230.38
              Subnet Mask:             255.255.255.0
              Default Gateway:         204.70.100.1
              DNS Server:              206.128.230.21
              Secondary DNS Server:    204.70.57.242
              Domain Name:             corecom.com
              Receive RIP:             Off
              Transmit RIP:            Off

              IP Encapsulation...      Ethernet
              IP BCast 1s or 0s...     Use Ones
```

```
Enter IP Address in this decimal and dot form: xxx.xxx.xxx.xxx
Set up the basic IP attributes of your Netopia in this screen.
```

The Netopia supports only RIP v1 and does not support static routing. All hosts on the single LAN segment should be configured to
use the Netopia as the default router, so there is no need to run RIP
(turning RIP off eliminates unnecessary LAN traffic).

The AppleTalk Setup is not included here, but is also available.[1] Dynamic IP Address Serving can be used to the modify DHCP configuration choices made through Easy Setup. The Scheduled
Connections menu can be used to restrict ISDN call placement by
day of week, time of day, call duration, and connection profile. Fil-
ter Sets (Firewalls) provide menus for constructing input and output traffic filters. The Trivial File Transfer Protocol (TFTP) menu is
used to set up the unit for transferring firmware or configuration
files to and from a TFTP server. The PC Card Config/X Modem File
Transfer and Console Configuration menus are used to configure
the optional analog modem and the console, respectively.

To monitor the unit using SNMP, we completed the SNMP Setup
menu as follows:

```
SNMP Setup

    System Name:                  myhost
    System Location:              Dresher, PA 19025 USA
    System Contact:               David Piscitello
    Read-Only Community String:   ourPublicCS
    Read/Write Community String:  ourPrivateCS

    Authentication Traps Enable:  On
    IP Trap Receivers...

    DDP (AppleTalk) Trap Receivers...

Return/Enter to view, modify, and delete DDP Trap Receivers.
Configure optional SNMP parameters from here.
```

---

[1] It should be noted that AppleTalk support is one of Farallon's fortes. We had occasion to try the LocalTalk-Ether-
Talk forwarding in a multizone, multirouter environment. The Netopia correctly discovered an existing seed
router and AppleTalk worked flawlessly.

IP Trap Receivers invokes a submenu to add, delete, and modify hosts that are to receive SNMP traps.

The Netopia provides some real-time statistical information through the Statistics submenus of the Statistics, Utilities, and Tests menu. Here, we illustrate the WAN statistics, LAN statistics, and Device and ISDN Event histories (submenus of Event Histories):

```
Statistics, Utilities and Tests

   Statistics                  WAN Statistics...
                               LAN Statistics...
                               Event Histories...
                               AppleTalk Routing Table...
   Utilities                   Date and Time...
                               Establish Connection...
                               Hang Up Connection...

                               Reset System
                               Revert to Factory Defaults...

   Tests                       ISDN Switch Loopback Test...

                          WAN Statistics

       Current B1 Channel Remote Network:       clear
       B1 Bytes Received:                       2606
       B1 Bytes Transmitted:                    2552
       B1 Packets Received:                     106
       B1 Packets Transmitted:                  117
       Current B2 Channel Remote Network:       clear
       B2 Bytes Received:                       564
       B2 Bytes Transmitted:                    799
       B2 Packets Received:                     27
       B2 Packets Transmitted:                  35
       Switch Detected Frame Errors (FEBE):     0
       Netopia Detected Frame Errors (NEBE):    0

       Conn--Connection Profile Name---------Rem. IP Address--State---
       clear
       clear


LAN Statistics
```

```
    Prot.---Pkts Rx----Pkts Tx-----+-General Statistics----------------
    EN IP    0         801      | EN Rx Packets          0
    ET II    0         791      | EN Rx Errors           0
    ET I     0         0        | EN Collisions          0
    LT       0         785      | LT Rx Bad Pkts         0

    IP Address Serving--------------------------------------------------
    Addresses Unused:  DHCP --    0        MacIP (Dynamic) --      0
```

Device Event History

```
  Time-----Date-----Event---------------------------------------------
  -----------------------------SCROLL UP-----------------------------
  11:47:35 02/19
  11:47:35 02/19/96 LocalTalk port active
  11:47:35 02/19/96 EtherTalk Phase 2 port active
  11:47:30 02/19/96 AppleTalk Stack Initialization Complete
  11:47:30 02/19/96 LocalTalk port up
  11:47:30 02/19/96 EtherTalk Phase 2 port up
  11:47:28 02/19/96 BOOT: Warm start
  11:43:15 02/19/96 AppleTalk Router Discovery Complete
  11:43:15 02/19/96 LocalTalk port active
  11:43:15 02/19/96 EtherTalk Phase 2 port active
  11:43:10 02/19/96 AppleTalk Stack Initialization Complete
  11:43:10 02/19/96 LocalTalk port up
  11:43:10 02/19/96 EtherTalk Phase 2 port up
  11:43:08 02/19/96 BOOT: Cold start
  13:21:28 02/16/96 AppleTalk Router Discovery Complete
  -----------------------------SCROLL DOWN----------------------------
```

Return/Enter for details about selection, Left/Esc to exit

Current Time -- 14:36:24

```
                         ISDN Event History    Current Date -- 2/20/96

  Time-----Date------Event-------------------------------Dir. Number---------
  -----------------------------SCROLL UP-----------------------------
  13:44:29 02/20/96 SPID Init Failed                 8301235
  13:44:29 02/20/96 SPID Init Failed                 8301234
  13:44:29 02/20/96 Line Deactivated
  13:01:50 02/20/96 Clear Request Issued             15102384164
  13:01:50 02/20/96 Disconnect Indication Received   15102384164
  13:01:48 02/20/96 Connect Indication Received      15102384164
  13:01:46 02/20/96 Setup Request Issued             15102384164
  13:01:05 02/20/96 Clear Request Issued             15102384164
```

```
13:01:05 02/20/96 Disconnect Indication Received        15102384164
13:01:03 02/20/96 Connect Indication Received           15102384164
13:01:01 02/20/96 Setup Request Issued                  15102384164
13:00:20 02/20/96 Clear Request Issued                  15102384164
13:00:20 02/20/96 Disconnect Indication Received        15102384164
13:00:18 02/20/96 Connect Indication Received           15102384164
13:00:16 02/20/96 Setup Request Issued                  15102384164
-----------------------------SCROLL DOWN-----------------------------

Return/Enter on event item for details or 'SCROLL [UP/DOWN]' item for scrolling.
```

It is also possible to test the ISDN line by attempting a loopback, or to place an ISDN call, from this menu.

Livingston PortMaster OR-U

Livingston offers three means of configuring and monitoring the office router: a command-line interpreter, a Windows-based utility called PMConsole, and a Windows-based configuration wizard. The Office Router Configuration Wizard for Windows 95 is a GUI-based application that methodically leads a user through a basic configuration suitable for Internet access.

The Configuration Wizard presents separate windows for:

- administrative password
- system (Ethernet) IP address and subnet mask
- ISDN switch type
- ISDN SPIDs and directory numbers
- security (if yes, four additional screens request the IP addresses of hosts that act as servers for FTP, HTTP, SMTP, and DNS)
- connection type (on-demand or continuous)
- ISDN speed (64K or 128K) and primary ISDN number to call
- ISP authentication information (PPP, PAP, or CHAP account username and password)

The windows provide highly descriptive and easy to follow instructions, as is illustrated by the Internet Address window:

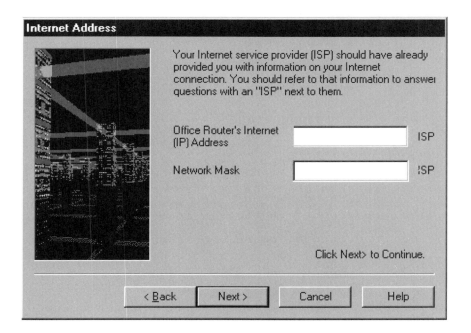

If these do not suffice, a very thorough hypertext help facility can
be invoked:

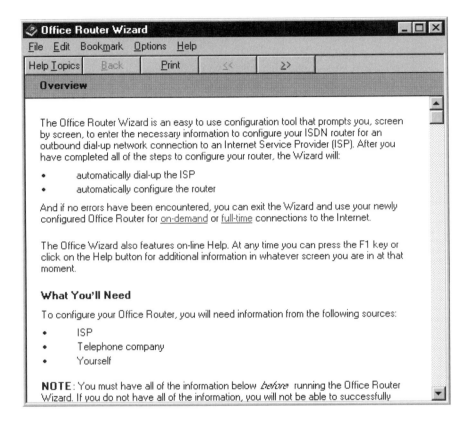

When the Wizard has finished gathering configuration information,
it displays a summary for the user to review. If the user is satisfied
with the configuration, the PC connects to the router, downloads
the configuration, reboots the router, re-establishes a connection
with the router, checks the ISDN connection, checks the routing,
and attempts to place a call to the primary ISDN phone number
identified during configuration.

A limited amount of additional reconfiguration can be accomplished using the Configuration Wizard (e.g., modification of the

parameters that the Wizard requests for initial configuration). Advanced configuration must be performed using the PMConsole application (UNIX or windows-based PC) or the command-line interpreter.

Livingston also provides a GUI-based application for Windows 3.x, Windows 95, and UNIX systems. PMConsole is essentially a graphical interpretation of the command-line interpreter. The Windows application provides the password-protected access to an office router from the PC. Configuration and modification of global and SNMP parameters, ports, locations, users, routes, hosts, and filters are performed through forms within sub-windows of the PMConsole application. The user can view the same statistics and configuration data from PMConsole as from the command line. Port and network connection statistics can be monitored in real time with variable refresh (seconds, minutes, hours). Router maintenance can also be performed from PMConsole (router reboot, configuration download and upload, and system upgrades can be performed from the PC).

The following example illustrates first-time configuration of a PortMaster OR-U router using the router's console command-line interface and the instructions provided in the users' guide.

Note that for a first-time configuration, the command-line interface must first be used to configure the LAN interface for IP routing. Use a terminal emulation program (e.g., ZTerm 0.91 on a Macintosh, or terminal.exe on a PC) on a PC serially connected to the console (S0) port of the PortMaster OR-U to configure the unit (or to configure the unit for PMConsole across a LAN).

Power on the unit. When the OR-U completes its initial boot sequence, a "login:" prompt is displayed. Log in as the PortMaster administrator, that is, the "!root" user (default password is <return>). A prompt "Command>" appears. To set the system password (highly recommended), system name (also used as the sysName SNMP Management object and the CHAP system name), IP address, subnet mask, default gateway, and DNS domain and name server address (optional), use the following commands via a console window:

```
login:!root
Password:
corecom> set password longpassword4you
!root password changed from  to longpassword4you
Command>set sysname corecom
System Name Successfully changed
corecom> set ether0 address 206.128.230.38
Local (ether0) address changed from  to 206.128.230.38
corecom> set ether0 netmask 255.255.255.240
ether0 netmask changed from  to 255.255.255.240
corecom> set gateway 204.70.100.1
Gateway changed from 0.0.0.0 to 204.70.100.1, metric = 1
corecom> set nameserver 206.128.230.21
Name Server changed from  to 206.128.230.21
corecom> set domain corecom.com
Domain changed from    to corecom.com
```

Next, set the ISDN parameters (switch type, SPIDS, DNS) using the following commands (or exit the terminal emulation application and use PMConsole):

```
corecom> set isdn-switch ni-1
ISDN switch type set to NI-1
corecom> set s1 spid 018301234000
SPID for port S1 changed from  to 018301234000
corecom> set s1 directory 8301234
Directory No for port S1 changed from  to 8301234
corecom> set s2 spid 018301235000
SPID for port S2 changed from  to 018301235000
corecom> set s2 directory 8301235
Directory No for port S2 changed from  to 8301235
```

Note that for the PortMaster OR-U, three physical ports (S0–S2) are available; S0 is the console port and can be used for asynchronous dial-in; S1 and S2 are used to represent the two B channels of the ISDN basic rate interface. Assign both S1 and S2 to a unique Dial Group so that they may be bonded for dial-out to a single location (i.e., multilink service) using the following commands:

```
corecom> set s1 group 1
Group number for port S1 changed from 0 to 1
```

```
corecom> set s2 group 1
Group number for port S2 changed from 0 to 1
```

Create a dial-out location using the access server information provided by your ISP, as follows:

```
corecom> add location weasle
Location weasle successfully added
corecom> set location weasle on_demand
weasle changed to On-Demand Dial
corecom> set location weasle destination 204.70.100.1
weasle destination changed from 0.0.0.0 to 204.70.100.1
corecom> set location weasle netmask 255.255.255.0
weasle netmask changed from 0.0.0.0 to 255.255.255.0
corecom> set location weasle netmask 255.255.255.0
weasle netmask changed from 0.0.0.0 to 255.255.255.0
corecom> set location weasle username corecom
New username successfully set for location weasle
corecom> set location weasle password my Password
New password successfully set for location weasle
corecom> set location weasle telephone 18008331234
New telephone successfully set for location weasle
corecom> set location weasle group 1
weasle group number changed from 0 to 1
corecom> set location weasle idletime 2
weasle idle timeout changed from 0 to 2 minutes
corecom> set location weasle maxports 2
weasle maximum port count changed from 0 to 2
corecom> set location weasle high_water 4000
weasle high water level changed from 0 to 4000
```

The preceding commands will allow multilink operation (max
ports set to 2) and "on demand" operation (i.e., IP packets arriving
via the Ethernet for destinations other than the Ethernet subnet will
cause an ISDN call to be placed if one is not in progress).

The set location <location-name> commands were entered individ-
ually, for illustration purposes. It is also possible to enter all the location parameters in a single set command of the form:

```
set location <loc-name> on_demand destination <ip-address> netmask <mask> group
<group-#> ...
```

When you have completed entering the location commands, save
the configuration, as follows:

```
corecom> save all
Saving global configuration
Saving ports
User table successfully saved
Hosts table successfully saved
Static route table successfully saved
Location table successfully saved
SNMP table successfully saved
Filter table successfully saved
New configurations successfully saved.
```

To confirm that you have entered the global parameters correctly,
use the sho all command:

```
corecom> sho all
Local Addr: 206.128.230.38            Default Host: 0.0.0.0
   Gateway: gw.myISP.net              Netmask: 255.255.255.240
DNS Server: 206.128.230.21            Domain: corecom.com
```

Port	Speed	Mdm	Host	Type	Status	Input	Output	Pend
S0	9600	on		Login	COMMAND	1907	22472	2
S1	64000	on	ptp3	Netwrk	ESTABLISHED	2321	2230	0
S2	64000	on		Login/	IDLE	0	0	0

To confirm that you have entered the location parameters correctly,
use the sho location <location-name> command:

```
corecom> sho location weasle
    Location: weasle                  Type: On Demand
 Destination: gw.myISP.net            Netmask: 255.255.255.0
    Protocol: PPP                     Options: Quiet, Compression, Multilink
       Group: 1                       Max Ports: 2
Idle Timeout: 2 minutes               High Mark: 4000 bytes
         Mtu: 1500                     Async Map: 00000000
    Username: corecom                 Password: my Password
   Telephone: 18008331234
```

To place a test call, use the "dial Location_Name [-x]" command;
that is, dial isp-svr.

In a multisegment LAN environment, add static routes through the add route command. In our example, we add a static route for the /16 subnet of the 206.128.230.0 network via gateway 206.128.230.34, then list the routing table to confirm that we have entered the route as intended. We then PING and trace the route to the name server host on that subnet to confirm that the configuration is correct.

```
corecom> add route 206.128.230.16 206.128.230.34 2
New route entry successfully added
corecom> sho route
Destination             Gateway              Flag Met  Interface
------------------      --------------------  ----  ---  ---------
0.0.0.0                 204.70.100.1          NS    1    ptp3
204.70.100.1            204.70.100.1          HL    1    ptp3
206.128.230.16          206.128.230.34        NS    2    ether0
206.128.230.32          206.128.230.38        NL    1    ether0
corecom> ping 206.128.230.21
206.128.230.21 is alive
corecom> traceroute 206.128.230.21
traceroute to  (206.128.230.21), 30 hops max
 1 206.128.230.34
 2 206.128.230.21
```

The PortMaster offers several useful diagnostic commands: ifconfig can be used to determine the protocols and routing protocols in use on a particular interface:

```
corecom> ifconfig
ether0: flags=106<IP_UP,IPX_DOWN,BROADCAST,PRIVATE>
        inet 206.128.230.38 netmask ffffff0 broadcast 206.128.230.47 mtu 1500
ptp3: flags=75<IP_UP,IPX_DOWN,POINT_TO_POINT,SUSPENDED>
        dest 204.70.100.1 netmask fffff00 mtu 1500
```

There is also a wealth of show commands that can be used to view active TCP/UDP connections (sho netconns), port connections (sho sessions), arp, user, and location table entries. For real-time monitoring, the ptrace command can be used in conjunction with packet filters that define the set of packets to view. A debug command is also available to monitor PPP negotiation and ISDN call progress. A sample debug output illustrating the PPP negotiation

between the PortMaster OR-U and an Ascend Max access server
follows:

```
corecom> set console s0
Setting CONSOLE to port S0
corecom> set debug 0x51
Setting debug value to 0x51
corecom> ping 204.70.100.1
sendthem (CRN18008331234)
expect   (=DCD=)
=DCD=got it
Chat Succeeded - Starting PPP
Sending LCP_CONFIGURE_REQUEST to port S1 of 10 bytes containing:
01 01 00 0a 05 06 a1 a1 6c e7
Sending LCP_CONFIGURE_REQUEST to port S1 of 10 bytes containing:
01 02 00 0a 05 06 a1 a1 6c e7
Received LCP_CONFIGURE_REQUEST on port S1 of 26 bytes containing:
01 02 00 1e 00 04 00 00 01 04 05 f4 03 05 c2 23
05 11 04 05 f4 13 09 03 00 c0 7b 4e df 88
Sending LCP_CONFIGURE_REJECT to port S1 of 8 bytes containing:
04 02 00 08 00 04 00 00
Received LCP_CONFIGURE_ACK on port S1 of 6 bytes containing:
02 02 00 0a 05 06 a1 a1 6c e7
Received LCP_CONFIGURE_REQUEST on port S1 of 22 bytes containing:
01 03 00 1a 01 04 05 f4 03 05 c2 23 05 11 04 05
f4 13 09 03 00 c0 7b 4e df 88
Sending LCP_CONFIGURE_REQUEST to port S1 of 25 bytes containing:
01 03 00 19 05 06 a1 a1 6c e7 11 04 06 1c 12 02
13 09 03 00 c0 05 03 02 c8
Sending LCP_CONFIGURE_ACK to port S1 of 26 bytes containing:
02 03 00 1a 01 04 05 f4 03 05 c2 23 05 11 04 05
f4 13 09 03 00 c0 7b 4e df 88
Received LCP_CONFIGURE_REJECT on port S1 of 2 bytes containing:
04 03 00 06 12 02
Sending LCP_CONFIGURE_REQUEST to port S1 of 23 bytes containing:
01 04 00 17 05 06 a1 a1 6c e7 11 04 06 1c 13 09
03 00 c0 05 03 02 c8
Received LCP_CONFIGURE_ACK on port S1 of 19 bytes containing:
02 04 00 17 05 06 a1 a1 6c e7 11 04 06 1c 13 09
03 00 c0 05 03 02 c8
S1: LCP Open
Sending IPCP_CONFIGURE_REQUEST to port S1 of 10 bytes containing:
01 01 00 0a 03 06 ce 80 e6 26
Received CHAP_CONF_CHALLENGE on port S1 of 29 bytes containing:
```

```
Sending CHAP_CONF_RESPONSE to port S1 of 28 bytes containing:
Sending LCP_PROTOCOL_REJECT to port S1 of 16 bytes containing:
08 02 00 10 80 fd 01 01 00 0a 11 06 00 01 01 03

Received IPCP_CONFIGURE_REQUEST on port S1 of 12 bytes containing:
01 02 00 10 02 06 00 2d 0f 01 03 06 cc 46 87 04

Sending IPCP_CONFIGURE_ACK to port S1 of 16 bytes containing:
02 02 00 10 02 06 00 2d 0f 01 03 06 cc 46 87 04

No answer from 204.70.100.1
corecom> Sending IPCP_CONFIGURE_REQUEST to port S1 of 10 bytes containing:
01 03 00 0a 03 06 ce 80 e6 26
Received IPCP_CONFIGURE_ACK on port S1 of 6 bytes containing:
02 03 00 0a 03 06 ce 80 e6 26
S1: IPCP Open
LCP IPCP Open
Connection Succeeded
```

Sample Configuration: ACC Congo and ACC Congo VoiceRouter

The ACC Congo Voice Router configuration follows, including information on theExpress ACCess configuration utility, the ACC router software release 9.5, and the Web-Wizard browser interfaces. The Express ACCess interviewer presents the user with a series of questions and builds an initial configuration based on the responses.

The initial display explains how to navigate the configuration system:

```
******  Welcome to Express Access for the ISDN Telecommuter  ******

Please answer every question before exiting.

NOTE: Some answers require information from your service provider(s).
      To re-enter Express Access login as NETMAN and type CONFIGURE.
---------------------------------------------------------------------
<ctrl>-B    backup to a previous question.
<ctrl>-F    forward to the next question.
```

```
<ctrl>-T    Top: return to first question.
<ctrl>-E    End: go to last question.
ESC         Exit interviewer without saving.
BACKSPACE   Delete previous character.
?           display this guide.


The asterisk (*) in the first column indicates the factory default setting.

The value shown in parentheses is the current value.

Press RETURN to accept the value displayed in parentheses and
proceed to the next question.
-------------------------------------------------------------------------
```

Prompts subsequent to the initial display ask for ISDN switch type, SPIDs, ISDN connection and service information (e.g., 2B+D), and (iteratively, for up to two calls) IP addressing, authentication, ISDN number information for the destination system (e.g., the ISP's access server) and phone numbers for the analog ports. The ISDN connection related questions are illustrated below (the values in parentheses are those used in the evaluation):

```
Select your ISDN switch type:
*  1 = NET3 (UK-EURO ISDN)
   2 = NI-1 (N. America)
   3 = 5ESS (N. America)
   4 = DMS-100 Custom (N. America)
   5 = VN3 (France)
   6 = KDD (Japan)
   7 = NTT (Japan)
   8 = Telia Access Duo (Sweden)
   9 = TPH1962 (Australia)
(2) >


Has your service provider given you a Service Profile Identifier (SPID)?
*  1 = yes
   2 = no
(1) >


How many Service Profile Identifiers (SPID) have you been given?
*  1 = 1 SPID
   2 = 2 SPIDs
(2) >
```

```
Enter the first SPID:
(015558392000) >

Enter the first Telephone Number
(5558392) >

Which phone port do you want calls for this number to ring?
  1 = PHONE1
  2 = PHONE2
(1) >

Enter the second SPID:
(015558907000) >

Enter the second Telephone Number
(5558907) >

Which phone port do you want calls for this number to ring?
  1 = PHONE1
  2 = PHONE2
(2) >

Describe your ISDN service provisioning
  1 = 1B+D
  2 = 2B+D
(2) >

Do you want to configure to send data to two different locations?
  1 = Yes
  2 = No
(2) >

Do you want to use Multilink to combine both the B-channels
for higher bandwidth (up to 128K)?
  1 = Yes
  2 = No
(1) >


Enter the first number you will be calling
(no dashes, no spaces; e.g., 18005551212):
(18005551212) >

Login name for this number (case sensitive, 63 characters max.):
(weasle) >
```

```
Password for this number (case sensitive, Maximum Length: PAP - 8, CHAP - 16):
(password4me) >


Select the authentication method to be used for this number
(The remote side must use the same method.):
* 1 = PAP  (Password Authentication Protocol, less secure)
  2 = CHAP (Challenge Handshake Authentication Protocol, more secure)
(2) >


Enter the second number you will be calling
(no dashes, no spaces; e.g., 18005551212):
(18005551213) >
```

The last set of questions is specific to the environment in which the Congo will operate: IP or IPX routed or bridging. For Internet access, it is necessary to enter the IP address of the LAN port and the subnet mask used in the Ethernet LAN environment. The choice of "unnumbered" IP for the ISDN interface is appropriate for the service provided by most ISPs. Answer "NO" to the bridge non-IP traffic question to avoid propagating packets other than IP packets onto the ISDN connection (such packets will be discarded but the traffic will result in unwanted ISDN calling charges if not filtered). The final question asks whether the configuration should be installed.

```
Select a routing protocol to configure or Bridging only:
* 1 = IP routing
  2 = IPX routing
  3 = IP/IPX routing
  4 = Bridging only
(1) >


Enter the IP address for your Ethernet port (e.g., 129.192.111.111):
(206.128.230.38) >


Enter the subnet mask for your Ethernet port:
(255.255.255.240) >


Will you be using unnumbered IP for your ISDN port
(if yes, both sides must use unnumbered IP):
* 1 = yes
  2 = no
(1) >
```

```
Do you want to bridge non-routed traffic?
  1 = yes
* 2 = no
(2) >

Do you want to set the router's name?
  1 = Yes
  2 = No
(1) >yes

Enter your router's name
(weasle) >

Do you want to install this configuration?
* 1 = yes
  2 = Exit without install
(1) >
...........

Configuration installed.
```

Once the configuration is installed, the Congo will begin processing. It is necessary to enter the command "set configuration save" to make permanent this or any subsequent change to the configuration entered. To use DHCP, the host must enable DHCP and the router must be set to the default factory settings. The IP address for the host need not be set.

Web-Wizard Configuration Tool

ACC provides a browser-based configuration tool for Windows 3.x and Windows 95-based PCs called the Web-Wizard. The Web-Wizard runs on the PC as a combination BOOTP/HTTP server, TFTP client and SNMP manager. From a Web browser such as Mosaic or Netscape Navigator, the user opens a URL to the PC's IP address (e.g., http://206.128.230.35/). From the home page, the user can read a mini-tutorial on ISDN, view a step-by-step, pictorial description of the hardware installation process, and then configure the Congo. A guide to troubleshooting and a glossary are also available. As an example, when help on B-channels is requested, the following screen is shown.

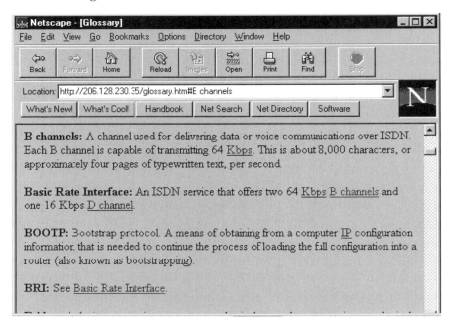

The Web-Wizard uses HTML forms to collect configuration data in the form of typed text, checkmarks, and radio button selection inputs. The Web-Wizard directs the user through the configuration process in much the same manner as the Express ACCess interviewer, but the look and feel is clearly designed to take full advantage of a user's familiarity (and fascination) with Web browsers. When the user asks to configure routing, the Wizard asks for:

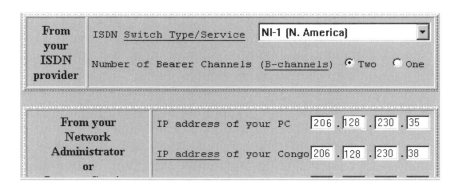

- ISDN Switch type and # of B channels
- IP address and mask of Congo VR and PC running Web-Wizard

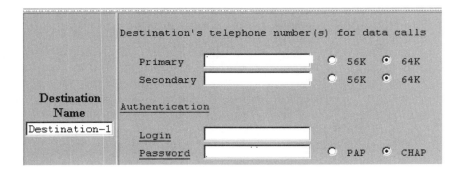

- SPID, telephone number, and phone assignment for primary and secondary ISDN numbers (we've left these blank as an exercise for the reader to complete). Assignments of ISDN numbers to phones is accomplished using radio buttons.

- Telephone number(s) and name of the destination to be called
- Data rate of calls (select radio button for 56K or 64K)
- Authentication information (login and password)
- Mode of authentication (radio button for PAP or CHAP)
- Whether multiple B channels are to be used (checkmark) item
- Selection of ISDN port for unnumbered TCP/IP. This implies that an IP address for the B channel interfaces need

```
☑  Multilink (combine) B-channels

☑  TCP/IP (Internet)

ISDN Port's IP Address Type

◉  Dynamic (Unnumbered or Negotiated)
◯  Static (Numbered)
    IP Address    [206].[128].[   ].[   ]
    Subnet Mask   [255].[255].[255].[0  ]
    Next Hop      [206].[128].[   ].[   ]
```

not be assigned. Instead, the IP address of the Ethernet port is used to connect to the remote network. This is made possible by Internet Protocol Control Protocol (IPCP) support. Based on the access server's willingness to negotiate IPCP parameters, the Congo will use Network Address Folding (NAF), which will perform network address translation on every source IP address on the remote LAN, and use only single IP addresses assigned by the ISP's access server to the Voice Router. Another useful feature of the Voice Router is default DHCP support, wherein an IP address may be assigned to each user from a pool of reserved IP addresses configured at the router (through the command line interface). DHCP provides IP addresses to PC and Macintosh clients that are configured to acquire addresses dynamically through DHCP. The IP address, the domain name, and the domain server address are supplied by the Congo.

The sample configuration can also be displayed and saved to a file. The Web-Wizard translates the forms input into a configuration, and the configuration file is TFTPed to the router. To test the router, a call can be placed through this interface.

Command Line Interpreter

A local management agent displays significant events to the console in the vernacular of the Simple Network Management Protocol (SNMP). A "PROMPT?" indicates that console access is available to an authenticated user. Use the login command to enter configuration mode (defaults shown). The "?" changes to a ">" once the user successfully logs in.

```
PROMPT?
*** TRAP from local agent at 01-Jan-80 00:00:00 uptime 0 Days, 00:00:00
*** RM: Setting the source address for M1 to IP address 206.128.230.38

PROMPT?
*** TRAP from local agent at 01-Jan-80 00:00:00 uptime 0 Days, 00:00:00
*** MLINK: M1: Link Up
PROMPT?
*** TRAP from local agent at 01-Jan-80 00:00:00 uptime 0 Days, 00:00:00
*** Link Up, ETH1
PROMPT? login netman
Password:
  login successful
System Description = IP/IPX ISDN Small Office, Home Office Access
Software Version   = 8.2 (ISDN Software Version 8.0)
```

To view the configuration file created by the software, enter the following command (response shown):

```
PROMPT> display file config filespec sys:config.scr
SET BRIDGE PORT COUNT 3
SET STP MODE OFF
SET BRIDGE MODE OFF
ADD BRIDGE PORT ENTRY ETHERNET 2 ETH1
SET BRIDGE PORT STATUS 2 ENABLED
ADD DIAL PORT ENTRY D01 WAN1
ADD DIAL PORT ENTRY D02 WAN1
SET DIAL PORT ADMIN STATE D01  ENABLED
SET DIAL PORT AUTHENTICATION METHOD D01 CHAP
ADD DIAL PORT CALL ADDRESS D01 "18005551212,CM56" "password4me" "weasle"
SET DIAL PORT ADMIN STATE D02  ENABLED
SET DIAL PORT AUTHENTICATION METHOD D02 CHAP
ADD DIAL PORT CALL ADDRESS D02 "18005551213,CM56" "password4me" "weasle"
ADD IP NETWORK ENTRY 206.128.230.38 255.255.255.240 ETH1
ADD IP NETWORK ENTRY M1
```

```
ADD IP ROUTE ENTRY 0.0.0.0 0.0.0.0 M1 1
SET ISDN SWITCH TYPE WAN1 BRI-NI1
ADD ISDN SPID ENTRY WAN1.1 "015558392000"
ADD ISDN SPID ENTRY WAN1.2 "015558907000"
ADD MULTILINK GROUP ENTRY M1
ADD MULTILINK GROUP PHYSICAL PORT M1 D01
ADD MULTILINK GROUP PHYSICAL PORT M1 D02
SET MULTILINK GROUP PROTOCOL M1 STANDARD
SET MULTILINK GROUP ADMIN STATUS M1 ENABLED
RESET
```

Note line 16 of the configuration. The default route for all but local network traffic is automatically forwarded out the ISDN multilink connection (M1). Note also that this configuration can be copied to a TFTP server for archiving or restoral.

In a LAN environment where RIP is operated, the configuration generated by Express ACCess is complete; no additional configuration is required (unless the SNMP agent is to be configured). In an environment where classless IP numbering is applied, the only remaining configuration information required is to introduce static routes. This is accomplished using the ADD IP ROUTE ENTRY command. To enable routing to a second LAN in our multi-LAN segment example via our dual Ethernet router through IP address 206.128.230.34, we enter the following:

```
ADD IP ROUTE ENTRY 206.128.230.16 255.255.255.240 206.128.230.34 1
```

The resulting routing table (DISPLAY IP ROUTE TABLE) is:

Destination	Route Mask	Next Hop	Port	Metr	Typ	Src	Age
0.0.0.0	0.0.0.0	M1	M1	1	DIR	MGMT	0
204.70.100.0	255.255.255.0	M1	M1	1	DIR	MGMT	0
206.128.230.16	255.255.255.240	206.128.230.34	ETH1	1	REM	MGMT	0
206.128.230.32	255.255.255.240	206.128.230.38	ETH1	0	DIR	LOC	25903
End of table							

The following commands are used to configure the SNMP agent (add trap entry identifies the trap host):

```
SET SYSTEM CONTACT "David M. Piscitello"
SET SYSTEM LOCATION "Core Competence, Inc., Dresher PA"
```

```
SET SYSTEM DOMAIN "weasle.corecom.com"
set snmp authentication trap mode enable
add trap entry 206.128.230.35 1
```

The Congo provides access to SNMP, interface, router, and system statistics through DISPLAY commands. For example, DISPLAY ISDN STATISTICS TAB shows the following:

```
ACCCONGO> display isdn statistics tab
Interface     = WAN1    InErrors = 14      OutErrors = 0
InPackets     = 4460    InOctets = 29911   InDiscards = 14
OutPackets    = 4460    OutOctets = 18630  OutDiscards = 0
UnsolResps    = 0       PeerSABME = 0      N200Errors = 1
NrSeqErrors   = 0       RecvdFRMR = 0      CntlErrors = 0
InfoErrors    = 0       WrongSize = 0      N201Errors = 0
CallsOrig     = 13      CallsOffrd = 0     CallsCompl = 13
CallsRouted   = 13      CallsAccpt = 0     CallsClear = 13
```

The HELP command can be used to identify parameters, and is in some cases more detailed and accurate than the documentation.

The Congo issues alarm or "trap" messages to the console for specific events, controlled by SET commands.

```
*** TRAP from local agent at 01-Jan-80 00:28:51 uptime 0 Days, 00:28:51
*** DIAL: D01: trying (18005551212,CM56) on port WAN1.1, retries left = 2
*** TRAP from local agent at 01-Jan-80 00:28:51 uptime 0 Days, 00:28:51
*** DIAL: D01: call initiated
*** TRAP from local agent at 01-Jan-80 00:28:51 uptime 0 Days, 00:28:51
*** DIAL: D01: event Dial from state Disconnected to state Dialing
*** TRAP from local agent at 01-Jan-80 00:28:51 uptime 0 Days, 00:28:51
*** ISDN: Calling 18005551213, WAN1 (WAN1.1)
*** TRAP from local agent at 01-Jan-80 00:28:53 uptime 0 Days, 00:28:53
*** ISDN: Call connected on channel B1, WAN1 (WAN1.1)ACCCONGO>
*** TRAP from local agent at 01-Jan-80 00:28:54 uptime 0 Days, 00:28:54
*** DIAL: D01: CHAP Authentication Success, WAN1.1
*** TRAP from local agent at 01-Jan-80 00:28:54 uptime 0 Days, 00:28:54
*** DIAL: D01: event LLUp from state Dialing to state Connected
*** TRAP from local agent at 01-Jan-80 00:28:54 uptime 0 Days, 00:28:54

*** MLINK: M1: Link D01 Accepted, Active Links:1
```

Proteon GlobeTrotter 70

Proteon offers three means of configuring and monitoring the Globe-Trotter 70. The Windows-based GlobeTrotter Setup Utility (Windows 3.11, Workgroups 3.11, Windows NT, and Windows 95), the Quick Config, and Command Line Interface.

Quick Config and the Command Line Interpreter

Quick Config is used to set an initial configuration for the router. Once the unit is named, the Quick Config interviewer organizes the configuration process.

The following sample quick configuration dialog illustrates a first-time configuration of a GT 70 router. This was generated using a VT 100 emulation from a PC serial port to the router console port.

Quick Configuration Utility

The interviewer identifies the physical interfaces available (Ethernet, ISDN) and then asks for:

- ISDN switch type (default NI-1)
- point or multipoint (default MP)
- local directory numbers (for our NI-1 switch, two)
- ISDN SPID (for our NI-1 switch, two)
- remote router name
- ISDN phone number used to call remote router (for our NI-1 switch destination, two)
- call placement directives (place outbound, accept inbound)
- multilink PPP and STAC compression selection (enable or disable)
- CHAP setup (local CHAP name, demand CHAP from remote, CHAP secret)

The initial configuration sequence is as follows:

```
*talk 6

Config>qc
```

Router Quick Configuration for the following:

- Router Name
- Interfaces
- Protocols
  IP (including RIP and SNMP)

Event Logging will be enabled for all configured subsystems with logging level 'Standard'

Local Router's Name: [] **weasle**

```
***********************************************************
Interface Configuration
***********************************************************

Type 'Yes' to Configure Interfaces
Type 'No' to skip Interface Configuration
Type 'Quit' to exit Quick Config

Configure Interfaces? (Yes, No, Quit): [Yes] Yes
Type 'r' any time at this level to restart Interface Configuration


Intf 0 is Ethernet

Intf 1 is ISDN

Switch Variant Model (5ESS, DMS100, NET3, INS64, USNI1, USNI2, VN3, AUS): [USNI1] USNI1

Point/Multi-Point Selection (PP, MP): [MP] MP

Enter Directory-Number-0 (number or number:extension): [] 5558320
Enter Directory-Number-1 (number or number:extension): [] 5558321

Enter Service Profile ID 0 (19 digits max): [] 015558320000
Enter Service Profile ID 1 (19 digits max): [] 015558321000

Specify remote router name (1-23 chars): [] myISP
Enter 'myISP' ISDN address (number or number:extension): [] 18005551212
Enter a second ISDN phone number? (Yes, No): [Yes] No

Place Outbound Calls (Yes, No): [Yes] Yes
Accept Inbound Calls (Yes, No): [Yes] No
```

```
Multilink PPP (Disable, Enable): [Disable] Enable
PPP STAC Data Compression (Disable, Enable): [Disable] Disable

Setup CHAP authentication? (Yes, No): [Yes] Yes

Local Name used for CHAP Identification: [weasle] weasle
Require CHAP from remote? (Yes, No): [No] No
Router myISP's CHAP Secret: [] mysecret

Setup PAP authentication? (Yes, No): [No] No

This is all configured device information:

Intf 0 is Ethernet
Ethernet, Connector (10baseT) auto-configured
Intf 1 is ISDN

Switch-Variant-Model:          USNI1
Multipoint Selection:          MP
DN0 (Directory-Number-0):      5558320
DN1 (Directory-Number-1):      5558321
Service Profile ID (SPID) 0:   015558320000
Service Profile ID (SPID) 1:   015558321000
Terminal Endpoint ID (TEI) 0:  AUTO
Terminal Endpoint ID (TEI) 1:  AUTO

Remote Router Name:            myISP
Remote Router Phone Number:    18005551212

Outbound Calls:                Enabled
Inbound Calls:                 Disabled
Multilink PPP:                 Enabled
PPP STAC Data Compression:     Disabled

CHAP options
------------
Local router identifier:       weasle
Require CHAP from remote?       No
my-access-server's Secret:     mysecret


Save this configuration? (Yes, No): [Yes] Yes

Device configuration saved
```

```
**********************************************************
Protocol Configuration
**********************************************************

Type 'Yes' to Configure Protocols
Type 'No' to skip Protocol Configuration
Type 'Quit' to exit Quick Config

Configure Protocols? (Yes, No, Quit): [Yes] Yes
Type 'r' any time at this level to restart Protocol Configuration

Configure IP? (Yes, No): [Yes] Yes
Type 'r' any time at this level to restart IP Configuration

Enable IP on this interface? (Yes,No) : [Yes] Yes

IP Address:[] 206.128.230.38

Address Mask:[255.0.0.0] 255.255.255.240

Use Unnumbered IP Addressing? (Yes,No): [Yes] Yes

Enable Dynamic Routing via RIP> (Yes,No): [Yes] Yes

Specify a Default Route? (Yes,No): [Yes] Yes

Default Route Gateway IP Address?[0.0.0.0] 206.128.230.38

Specify default route via an Unnumbered Interface? (Yes,No): [Yes] Yes

Which interface is the default route? (0-1):[1] 1

Quick Config Done
Restart the router for this configuration to take effect
```

The resulting configuration is then saved and the router is restarted for the configuration to take effect.

```
Restart the router? (Yes, No): [Yes] Yes


RESTARTING THE ROUTER........
```

This configuration worked with the initial rate of 64K.

GlobeTrotter Setup Utility

The windows-based GlobeTrotter Setup Utility allows the user to create a new (initial) configuration, modify a configuration file stored on the PC, and upload the current setup data from a Globe-Trotter via the local console port or the Ethernet. Serial download of the configuration file from a PC to the console port through Setup is straightforward, but to download an initial configuration for a router across the Ethernet, you must enable IP and an SNMP write community string on the router using the command line interface before the GUI application can communicate with the GlobeTrotter.

The GlobeTrotter Setup begins by requesting that the user identify the router type (e.g., GlobeTrotter 70, 72, etc.). Subsequent windows for the GlobeTrotter 70 (selected) are styled as index cards and request:

- Router Info/Console Login: two index cards with embedded forms fields request router name, Location and Contact (used for SNMP agent), and router security (user/password pairs for three levels of user permission: monitor, administrator, operator).
- LAN configuration: IP address and subnet mask for the Ethernet interface. Setup presets the mask to an appropriate Class-full mask, and the user may modify this for classless addressing.
- WAN port: this window establishes the data link encapsulation for WAN circuits and is preset to PPP for the GlobeTrotter 70.
- ISDN phone book: ISDN call destination names and telephone numbers entered here are stored in a phone book. The terminology in this window was rather confusing, but the Getting Started Guide and the second-level online help confirmed that these were indeed the names and directory numbers for destinations (called remote routes).
- ISDN circuit configuration: a separate circuit must be created for each destination to be called by the Globe-Trotter. For each circuit, the user selects a calling profile

(an inbound/outbound/inbound and idle time), and can optionally edit an access list (packet filters). A second index card allows PPP NCP configuration. A third index card requests ISDN switch-type, DNs and SPIDs. A fourth index card can be used to select unnumbered or numbered IP operation (default: unnumbered).

- Routing and SNMP agent: identification of default gateway, selection of IP RIP routing and enabling of SNMP is performed using these two index cards.
- Advanced Configuration Options: from this window, the user can view and customize the configuration created.
- Export Configuration: from this window, the user can save the configuration file, or attempt to export it to the router over the serial (console) port or the Ethernet.

This configuration also worked with an initial rate of 64K.

Command Line Interpreter

The interpreter provides access to configuration, monitoring and logging facilities, which are run as independent processes on the router. Complete configuration information, statistics, and monitoring utilities (PING, traceroute) can be viewed through the GWCON process. The CONFIG process provides access to the Quick Config utility; changes to individual configuration parameters are performed from the command line through this process. The Event Logging System can be configured to display selected messages logged as a result of router activity.

Summary

You're a business person; therefore, you know that nothing works perfectly the first time you try it. Murphy's law just won't let that happen. So try to be patient and check your setup parameters carefully when you enter them. Proceed deliberately, step by step. Test after each step. Write everything down as if you were the one writing this book for someone else to follow for a first-time installation.

If you have problems, Chapter 14 may help you. Also, call your ISP if the problems are in connecting to their Internet system. If your POTS phone won't work at all, give the phone company a call. They can use their computers to check your ISDN line fairly far up toward your location without sending anyone out. Also, check out Chapter 15 for helpful tips and ideas on making your ISDN service more useful and more reliable once you get it up and running.

14

Troubleshooting, Tips, and Testing

Troubleshooting Your ISDN System

When it comes to dealing with trouble on an ISDN system, it's wise to recall the organization of the Open Systems Interconnection (OSI) Reference Model, which starts at the physical layer and works its way up through data link, network, transport, session, presentation, and application layers on its way from the networking hardware to the software that's trying to use the network.

In general, most problems tend to occur lower in the model than at higher levels. That's certainly borne out by the most common cause of networking problems of any kind, namely loose or damaged cables. If you'll take the time to work your way through the following troubleshooting steps, you'll find that most problems will pop out on their own. Although it may be time consuming to follow this recipe, it provides the best guarantee not only that you'll be able to identify the source of your problems but also that you'll be able to fix them.

1. If the hub, PC, and router have visual indicators that show whether signal is present, are the lights for each port on? If not,
   • Are the cables properly situated in RJ-45 female connections (snap them out and back in again)?
   • Is the cable from PC to hub OK (cable tester required)?
   • Is the cable from router to hub OK?
2. Now that you are confident your local area network (LAN) wiring is OK, check the status of the Ethernet interfaces on your PC(s) and router, in particular:
   • Are the Ethernet ports administratively up?
   • Can you perform a successful loopback (self-test)?
3. If Ethernet self-tests pass, try PINGing the router from the PC (identify applications). If PING fails, examine these possibilities:
   • Are the Internet Protocol (IP) addresses correctly entered for the PC and the router?
   • Is the default gateway parameter in the PC correctly set?
   • Are both the router and PC configured with the same IP subnet mask?
   • Is IP enabled on the Ethernet port of the router?
4. If PING succeeds to the router, can you PING the IP address of your Internet service provider's (ISP's) access server? If not, debug facilities like those in Cisco's IOS operating system ("debug ISDN events, debug ISDN q931, debug ISDN q932") or "set ISDN message level 5" from ACC's command interpreter can be really helpful. With these, you can check the following:
   • Does your router detect a physical signal (are you sure you have an internal NT1 in that unit, bunky?)?
   • Did your router ISDN interface succeed in switch, service profile identifier (SPID), and terminal endpoint identifier (TEI) registration?
   • Is the called ISDN telephone number configured in your router the number for your ISP access server?
5. If ISDN is properly configured, are your Point-to-Point Protocol (PPP) parameters correct? Again, using debug facilities (in Cisco IOS, "debug PPP negotiation, debug PPP events, debug PPP packet") will help you determine whether your local router

identity, remote router identity, and Challenge Handshake Authentication Protocol (CHAP) secret or Password Authentication Protocol (PAP) password are incorrectly configured.

6. If PPP is correctly configured:
   - Look at the router's local IP routing table. Is your router configured to forward all nonlocal traffic to the ISP's access server?
   - Is your router configured to place ISDN calls on demand? Is your router configured to interpret all IP packets as reasons to place an on-demand call?
7. If your routing is correctly configured and the PING succeeds, try PINGing a host on the Internet. If you cannot PING the host, try a traceroute. If you get only to the ISP's access server and no further, call your ISP to see if the ISP's access server or backbone is routing your subnet properly.
8. If you succeed in PINGing or tracing to a remote host, try running an application to that host using the host's domain name. If this fails, check to see that you have properly configured the domain name server (DNS) entry in your PC.

At this point you ought to be up and running!

ISDN Line Problems

ISDN lines fail differently from analog lines. With an analog line, you can get poor voice reception, noisy lines, and even crossover to other conversations. With an ISDN line, you may occasionally get a "pop" or "snap" on the line, but when an ISDN line fails, it usually won't work at all.

If you're not sure if your ISDN line is down, or your NT1 or TA isn't working properly, try plugging your POTS phone into the ISDN jack. If you hear "white noise," the ISDN line is still there, in some fashion. If it is dead calm, the ISDN line is completely out and it's time to call your local phone company's repair number.

If your PC ISDN drivers try to load and give you a layer 1 failure error, there is probably something wrong with the ISDN line itself.

If you get a layer 2 failure error, the problem is probably with the provisioning of the phone company's switch for your service.

In testing your TA, you may be instructed to perform a "self-call" test. Some instructions have you call your secondary ISDN number via your primary number. For some reason, this may not work, although if you try to call your primary ISDN number, it will work. Try both and see what happens. This is probably a function of the way the ISDN service is provisioned for data. Call your ISDN provider if neither works and you can't get any data call to function.

Most TA software packages include a "logging" function, which is useful for tracking down problems (see Chapter 12). The log files keep a running account of what happens during your ISDN sessions. They generally contain the following type of information (as shown in this example taken from our ISC SecureLink log):

```
06/26/95 11:18:45 *** Logging STARTED ***
06/26/95 11:18:45 SecureLink(TM) ISDN Adapter, Version 3.00b Feb 09 1995
06/26/95 11:18:45 TAPI Version 3.00b Feb 09 1995
06/26/95 11:18:45 Switch type: National ISDN-1
06/26/95 11:18:45 Board 1:
06/26/95 11:18:45   S/T interface, iobase = $2a0, IRQ = 11, address = $cc00
06/26/95 11:18:45     SPID #1 = 512123123401
06/26/95 11:18:45     SPID #2 = 512123123501
06/26/95 11:18:46 Physical layer connection established for board 1
06/26/95 11:18:46 Layer 2 connection established for board 1, TEI 105
06/26/95 11:18:46 Layer 2 connection established for board 1, TEI 106
06/26/95 11:18:46 SPID #1 accepted for board 1
06/26/95 11:18:46 SPID #2 accepted for board 1
06/26/95 11:18:46 Initialization successful.
06/26/95 11:18:58 Attempting to establish PPP connection to REALTIME.
06/26/95 11:19:01 Call established (64 Kbps) to REALTIME at 3774141.
06/26/95 11:19:01 PPP - Authentication Complete to REALTIME.
06/26/95 11:19:01 PPP - IP Link UP to REALTIME (213.88.3.133)
06/26/95 11:19:01         Local IP Address (213.88.3.124) was configured.
06/26/95 11:20:03 Call down (64 Kbps) to REALTIME at 3774141.
06/26/95 11:20:03     Reason -> NORMAL.
06/26/95 11:20:03 PPP connection terminated to REALTIME.
06/26/95 12:18:03 Attempting to establish PPP connection to REALTIME.
06/26/95 12:18:04 Call established (64 Kbps) to REALTIME at 3774141.
06/26/95 12:18:04 PPP - Authentication Complete to REALTIME.
06/26/95 12:18:04 PPP - IP Link UP to REALTIME (213.88.3.133)
```

```
06/26/95 12:18:04        Local IP Address (213.88.3.124) was configured.
06/26/95 12:19:07 Call down (64 Kbps) to REALTIME at 3774141.
06/26/95 12:19:07     Reason -> NORMAL.
06/26/95 12:19:07 PPP connection terminated to REALTIME.
```

The log includes any error messages that occur during operation. These will hopefully be defined—with suggestions on how to remedy the problem—in your card's users' manual. You can always give the vendor or manufacturer or your ISDN TA a call on your working POTS line to help you diagnose and repair your problem.

IRQ, Address, SRAM, and Other Hardware Conflicts

Newer PCs have various built-in system diagnostics and settings that are designed to provide faster, smoother operation. But when you start adding complicated network cards and drivers, some conflicts may occur. The standard IRQs, I/O addresses, and SRAM (scratch random-access memory) conflicts are usually noticed by the installation program from the ISDN card, or will be handled automatically on a plug-and-play system like Windows 95. Alternatively, you can use the Microsoft diagnostic program (MSD.EXE) or a Windows-based diagnostic program to determine your current hardware and software settings and usage, and then configure the card manually to avoid conflicts.

Conflicts with the PC's BIOS and CMOS settings are much harder to find. It generally requires using a process of elimination by testing one setting at a time until the conflict is located (or fixed). Since this requires that you reboot your computer each time you try a different setting, it is very time consuming.

Comments from users of various WfW systems have pointed to the following known conflicts, so you might start by disabling these settings if they are present on your computer:

- Auto Config Function: AMIBIOS ADVANCED CHIPSET SETUP
- Hidden Refresh: AMIBIOS ADVANCED CHIPSET SETUP

These two functions, when enabled, kept WfW from loading properly with the ISC SecureLink card and Network Device Interface Specification (NDIS) drivers. When disabled, the system worked just fine with no noticeable degradation in functionality, which makes you wonder what enabling the two "features" really did in the first place.

Read-only memory (ROM) shadowing in a Compaq ProSignia seemed to cause memory conflict problems when installing the drivers for a Digi PCIMAC/4 board under the Windows NT Server.

If you don't know how to check your CMOS settings, give your hardware vendors a call and ask for help. They deal with these problems every time they change a modem or another I/O card in a PC. If you think you know enough to try to fix your system yourself, remember to write everything down on screen prints of the settings, to change only one setting at a time, and to cold boot your computer after each change. Entering Ctrl + Alt + Delete may not reset the hardware, and pushing the reset button may not completely clear the RAM in some computers. Always turn your machine off for at least 10 seconds before restarting it.

Windows for Workgroups and Windows NT Problems and Solutions

If you installed a network ISDN TA/NT1 card or router and notice that your network occasionally creates periodic ISDN connections to your ISP for no apparent reason (we mean here that you'll observe a connection being established every one to five minutes). If your minimum time-out is one minute and your system automatically reconnects one minute after it has been disconnected, you will be "on line" for about 30 out of every 60 minutes. This adds rapidly to any per-minute toll charges from both your ISDN and Internet providers.

Several causes, and a couple of solutions, have been suggested for this problem. On systems using Windows NT, the NetBIOS-based browser service looks for other NT machines in your workgroup or domain at regular intervals. Since you have an ISDN interface that looks like any other NIC card as far as the system is concerned, when it sends local subnet broadcasts, your ISDN link tries to call the other end of the line to pass that information along.

The solution is easy, because NT has a neat configuration screen in the Network Control Panel. Start Control Panel, and open the Network panel. Then click on "Bindings." On this screen, items on the left represent services, protocols, and so on. Items on the right represent interfaces and lower level protocols. If the light bulb is on, the software pieces are talking to each other. If the bulb is dim, they aren't. You want to turn off all the bulbs other than TCP/IP that lead to your ISDN interface. Just figure out which ones these are and double-click them to do so. Bindings can be manipulated in much the same way (Start, Control Panel, Network, Bindings tab) for Windows 95 as well.

On WfW systems, the solution isn't as simple. The only solution one user has found is to use the Network Settings section of the Windows Setup program to turn off sharing for both files and printers on the ISDN-equipped PC. This stops spurious connections, but it also keeps other PCs from sharing files and printers, which is why you installed WfW in the first place. Maybe someone will come up with a better solution; otherwise, we have to live with it until we switch to Windows 95 (which we hope won't have the same problem). So far, nobody has brought this problem up on the newsgroups for Windows 95.

On routers and bridges, these problems can be caused by routing and "service advertisement" protocols, especially if you are running protocols other than TCP/IP, such as Novell Netware or AppleTalk. The solutions to eliminating unwarranted ISDN calls typically involve correctly identifying which traffic is permitted and controlling these through proper configuration.

Tips for Better ISDN Use

In the sections that follow, we try to present some ideas for better ways to use your ISDN service in your small office or home office environment. Some will help you avoid potential sources of trouble, others potential unexpected expenses.

Would ISDN work to replace my house's POTS service?

If one person is using an ISDN phone and someone in another room picks up an ISDN phone and attempts to access the same B channel, will this work? How is the whole family supposed to talk to Grandma on an ISDN line? Use a speakerphone? Crowd around the same handset?

These are some of the primary reasons that ISDN isn't recommended for general home use. If you just wanted to use your ISDN basic rate interface (BRI) service for all of your home needs, you could install a TA or an NT1 with a POTS jack. Then you'd plug the existing house phone wiring into one of the POTS jacks (instead of into the demarc outside your house), thereby keeping your house phone system analog up to the TA or NT1. As long as your TA or NT1 remains powered up, your home analog phones still work the same way as before, except that you can call them with one of your ISDN line numbers and they won't ring. The ring voltage isn't usually passed on from the TA or NT1, which is yet another reason not to replace your home POTS with ISDN.

If you're using only ISDN telephones in your house, with the proper wiring and necessary number of S/T jacks on TAs, then ISDN allows multiple directory numbers and multiple call appearances for each number. With a keyset feature option, the same number can appear on both phones, but for both to be on the SAME call at once, a conference bridge is required (this is automatic with the feature). Also note that it requires two SPIDs and is usually implemented with two lines, although two SPIDs can share a line and support a conference bridge (at least with AT&T, probably NI too).

When you "bridge on" to the call by pressing the lighted button, the central office (CO) switch automatically picks out a conference bridge. This is required because ISDN sets are digital. On an analog line, you can put two phones in parallel and their microphone audio signals (analog) will add together, creating a composite. On a digital line, that wouldn't work: Adding 1s and 0s together would create random noise at best. So the switch "magically" inserts a bridge when you press a common line appearance on two sets.

How can I most efficiently use my current analog modem with my ISDN service?

You can plug your current analog modem into the POTS jack of your NT1 or your TA and use it in exactly the same way that you currently use it for outgoing calls. If you have a fax or modem, you can use it in the same way, too. But the receipt of calls changes with some NT1s and TAs: Most fax/modem cards or stand-alone devices rely on the analog ring voltage to initiate their answering responses. Because some of the NT1s and many of the combined TA/NT1 cards don't pass the analog ring voltage (about 110 volts) through to the analog circuit, this keeps the fax or modem from knowing that there is a phone ringing for them.

If you receive a fax only after someone calls you on your voice line to tell you it's on the way, you can always manually run your fax software and click the manual receive button when you hear your TA card "ring." If you really need unattended fax receipt using your ISDN line, you should either purchase an NT1 that passes the ring voltage through to your analog fax machine or purchase an ISDN fax device that plugs into the S/T jack on your TA.

How can I keep my Internet connect time to a minimum?

Since your ISDN service can connect in just a second or three, you don't need to be continually logged into your Internet account. Set the time-out on your ISDN equipment's software to a short time (many offer one-minute increments only, with one minute the shortest allowable time-out). If you're being charged by the minute, this doesn't pose a problem, but if you're being charged by the second, you might try to find software with a shorter time-out, or try to get your software provider to reduce its minimum settings in their next upgrade. A time-out setting of 10-60 seconds is reasonable for an ISDN line.

Using an offline news reader can also greatly reduce your connect time if you subscribe to many newsgroups. The FreeAgent news reader from Forté (http://www.forteinc.com) quickly downloads article headers from the newsgroups you select. You can scroll through them while it is still downloading others; it can also download the bodies for selected articles while you are reading others. FreeAgent keeps a database of headers and articles on your hard disk so that you can read them at your leisure after you have disconnected from the ISDN provider, thereby stopping both your ISDN and your ISP charges.

Download large files during low-traffic times on the Internet. Because your ISDN line provides such fast transfer speed, your overall transfer rate may be slowed by bottlenecks on the Internet itself, or on the server from which you are retrieving the file. Try to determine an off-peak time of the day or night for that server (don't forget about time differences, either) and proceed accordingly.

You can always turn your Web browser's image display off, too. Of course, images do appear more quickly via your ISDN line, but copying and rendering images still take time. If you want to see them, you can always just click the images button (or whatever similar command your browser requires) and they will be quickly transferred and displayed. Turning off image display can cut your Internet connect time by as much as a third, so unless you're working on a topic that absolutely requires images to be displayed, leaving them turned off can save you money!

ISDN Line Testing Equipment

Although you may desire your very own BRI analyzer, the truth is you will probably never really need one. If you suspect your line isn't working properly, a quick call to your phone company's repair line will get it checked and fixed right away in most cases and at a much lower price, if any, than the lowest-priced BRI analyzer. The only BRI analyzer that costs under $3000 that we've found is the PA 100 protocol analyzer at $2495. Until it arrived, ISDN protocol analyzers were typically priced from $8000 to over $35,000. This made it difficult to justify their purchase, especially if you just needed one occasionally.

Without a protocol analyzer, it is almost impossible to resolve the "finger pointing" that commonly occurs between the service provider and the equipment vendor or the customer. If you are in a company that's plagued by ISDN problems, a knowledgeable technician with a protocol analyzer may be able to resolve these problems quickly and at a lower cost than the opportunity costs for the time and productivity lost because of an inoperative ISDN line.

The UPA 100 is a compact unit ($9.5 \times 7.5 \times 1.5$ inches) that connects to the serial port of an IBM-PC compatible or Mac computer. It captures the messages passing between the subscriber's equipment and the network, decodes them into plain English, displays them on screen, and places them in a buffer for later analysis. Circuit-switched and packet-switched decodes for National ISDN, Northern Telecom DMS 100 Custom, and AT&T #5ESS ISDN are supported. When you need a piece of equipment like this, nothing else will do (so you might want to see if any service companies in your area can provide one with a technician for an hourly rate, or check to see if a short-term rental or lease might be available).

Summary

The best advice for keeping your ISDN problems to a minimum, solving the ones you do have quickly, and maximizing the use of your ISDN service can be stated quite simply: "Read the *comp.dcom.isdn* newsgroup regularly." Ask for help from your ISP, your ISDN service provider, your ISDN hardware vendor, or the folks on the *comp.dcom.isdn* newsgroup.

Remember that nobody can help you diagnose a problem that you can't explain in adequate detail. Nobody will even want to try to help you if you tell them, "Yes, there was an error message on the screen but I don't remember what it said and I didn't write it down." Write everything down, including the circumstances under which the problem occurred, your hardware and software settings and configuration, and anything else you can think of that might possibly affect the situation. Let the experts ignore the parts that aren't germane to the problem. Good luck!

15

Frequently Asked Questions and Answers

The questions and answers in this chapter have been excerpted primarily from the *comp.dcom.isdn* newsgroup and its frequently asked questions (FAQ). The authors have edited the material to make it more useful to novice ISDN users. Our thanks to all of the subscribers to *comp.dcom.isdn* for their great questions and cogent answers. Special thanks are needed for a few of the professionals who always seem to be available to answer the questions patiently, day after day, with great skill and forbearance. They are Chuck Sederholm, IBM Corp., Laurence V. Marks, IBM Corp., Fred R. Goldstein, Bolt Beranek & Newman Inc., and Pat Coghlan, Newbridge.

341

Chapter Contents

- Can I put more than two ISDN devices on my BRI line?
- Is it possible to connect more than one NT1 to the U point/ISDN-2 wire line?
- Are there any ISDN bulletin board services (BBSs) in the United States?
- Can my existing analog telephone lines be used for ISDN?
- How does ISDN compare to regular (analog) telephone lines?
- Is caller ID available on ISDN?
- What do ISDN phones cost?
- What is National ISDN?
- What is the NIUF?
- What is ATM?
- What is B-ISDN?
- What is BONDing?
- Is full-motion video offered over ISDN?
- What is a SPID? Why won't my ISDN device work without one?
- Can I purchase European ISDN devices and use them successfully in the United States?
- Do different manufacturers' terminal adapters interoperate when used asynchronously?
- What are the differences between a BONDed 128 KB ISDN connection and a switched 56 line?
- How long should call setup take when using a TA?

Can I put more than two ISDN devices on my BRI line?

Q: Is it possible to put three ISDN phones (using the S/T bus) on one BRI ISDN line? Ameritech states that there is a limit of two devices that can use the same B channel. It's true that you can't use more than two B channels at one time, but since we don't plan to use more than one or two phones at the same time, why it isn't possible to have up to eight ISDN phones installed? Don't they just monitor the D channel for signaling information and use up only one B channel when you pick up the phone? By the way, the ISDN line in question is provisioned by an AT&T 5ESS switch, if that makes any difference.

A: Your problem is not a technical one, it is a policy issue. Your technical assumptions are entirely correct, and you should be able to have eight phones on an AT&T 5E provided BRI.

Your provider may have set a policy that they will not provide a service to a customer served by one switch type when that service is not available to all switch types. Therefore, since a DMS 100 is not capable of more than two devices per B channel, they will not offer more than two on any switch type.

Their logic is that this will prevent someone served by a DMS 100 from demanding an FX'ed line off a 5E switch. Also, we understand that DMS 100s are much cheaper, and they don't want people to get used to the superior 5E. Hopefully, this policy will go away when (and if) NI-2 becomes available on the DMS (but we wouldn't bet on it). We also imagine they hope people will buy more lines.

Is it possible to connect more than one NT1 to the U point/ISDN-2 wire line?

No. The U loop terminates a single NT1 (network termination) device per ISDN U line. Therefore if the NT1 functionality is built into the ISDN equipment, a telephone set, or a data terminal adapter, no additional NT1s can be attached to that ISDN U line. The ISDN equipment with the integrated NT1 would need to have an S/T bus output connection to allow additional ISDN equipment to be attached via an S/T interface.

As a product example, IBMs TE 7845 provides integrated NT1 functionality together with an analog POTS connection that can use one of the ISDN B channels for voice. The second B channel is then made available via an S/T bus connector, so an additional ISDN S/T bus device can be connected. In general, the only way to support multiple ISDN devices on a single ISDN U line is by using an NT1 and then connecting the multiple ISDN equipment at the S/T bus connector.

Are there any ISDN BBSs in the United States?

The NORTEL Digital Velocity BBS has an ISDN BBS list. You can access this ISDN BBS at http://www.isdn.nortel.net and Telnet in, or make an ISDN call to (919) 992-0407 for ISDN access up to 115.2 Kbps using the V.120 communications protocol.

Can my existing analog telephone lines be used for ISDN?

According to Bellcore, usually yes. Most of the analog lines currently in service do not require any special conditioning. However, if a line has load coils or bridge taps installed, your telephone company installation person will be able to "decondition" the line for ISDN use, usually without your knowledge or intervention. In North America, about 90 percent of existing telephone lines need no deconditioning in order to be used for ISDN BRI service.

How does ISDN compare to regular (analog) telephone lines?

A "single" ISDN BRI line may act like two independent analog phone lines with two numbers and be capable of handling data transmission at 64 Kbps per line (B channel). Depending on the central office (CO) equipment, many "special" features may be available (conferencing in the telephone switch). BRI ISDN phones can support key-set features like those you would expect to get on an office private branch exchange (PBX), including the following:

Multiple directory numbers per line	Speed call
Multiple lines per directory number	Call park
Conferencing features	Call pickup

| Forwarding features | Ring again |
| Voice mail features | Status displays |

Is caller ID available on ISDN?

Caller ID (name or number display) may be supported (depending on the CO setup). The availability of caller ID for residential phones would depend on the capabilities of the local phone network. The availability of caller ID relies on the underlying switching protocol used by the switches that make up the telephone system. If caller ID is available to your Internet service provider (ISP), it should be used to help secure your account. Having the ISP's system check to see if the ISDN call requesting your account is coming from either of your ISDN phone numbers greatly increases your security. It's practically impossible for someone who has stolen your account name and password to get around the caller ID number check.

What do ISDN phones cost?

The ISDN sets can cost between $180 for an AT&T 8503T ISDN phone from Pacific Bell up to $1900, depending on what and how many features are needed. A recent report states that the price is $536.90 for an AT&T 7506 with the RS-232 port on the back and $102.70 to get the 507A adapter to hook analog devices to the 7506. Recent quotes were $170 for a Coretelco 1800 and $500 for a Fujitsu SRS 1050.

What is National ISDN?

Because of the breadth of the international ISDN standards, vendors of ISDN equipment can make a number of implementation choices. Given the number of choices available to vendors, different vendors' equipment may not interoperate. In the United States, Bellcore has released a series of specifications to try to avoid such interoperability problems, including the National ISDN specifications. Contact the Bellcore ISDN hot line for more information (see the vendor list for the number).

What is the NIUF?

North American ISDN Users Forum (NIUF) is an organization of ISDN-interested parties, coordinated by NIST (National Institute of Standards and Technology), which promotes the use of ISDN and provides a great deal of information about ISDN to anyone who asks for it. Contact:

NIUF Secretariat
National Institute of Standards and Technology
Building 223, Room B364
Gaithersberg, MD 20899
Tel: (301) 975-2937
Fax: (301) 926-9675
(301) 869-7281 BBS 8N1 2400 bps

What is ATM?

ATM (asynchronous transfer mode) is a switching/transmission technique in which data is transmitted in small, fixed-size cells (5 byte header, 48 byte payload). The cells lend themselves both to the time division multiplexing characteristics of the transmission medium, and the packet-switching characteristics desired from data networks. At each switching node, the ATM header identifies a "virtual path" or "virtual circuit" for which the cell contains data, enabling the switch to forward the cell to the correct next-hop trunk. The virtual path is set up through the involved switches when two endpoints wish to communicate. This type of switching can be implemented in hardware, almost essential when trunk speeds range from 45 Mbps to 1.2 Gbps.

One use of ATM is to serve as the core technology for a new set of ISDN offerings known as broadband ISDN (B-ISDN). For more information, read *comp.dcom.cell-relay*. This group has a frequently asked questions list; it is posted to *news.answers* and is in various archives as "cell-relay-faq".

What is B-ISDN?

Broadband ISDN refers to services that require channel rates greater than that of a single primary rate channel. Although this does not specifically imply any particular technology, ATM will be used as the switching infrastructure for B-ISDN services.

B-ISDN services are categorized as follows:

Interactive

- Conversational, such as videotelephony, videoconferencing
- Messaging, such as electronic mail for images, video, and graphics
- Retrieval, such as teleshopping, news retrieval, remote education

Distribution

- Without user presentation control: electronic newspaper, TV distribution
- With user presentation control: remote education, teleadvertising, news retrieval

What is BONDing?

BONDing is a set of protocols developed by the United States inverse multiplexer that supports communication over a set of separate channels as if their bandwidths were combined into a single coherent channel. For example, BONDing supports a single 128 Kbps data stream over two 64 Kbps channels.

The specification defines a way of calculating relative delays between multiple network channels and ordering data so that what goes in one end comes out the other. Most vendors also have their own proprietary methods that usually add features and functions not present in BONDing mode 1. Mode 1 is the mode used for recent interoperability testing between vendors.

Is full-motion video offered over ISDN?

In ISDN, video isn't a "service being offered," at least not for low to midrange quality. To get full-motion video via ISDN, just buy the proper equipment for both subscribers, plug it in, and place the call yourself.

Video telephony over narrowband ISDN is governed by a suite of International Telecommunications Union-Telecommunications (ITU-T) (formerly CCITT) interoperability standards. The overall video telephony suite is known informally as p * 64 (and pronounced "p star 64"), and formally as standard H.320. H.320 is an "umbrella" standard: It specifies H.261 for video compression; H.221, H.230, and H.242 for communications, control, and indication; G.711, G.722, and G.728 for audio signals; and several others for specialized purposes. A common misconception, exploited by some equipment manufacturers, is that compliance with H.261 (the video compression standard) is enough to guarantee interoperability.

Bandwidth can be divided up among video, voice, and data in a bewildering variety of ways. Typically, 56 Kbps might be allocated to voice, with 1.6 Kbps for signaling (control and indication signals) and the balance allocated to video.

An H.320-compatible terminal can support audio and video in one B channel using G.728 audio at 16 Kbps. For a 64 Kbps channel, this leaves 46.4 Kbps for video (after subtracting 1.6 Kbps for H.221 framing).

The resolution of an H.261 video image is either 352×288 (known as common intermediate format) or 176×144 (known as quarter-CIF or QCIF). The frame rate can be anything from 30 frames/second and down. Configurations typically use a 2B (BRI) or a 6B (switched-384 or 3×BRI with an inverse multiplexer) service, depending on the desired cost and video quality. In a 384 Kbps call, a videoconferencing system can achieve 30 frames/second at CIF and looks comparable to a VHS videotape picture. In a 2B BRI call, a standard video phone can achieve 15 frames/second at CIF.

Those who have seen the 1B video call in operation generally agree that the quality is not sufficient for anything useful like computer-based training; it is only for the social aspect of being able to "see" Grandma as well as hear her (sort of like the snapshot pictures you make with that $5 camera with no controls).

A 2B picture, on the other hand, is for all practical purposes sufficient for remote education, presentations, and so on. Rapidly changing scenes are still not very well handled, but as soon as the picture calms down, the sharpness and color quality are impressive (considering that only two plain phone channels are being used). With 2B + D as the standard BRI, this kind of picturephone will be usable "everywhere" (including private homes).

However, it should still be noted that 6xB or H0 does allow dramatic improvement in picture quality compared with 2xB. In particular, H.320 video/audio applications will often allocate 56 Kbps for audio, leaving only 68.8 Kbps for video when using 2xB. On the other hand, using H0 would get you 326.4 Kbps for video with 56 Kbps for audio. Alternative audio algorithms can improve picture quality over 2xB by not stealing as many bits. Note that 6B is not identical to H0; the latter is a single channel that will give you 80 Kbps above that of six separate B channels. Inverse multiplexers can be used to combine B channels.

What is a SPID? Why won't my ISDN device work without one?

SPIDs are service profile IDs. SPIDs are used to identify the sort of services and features the switch provides to the ISDN device. Currently they are used only for circuit-switched service (as opposed to packet-switched service). Annex A to ITU recommendation Q.932

specifies the (optional) procedures for SPIDs. They are most commonly implemented by ISDN equipment used in North America.

When a new subscriber is added, the telephone company personnel allocate a SPID just as they allocate a directory number. In many cases, the SPID number is identical to the (full 10 digit) directory number. In other cases it may be the directory number concatenated with various other strings of digits, such as digits 0100 or 0010, 1 or 2 (indicating the first or second B channel on a non-Centrex line), 100 or 200 (same idea but on a Centrex line), or some other, seemingly arbitrary string. Some people report SPIDs of the form 01nnnnnnn0 for AT&T custom and 01nnnnnnn011 for NI-1, where n is the seven digit directory number. It is all quite implementation-dependent.

Subscribers need to configure the SPID into their terminals (e.g., computer or telephone, not NT-1 or NT-2) before they will be able to connect to the central office switch. When the subscriber plugs in a properly configured device to the line, layer 2 initialization takes place, establishing the basic transport mechanism. However, if the subscriber has not configured the given SPID into the ISDN device, the device will not perform layer 3 initialization and the subscriber will not be able to make calls. This is, unfortunately, how many subscribers discover they need a SPID.

Once the SPID is configured, the terminals go through an initialization/identification state that has the terminal send the SPID to the network in a layer 3 INFOrmation message, whereupon the network responds with an INFO message with the Equipment Identifier (EID) information element (ie). Thereafter the SPID is not sent again to the switch. The switch may send the EID or the called party number (CdPN) in the SETUP message to the terminal for the purpose of terminal selection.

SPIDs should not be confused with TEIs (terminal endpoint identifiers). TEIs identify the terminal at layer 2 for a particular interface (line). TEIs will be unique on an interface, whereas SPIDs will be unique on the whole switch and tend to be derived from the primary directory number of the subscriber. Although they are used at different layers, they have a one-to-one correspondence, so mixing them up isn't too dangerous. TEIs are dynamic (different each time the terminal is plugged into the switch) but SPIDS are not. Following the initialization sequence, the one-to-one correspondence is established. TEIs are usually not visible to the ISDN user so they are not as well known as SPIDs.

The "address" of the layer 3 message is usually considered to be the call reference value (also dynamic but this time on a per-call basis) as opposed to the SPID, so the management entity in the ISDN device's software must associate the EID/CdPN on a particular TEI and Call Reference Number to a SPID.

Some standards call for a default service profile, in which case a terminal doesn't need to provide a SPID to become active. Without the SPID, however, the switch has no way of knowing which terminal is which on the interface, so for multiple terminals an incoming call would be offered to the first terminal that responded, rather than to a specific terminal.

Can I purchase European ISDN devices and use them successfully in the United States?

There are four major problem areas regarding interoperability of ISDN equipment between countries.

The first has to do with voice encoding and is a problem only if the equipment is a telephone. Equipment designed for use in North America and Japan uses mu-law encoding when converting from analog to digital, whereas the rest of the world uses A-law. If the equipment has a switch for selecting one or the other of these encoding types, there will not be a problem with the voice encoding.

The second has to do with the way the equipment communicates with the telephone exchange. There are interoperability problems because there are so many different services (and related parameters) that the user can request, each country can decide whether or not to allow the telephone exchange to offer a given service, and the specifications that describe the services are open to interpretation in many different ways. So, as with other interoperability problems, you must work with the vendors to determine whether the equipment will interoperate. This is a basic problem; it affects all ISDN equipment, not just voice equipment.

The third has to do with homologation, or regulatory approval. In most countries in the world the manufacturer of telephone equipment must obtain approvals before the equipment may be connected to the network. So, even if the equipment works with the network in a particular country, it isn't OK to hook it up until the manufacturer has jumped through the various hoops to demonstrate safety and compliance. It is typically more expensive to obtain worldwide homologation approvals for a newly developed piece of ISDN equipment than it is to develop it and tool up to manufacture it.

A fourth issue is that in the United States the TA and NT1 are both provided by the customer, whereas in Europe the NT1 is provided by telephone company. Stated differently, if you walk into a store in the United States and buy something to plug into an ISDN line it may be designed as a one-piece unit that connects to point U. In Europe you would get something that plugs into point T. Thus you might take a piece of U.S.-originated equipment to Europe and find that it won't work because the jack in Europe is a T interface and the plug on your U.S. equipment is a U interface.

There are attempts to remedy this situation, particularly for BRI ISDN. The North American ISDN Users Forum is coming up with standards to increase the uniformity of ISDN services. In Europe, a new standard called NET3 is being developed.

Do different manufacturers' terminal adapters interoperate when used asynchronously?

There is a standard up to 19.2k (V.110), but above that no real standard is implemented. However, in practice there is a fair degree of interoperability (even when the TA's manual tells you otherwise) because many TAs use the same chip set (supplied by Siemens), which happily goes up to 38.4. TAs from different suppliers that are using the Siemens chips have a fair chance of interoperating at up to 38.4k.

What are the differences between a BONDed 128 KB ISDN connection and a switched 56 line?

Switched 56 and ISDN are both dial-up services. Given a choice of ISDN or Sw56, go with ISDN. Switched 56 is an earlier, predecessor service that is being phased out in favor of ISDN. The two interwork freely (call each other), but ISDN gives you two B channels, usually for a lower price than one Sw56 line. The delay is about the same, unless you're closer to one service's switch than the other.

How long should call setup take when using a TA?

The "less than a second" call setup sometimes claimed seems to be rare. TAs have a negotiation phase, and it typically takes about four to six seconds to get through to the remote site.

A

ISDN Dial Tone Service Providers

This information was prepared by Core Competence, Inc., and updated January 6, 1997. ISDN dial tone service providers and Internet service providers change frequently, as do their offerings and charges. Core Competence periodically updates this information on their Web site. Visit http://www.corecom.com/html/ISPlist/html regularly for more information.

Bellcore (Bell Communications Research)

National ISDN HotLine	1-800-992-ISDN
Fax	201.829.2263
E-mail	isdn@cc.bellcore.com
URL	http://info.bellcore.com
System prompt	ftp info.bellcore.com

Table A.1 ISDN contacts in the United States.

Company	Contact	Telephone No.
Ameritech	National ISDN Hotline	1-800-TEAMDATA (1-800-832-6328)
Bell Atlantic In New Jersey, call your local telephone office	ISDN Sales and Tech Center For small businesses	1-800-570-ISDN 1-800-570-4736) 1-800-843-2255
Bell South	ISDN Hotline	1-800-428-ISDN (1-800-428-4736)
Cincinnati Bell	ISDN Service Center	513-566-DATA (513-566-3282)
GTE	Menu-driven information Florida, North Carolina,Virginia, and Kentucky Illinois, Indiana, Ohio, and Pennsylvania Oregon and Washington California Hawaii Texas	1-800-4GTE-SW5 1-800-483-5200 1-800-483-5600 1-800-483-5100 1-800-483-5000 1-800-643-4411 1-800-483-5400
Nevada Bell	Small business Large business	702-333-4811 702-688-7100
Nynex	ISDN Sales Hotline New England states	1-800-GET-ISDN 1-800-438-4736 617-743-2466
Pacific Bell	ISDN Service Center 24-hour automated ISDN available hotline ISDN Telemarketing	1-800-4PB-ISDN 1-800-472-4736 1-800-995-0346 1-800-662-0735
Rochester Telephone	ISDN Information	716-777-1234
SNET	Donovan Dillon	203-553-2369
Stentor (Canada)	ISDN "Facts by Fax" Steve Finlay Glen Duxbury	1-800-578-ISDN 604-654-7504 403-945-8130
Southwestern Bell	Austin, TX Dallas, TX North Houston, TX South Houston, TX San Antonio, TX For ISDN availability for remaining locations please contact the Bellcore ISDN HotLine at	1-800-SWB-ISDN 214-268-1403 713-537-3930 713-567-4300 210-351-8050 1-800-992-ISDN

Table A.1   Continued

Company	Contact	Telephone No.
U S West	Ron Miller	303-965-7153
	Ron Woldeit	206-447-4029
	Denver, CO	1-800-246-5226
	Julia Evans	303-896-8370

National ISDN Long-Distance Carrier Contacts

Company	Contact	Telephone No.
AT&T	AT&T Front End Center	1-800-222-7956
GTE	Nationwide availability/pricing	1-800-888-8799
	Ron Sterreneberg	214-718-5608
MCI	Tony Hylton	214-701-6745
	ISDN availability	1-800-MCI-ISDN
US Sprint	Rick Simonson	913-624-4162
LDDS-Worldcom	Justin Remington	918-588-5069

ISDN Internet Service Providers (ISPs)

A growing number of commercial ISPs offer ISDN-based access to the Internet. The cost-conscious consumer faces quite a challenge when selecting an ISDN ISP. ISDN service offerings and prices vary widely. Finding a list of candidate ISPs may be as simple as culling local newspaper advertisements for the keyword "ISDN" or searching online lists such as Dan Kegel's ISDN page, http://www.alumni.caltech.edu/dank/isdn/index.html. However, this represents only a starting point, akin to arriving at the shopping mall, wish list in hand. Selecting the right ISP requires careful consideration of many factors, including location, pricing alternatives, service bundling, hardware compatibility, and connectivity needs. Ferreting out technical nuances and appreciating the often subtle implications that differentiate one ISDN service offering from another can be difficult. We offer the following guidance to assist in this selection process.

Location of ISDN Points of Presence (POPs)

In all but the largest of cities, the list of candidate ISPs can be quickly trimmed by identifying ISDN POPs and determining their location relative to your own. The ISDN POP is the ISDN telephone number your ISDN card, TA, or router will dial to obtain Internet access. As with analog telephone service, surcharges apply to ISDN calls placed to destinations beyond your local calling area. Toll-free ("800") ISDN POPs exist but are still rare. Ideally, candidate ISPs should be located within your local calling area. In many rural or suburban areas, local ISDN POPs may not exist. Obtain the list of ISDN POPs from each candidate ISP and consult your telephone company or ISDN "dial tone" provider to obtain the charges associated with ISDN calls between your ISDN number and each POP. Be careful to obtain the list of ISDN POPs, typically much shorter than the same ISP's list of analog dial POPs. Do not assume that a local analog destination will also be a local ISDN destination: in some regions, "extended" local calling areas do not apply to ISDN. Also beware that your and/or your ISP may be assigned an off-premise exchange (OPX) if the nearest telephone central office is not equipped to support ISDN subscribers. In this case, your ISDN calls are treated as though placed from another (more distant) location and may therefore be subject to unanticipated surcharges. Use the actual rate information and your anticipated online time to narrow down your list to ISPs who are within your calling budget.

Dedicated or Dial-up ISDN

With an ISDN dial-up account, the ISP dynamically assigns an access server port to each caller, as needed, for the duration of the call. After the call is completed, the port is available for use by another caller. Dial-up accounts allow ISPs to "oversubscribe" their access servers, selling many more subscriber accounts than there are ports available, on the premise that each account is active only some of the time. Oversubscription also allows the ISP to economize on the number of access lines purchased from its own ISDN dial tone provider and can result in conservation of IP address space when coupled with dynamic address assignment. The ISP uses anticipated calling behavior, call duration, calling time, and call frequency to calculate the resources required to provide a reasonable quality of service. Accordingly, dial-up accounts are much less expensive than dedicated or Centrex accounts and will be the most economic alternative for the vast majority of ISDN users.

ISPs impose usage limits or charges on dial-up ISDN accounts. For example, 20 "B" hours per month may be included in the ISDN account fee. This entitles the subscriber to 20 "free" hours (one B channel) or 10 "free" hours (two B channels, BONDed) of Internet access per month. Depending on the ISP, the subscriber may be cut off after reaching this limit or (more often) charged per minute for usage beyond 20 hours. Note that with ISDN dial-up accounts, blocking may occur during peak calling hours. A good ISP will ensure that this happens infrequently.

If your anticipated online usage is very high, you may need to consider purchasing a dedicated or Centrex ISDN account. With both of these accounts, the ISP permanently assigns or "dedicates" an access server port for your use. The ISP does not impose any usage charges or limit; monthly B hours are unlimited. However, even with a dedicated ISDN account, your card, TA, or router still places ISDN calls to the ISP. Usage charges imposed by your telephone company or ISDN dial tone provider still apply. Thus, a dedicated ISDN account makes sense when anticipated online usage is fairly high, but local access charges are still reasonable.

Alternatively, a Centrex ISDN account provides what can be thought of as one long, continuous call between your ISDN number and the ISP's POP. The Centrex "call" is purchased from your telephone company or ISDN dial tone provider for a flat rate (fixed fee per month). Centrex rates vary but are typically less than the metered charges associated with full-time use of a "normal" ISDN line. Centrex is an option only when the call origin and destination can be provisioned through the same telephone central office. A limited number of ISPs, mostly located in urban areas, provide Centrex ISDN accounts. In addition to reduced cost, Centrex subscribers benefit from continuous Internet presence (see the discussion of call-back under Host or LAN ISDN, later). In summary, this alternative makes sense only if your online requirements approach full-time and you are close to an ISP that offers Centrex ISDN. Of course, if your online usage is really this high, you should also consider other access alternatives such as Frame Relay, Asymmetrical Digital Subscriber Line (ADSL), or the newly emergent ISDN Digital Subscriber Line (IDSL) (a hybrid of ISDN and ADSL).

One Lump or Two?

As already noted, ISDN dial-up accounts meter and charge for B channel hours. Theoretically, using two B channels, BONDed, to download a file or browse a Web site should require half the time, right? Wrong. This economy is realized only when both B channels are fully loaded for a sustained period. Web browsing, news, e-mail, DNS lookups, and many other casual Internet activities are interactive, resulting in bursty traffic patterns that utilize a second B channel for relatively brief durations. Although the second B channel may prove useful when dropping in on a Web site filled with high-resolution graphics, this may not be very cost effective. Some ISPs charge extra for setup of a second B channel; other ISPs charge more for use of the second B channel. Obviously, dedicated ISDN accounts involving two B channels impose the highest surcharge for multichannel BONDing. If the ISP supports compression (see Hardware Compatibility), this may prove more economical than purchasing a second B channel. (Check out the 1996 ISDN router and bridge evaluation compression test results described on http://www.corecom.com/nscape/html/testing_&_evaluation.html). Remember that your telephone company or ISDN dial tone provider is likely to charge for calls *per B channel*. If your anticipated usage justifies purchase of a second B channel, keep this requirement in mind when comparing ISP pricing so that you can factor in associated costs.

Packaging of Internet Application Services

Many ISPs provide much more than Internet access; they provide a plethora of Internet Application Services such as e-mail (SMTP or POP accounts), shell accounts, storage space for Web or FTP sites, a news feed or NNTP access, and naming services associated with hosting your domain (sometimes called a "virtual domain" service).

Many of these Internet Application Services are "bundled" with dial-in accounts; that is, they are included with your Internet access under a single monthly fee. For example, a typical analog dial-in account includes a shell account and one e-mail account. By extension, it is not uncommon to find entry-level ISDN dial-in accounts bundled with the same set of basic Internet Application Services.

More sophisticated home users and small businesses may want to purchase space in which to store their Web site or provide anonymous FTP access to files. Typically, such a Web site has an address of the form *myISP.net/~myname*. Other companies may prefer to register their own domain name, *myname.com*. Without a continuous Internet presence, such a company might purchase a "virtual domain" service that handles e-mail addressed to *user@myname.com* and supports Web hits on *www.myname.com*. The combinations and permutations of Internet Application Services are endless, and we cannot exhaustively enumerate the options you may find here (see also Host or LAN ISDN, later). Suffice it to say that these services should be negotiated as part of your Internet access account. Many ISPs are willing to "throw in" what you need: Don't be afraid to ask just because you don't see it listed, and don't pay for services you don't need.

Hardware Compatibility

Many ISPs readily recommend ISDN hardware to subscribers in order to avoid or reduce interoperability problems. Some ISPs even go the extra mile and resell ISDN hardware or package it with their service offerings, often at a reduced cost. If you don't already own ISDN access gear, seriously consider purchasing the hardware recommended by your ISP of choice, and factor this cost in when comparing ISPs. If you already own ISDN hardware, ask the ISP whether they have previously demonstrated interoperability with the ISDN product you've selected, and request sample configurations and parameter settings appropriate for your use with your hardware. If possible, choose the ISP that has a proven track record interoperating with your hardware. Ask about features such as compression and multichannel BONDing. It is important to note that compression, BONDing, and bandwidth allocation algorithms must match at both endpoints. Odds that an interoperability problem will occur are reduced when both you and the ISP use ISDN hardware from the same vendor, but this should be considered a plus, not a requirement.

Quality of Service, Reliability, and Support

Internet access is fast becoming a commodity market, even for ISDN access. Not all ISPs are made alike when it comes to quality of service: Factors such as oversubscription ratio, the type and number of access servers, Internet backbone connectivity, and the competence of network operations staff affect how often your ISDN calls will be disconnected or go unanswered.

When problems do occur, the level of support provided by the ISP is critical to timely and satisfactory resolution. Does the ISP provide support 24 hours a day, 7 days a week, 365 days a year? Does the ISP employ a network operations staff that is large and skilled enough to meet customer support needs? Will the ISP still be there six months from now? A year from now? The best rule of thumb here is to try before you buy. Consider purchasing an inexpensive analog dial account for a brief trial period, and use this opportunity to assess the quality of service provided for this, the tiniest of accounts. Chances are that, if you are uncomfortable with the service provided during this trial, you will be equally (if not more) unhappy with the service provided for larger ISDN accounts.

If you intend to become a high-end (especially dedicated or Centrex) user, insist on speaking with the network operations staff who will be responsible for supporting you, and verify that they understand and can meet your ISDN requirements. Finally, check references, including those supplied by both the ISP and other subscribers you might identify by browsing the ISP's Web site.

Host or LAN ISDN

The typical home user or telecommuter requires access from a single host (PC or workstation) to the Internet. Host ISDN accounts are relatively low in cost, perhaps twice as expensive as a 28.8 Kbps analog dial-up account from the same ISP. A typical host ISDN account is bundled with a shell account, one e-mail account, news access, and perhaps a modest amount of Web/FTP storage space intended for personal use. A host ISDN account is associated with a single IP address, which may be statically or dynamically assigned. If you have a PC or workstation and an ISDN card or TA, an ISDN host account is probably the right choice for you. ISPs that offer this type of account are easily found, and competition on price and features is high. Shop around.

A small business, remote office, or high-end home user may need to connect several computers located on one or more local area networks to the Internet. A LAN ISDN account provides this type of connectivity, often at a much higher cost than host ISDN accounts. However, a single LAN ISDN account can be cost effective because the cost of a single ISDN line and call charges are shared across LAN users rather than duplicated for each user. A typical LAN ISDN account is targeted for a given LAN size (for example, up to five hosts on a LAN), and Internet Application Services are packaged accordingly: five e-mail accounts, six IP addresses (one for the router), perhaps DNS support for a virtual domain, and sufficient Web/FTP storage for commercial use. A LAN ISDN account is associated with a range of IP addresses—occasionally an entire class C IP address, more often a "splinter" of addresses (for a discussion of IP addressing, see http://www.corecom.com/nscape/html/tcp_ip.html).

The key feature that differentiates a LAN ISDN account from a host ISDN account is the requirement to route Internet traffic destined to IP addresses on your LAN through your ISDN router. All LAN ISDN accounts do this when the ISDN call is active. Some LAN ISDN accounts provide "callback," where the ISP initiates a call to your ISDN router when traffic arrives destined for your LAN and no call is in progress. This feature is relatively uncommon and more expensive but must be considered if you require "continuous" Internet presence (for example, to host your own Web or FTP site). Callback is not required for Centrex LAN ISDN accounts. A LAN ISDN account is usually supported by an ISDN router rather than an ISDN card or TA.

ISPs that offer LAN ISDN are more difficult to find, and the feature choices more difficult to make, than for host ISDN. Table A.2 (prepared by Core Competence, Inc., and updated January 6, 1997) provides a sampling of ISPs that offer LAN ISDN accounts, either dedicated or dial-up. This list is representative of the diversity of features, prices, and packaging currently available for LAN ISDN service throughout the United States. Please refer to Dan Kegel's ISDN page for additional ISPs that offer LAN ISDN.

Disclaimer: Table A.2 provides a summary of LAN ISDN services and prices obtained from commercial ISP Web sites and "info" e-mail responses. We cannot be responsible for errors, omissions, or changes. Prices and service offerings change frequently; contact the affected ISPs for current information.

Table A.2   Summary of LAN ISDN services and prices

Internet Service Provider	LAN-ISDN Install Charge[1]	LAN-ISDN Recurring Charge[1]	ISDN Access Area(s)	Permanent IP Addresses	Hardware Pairings[2]	Network Services[3, 4]	Other Comments
Ablecom www.ablecom.net	1B $325	1B $275/mo	Bay Area	Yes		WWW E-mail News	Dedicated, includes callback
Aimnet www.aimnet.com	2B $175	2B $150/mo includes 150 B hr	Bay Area	Yes	Farallon Netopia	DNS NOC access	ISDN Centrex and callback also available
Alternate Access www.aa.net	1B $250 2B $500	1B $150/mo 2B $300/mo	Seattle	Yes Multiple IP addr	Ascend, Motorola, 3Com		Non resellable
A-Link www.alink.net	1B $195	1B $99/mo includes 80 B hr $1.50/hr thereafter	Bay Area	Yes 5 IP addrs	Ascend P25/50 Farallon Netopia	E-mail POP DNS	Virtual domain included, larger LAN and flat rate packages also available
Brainstorm Networks www.brainstorm.net	1B $295 2B $495 $250 per addtl. BRI (up to 4)	1B $278/mo 2B $378/mo or 2 cents/min $200/mo per addtl BRI	Bay Area	Yes 32 IP addrs	Ascend P25/5075	News E-mail	Metered ISDN also available, virtual domain included

Table A.2   Continued

Internet Service Provider	LAN-ISDN Install Charge[1]	LAN-ISDN Recurring Charge[1]	ISDN Access Area(s)	Permanent IP Addresses	Hardware Pairings[2]	Network Services[3,4]	Other Comments
CERFNet www.cerf.net	2B $250	1B $149/mo includes 99 B hr $79 for 99 addt'l hr	CA	Yes 16 IP addrs		WWW DNS News	SBA plan,
Colorado Internet Coop www.coop.net	1B $2700 2B $2700	1B $200 2B $300	Denver			None	Dedicated access, not-for-profit coop
ConnectNet www.connectnet.com	2B $99	$99/mo 2-6 hosts includes 99 B hr $0.75/hr thereafter	San Diego	Yes		E-mail DNS	ISDN Centrex, larger networks, dial-back also available
Direct Network Access www.dnai.com	2B $150	2B $25/mo includes 50 B hr $0.75/hr thereafter	Bay Area	Yes 5 IP addrs	Farallon Netopia	E-mail WWW FTP DNS	Virtual domain included, larger networks also available
Digital Telemedia www.dti.net	1B $95 2B $95	1B $95/mo 2B $195/mo 2B + callback $295/mo	NY	Yes 14 IP addrs	Ascend P25/50	E-mail	Flat rate also available
emf.net www.emf.net	2B $300	2B $99/mo includes 160 B hr $1.95/hr thereafter	Bay Area	Yes 5 IP addrs	Ascend P50 (can be purchased from ISP)	WWW E-mail FTP	Virtual domain included, larger LAN packages also available
Fastlane www.fastlane.net	1B $150 2B $200	1B $150/mo 2B $200/mo	Fort Worth and Dallas,TX	Yes 30+ IP addrs	Ascend P50 or Motorola	WWW E-mail	Dedicated access also available
GoFast.Net www.gofast.net	2B $249	1B $129/mo 2B $169/mo 200 hr/mo	MN Twin Cities	Yes 13 IP addrs	Ascend P50/75	E-mail News	On-site install included, callback also available

continued

Table A.2   Continued

Internet Service Provider	LAN-ISDN Install Charge[1]	LAN-ISDN Recurring Charge[1]	ISDN Access Area(s)	Permanent IP Addresses	Hardware Pairings[2]	Network Services[3,4]	Other Comments
ICO Networks www.ico.net	2B $120	2B $60/mo includes 60 B hr $2/hr thereafter	Monterey Bay	Yes 5 IP addrs	Livingston Ascend P25/50 Cisco 2503	E-mail FTP WWW (added cost)	Larger LAN packages also available
Internet Atlanta www. com/atlanta	1B $495 2B $995	1B $240/mo 2B $480/mo	GA	Yes IP Addr block	Ascend P50	DNS News	Dedicated, install charges reduced or waived for 6-12 month prepay
Market.NET www. market.net	1B $300 2B $300	1B $200/mo 2B $250/mo	Bay Area	Yes 1 Class C		Available with virtual host account	Centrex available, discount for quarterly pmts
NetReach www. netreach.net	1B $400	1B $150/mo includes 20 B hr	Philadelphia	Yes 32 IP addrs	Livingston	WWW E-mail DNS FTP News	Sample quote, price varies per customer/ config., discount for 12 month prepay
OnRamp www. onramp.net	1B $250 2B $498	1B $250/mo 2B $498/mo	TX		Ascend, Trancell, Farallon, Cisco 760 and 2500	WWW News	8 B channel package also available
OARnet www.oar.net	2B $395	2B $395/mo for "shared access"	Ohio	Yes upon request	Cisco, Adtran	None	Dedicated also available
PSINet www.psi.net	2B $495	2B $245/mo	US	Yes CIDR block		DNS News	Up to 254 hosts included
QuakeNet www. quake.net	2B $250	2B $85/mo includes 85 B hr 1.25/ hr thereafter or $225/mo unltd	Bay Area	Yes 5 IP addrs		E-mail DNS News	Larger LAN packages also available

Table A.2   Continued

Internet Service Provider	LAN-ISDN Install Charge[1]	LAN-ISDN Recurring Charge[1]	ISDN Access Area(s)	Permanent IP Addresses	Hardware Pairings[2]	Network Services[3,4]	Other Comments
RustNet www.rust.net	1B $150 2B $310	1B $210 2B $410	Michigan		Livingston	E-mail News WWW	Dedicated 8-15 users
Scruz-Net www.scruz.net	2B $25	2B $50/mo includes 100 B hr or $125/mo unltd	Santa Cruz and Bay Area	Yes 6 IP addrs	Ascend Motorola	E-mail News WWW	Centrex also available
Slip.Net www.slip.net	2B $150	2B $100/mo includes 100 B hr $1/hr thereafter or $125/mo unltd	Bay Area	Yes 5 IP addrs	Ascend P25/50 Farallon Netopia	E-mail FTP WWW	
Surf Communications www.surf.com	2B $499	2B $49/mo includes 49 B hr $1/hr thereafter max $250/mo	Bay Area	Yes 6 IP addrs	USR with EasyLAN software	WWW FTP	Virtual domain included, larger LAN packages also available
The Internet Access Co. www.tiac.net	2B $2999 includes router and Nynex access fees	2B $599/mo	MA, RI, NY, NH, CT		Ascend P50 included with service offering		All NYNEX access fees paid by ISP 1 year contract required
Third Planet www.3rdplanet.com	2B $100	2B $72 100/hr/mo or $129 200/hr/mo	Oregon	Yes	Livingston OR Ascend P25	E-mail WWW DNS	Discounts for 3/6/12 mos
ThoughtPort www.thoughtport.com	1B $250 2B $425	1B $250/mo 2B $400/mo	NY, Chicago	Yes 6 IP addrs	Ascend P25/50	E-mail News	DNS additional charge, timed services also available

continued

Table A.2 Continued

Internet Service Provider	LAN-ISDN Install Charge[1]	LAN-ISDN Recurring Charge[1]	ISDN Access Area(s)	Permanent IP Addresses	Hardware Pairings[2]	Network Services[3],[4]	Other Comments
UUNET (Alternet) www.uu.net	$295	$115/mo includes 50 B hr $2/hr thereafter for "Flex-Time" 2nd B channel subject to demand	US 800 access at $6/hr surcharge	Yes Class C addrs	Ascend PL50	DNS News E-mail WWW	Prime/full-time plans available, Novell LAN to Internet available, discounts available for 1-2 year contract

[1]All prices are as indicated by ISP's Web site, January 6, 1997. Unless otherwise noted, LEC charges for ISDN installation and service are not shown.

[2]Unless otherwise noted, hardware pairing represents a recommendation by the ISP, sometimes available for purchase through ISP at additional cost.

[3]The notation WWW or FTP indicates that the ISP includes space for the subscriber's Web or FTP site with the LAN ISDN account.

[4]The notation E-mail indicates that the ISP includes SMTP and/or POP support for local mailboxes with the LAN ISDN account.

B

Vendor Information

3Com Corporation
Great America Site
5400 Bayfront Plaza
Santa Clara, CA 95052
Tel: (408) 764-5000
Fax: (408) 764-5001
Web: http://www.3com.com

AccessWorks Communications Inc.
670 North Beers St.
Holmdel, NJ 07733
Tel: (800) 248-8204 or (908) 721-1337
Fax: (908) 888-4456
E-mail: info@accessworks.com

ADC Kentrox
14375 NW Science Park Dr.
Portland, OR 97229
Tel: (503) 643-1681
Web: http://www.kentrox.com

Adtran, Inc.
901 Explorer Blvd.
Huntsville, AL 35806-2807
Tel: (205) 971-8000
Fax: (205) 971-8030
Web: http://www.adtran.com

Advanced Computer Communications (ACC)
340 Storke Rd.
Santa Barbara, CA 93117
Tel: (805) 685-4455
Fax: (805) 685-4465
Web: http://www.acc.com

Advanced Micro Devices
901 Thomson Pl.
Mailstop 126
Sunnyvale, CA 94086
Tel: (408) 732-2400 or (800) 538-8450
Web: http://www.amd.com/Welcome.html

Alpha Telecom, Inc.
7501 S. Memorial Pkwy., Ste. 212
Huntsville, AL 35802
Tel: (205) 881-8743
Fax: (205) 880-9720
Web: http://www.alpha-tele.com

America Online
22000 AOL Way
Dulles, VA 20166
Tel: (800) 827-6364 or (703) 448-8700
Fax: (703) 883-1509
Web: http://www.aol.com

Ameritech
30 South Wacker
Floor 34
Chicago, IL 60606
Tel: (800) 327-9346
Web: http://www.Ameritech.com/
E-mail: share.owners@ameritech.com

ANDO
7617 Standish Pl.
Rockville, MD 20855
Tel: (301) 294-3365
Fax: (301) 294-3359
E-mail: mgriffin@access.digex.net

Apple Computer, Inc.
1 Infinite Loop
Cupertino, CA 95014
Tel: (800) 776-2333 or (408) 996-1010
Fax: (408) 996-0275
Web: http://www.apple.com

Ascend Communications, Inc.
One Ascend Plaza
1701 Harbor Bay Parkway
Alameda, CA 94502
Tel: (510) 769-6001
Fax: (510) 814-2300
Web: http://www.ascend.com
E-mail: info@ascend.com

AT&T
Front End Center: (800) 222-7956

AT&T
Visual Communications Products
8100 East Maplewood Ave., 1st Floor
Englewood, CO 80111
Tel: (800) 843-3646 or (800)VIDEO-GO Prompt 3

Bay Networks, Inc.
4401 Great America Parkway
Santa Clara, CA 95054
Tel: (800) 8BAYNET
Web: http://www.baynetworks.com

Bell Atlantic
ISDN Sales & Tech Center: (800) 570-ISDN

BellSouth
ISDN HotLine: (800) 428-4736

BinTec Computersysteme GmbH
Willstaetter St. 30
D-90449 Nuernberg, Germany
Tel: +49.911.9673-0
Fax: +49.911.6880725
E-mail: vertrieb@bintec.de

Booklinks, Inc.
Web: http://www.booklink.com/

Cardinal
1827 Freedom Rd.
Lancaster, PA 17601
Tel: (800) 775-0899 or (717) 293-3000
Fax: (717) 293-3055
Web: http://www.cardtech.com

Cello
Web: http://www.law.cornell.edu/cello/cellotop.html

Cincinnati Bell
ISDN Service Center: (513) 566-3282

Cisco Systems
170 West Tasman Dr.
San Jose, CA 95134
Tel: (800) 553-6387 or (408) 526-4000
Fax: (408) 526-6387
Web: http://www.cisco.com

Combinet
333 West El Camino Real, Ste. 240
Sunnyvale, CA 94087
Tel: (408) 522-9020 or (800) 967-6651
Fax: (408) 732-5479

Compaq
8404 Esters Blvd.
Irving, TX 75063
Tel: (800) 544-5255 or (972) 929-1700
Fax: (972) 929-1720
Web: http://www.compaq.com

CompuServe
5000 Britton Rd.
Hilliard, OH 43026
Tel: (800) 848-8199 or (614) 457-8600
Fax: (614) 723-1660
Web: http://www.compuserve.com

Connective Strategies, Inc. (CSI)
4500 Southgate Pl., Ste. 100
Chantilly, VA 22021
Tel: (703) 802-0023
Fax: (703) 802-0026
E-mail: info@csisdn.com

Conware Computer Consulting GmbH
Killisfeldstr. 64
D-76227 Karlsruhe, Germany
Tel: +49.721.9495-0
Fax: +49.721.9495-130
E-mail: vertrieb@conware.de

Core Competence
1620 Tuckerstown Rd.
Dresher, PA 19025
Tel: (215) 830-0692
Fax: (215) 830-7393
Web: http://www.corecom.com/
E-mail: info@corecom.com

Cornell
Web: http://www.cornell.edu/.

CPV-Stollmann Vertriebs GmbH
Gasstrasse 18
D-22761 Hamburg, Germany
P.O. Box 50 14 03
D-22714 Hamburg, Germany
Tel: +49-40-890 88-0
Fax: +49-40-890 88-444
E-mail: Info@Stollmann.DE (general inquiries)
Helge.Oldach@Stollmann.DE (IPX router technical contact)
Michael.Gruen@Stollmann.DE (IP router technical contact)

CyberBiz
Web: http://www.cybertoday.com/cybertoday/ISPs/
    Products.html#ISDN

Datacom
11001 31st Place, West
Everett, WA 98204
Tel: (800) 468-5557 or (206) 355-0590
Fax: (206) 290-1600
Web: http://www.datacomtech.com

DGM&S
1025 Briggs Rd., Ste. 100
Mt. Laurel, NJ 08054
Tel: (609) 866-1212
Fax: (609) 866-8850
Web: http://www.dgms.com

Diamond Multimedia Systems, Inc.
2880 Junction Ave.
San Jose, CA 95134
Tel: (408) 325-7000
Fax: (408) 325-7411
Web: http://www.diamondmm.com

diehl isdn GmbH
Bahnhofstrasse 63
D-7250 Leonberg, Germany
Tel. +49-7152-93 29-0
Fax. +49-7152-93 29-99
E-mail: bode@diehl.de

Digi International
11001 Bren Rd. East
Minnetonka, MN 55343
Tel: (612) 912-3444 or (800) 344-4273
Fax: (612) 912-4952
Web: http://www.digi.com

DigiBoard
6400 Flying Cloud Dr.
Eden Prarie, MN 55344
Tel: (612) 943-9020 or (800) 344-4273
Fax: (612) 643-5398
E-mail: info@digibd.com

Eicon
14755 Preston Rd., Ste. 620
Dallas, TX 75240
Tel: (214) 239-3200
Fax: (214) 239-3304

Euro-ISDN
53 Third Ave.
Burlington, MA 01803-4491
Tel: (800) 225-3317 or (617) 272-8140
Fax: (617) 273-5392
Web: http://www.xylogics.com

EuRoNIS
166 rue Montmartre
75002 Paris, France
Tel: +33 (1) 44 82 70 00
Fax: + 33(1) 42 33 40 98
E-mail: euronis@applelink.apple.com

Farallon Communications, Inc.
2470 Mariner Square Loop
Alameda, CA 94501
Tel: (510) 814-5100
Fax: (510) 814-5020
Web: http://www.farallon.com

Forté
2141 Palomar Airport Rd., Ste. 100
Carlsbad, CA 92009
Tel: (619) 431-6400
Fax: (619) 431-6465
Web: http://www.forteinc.com

FTP Software, Inc.
100 Brickstone Sq., 5th Fl.
Andover, MA 01810
Tel: (800) 282-4FTP or (508) 685-4000
Fax: (508) 794-4488
Web: http://www.ftp.com

Gandalf Technologies
130 Colonnade Rd. South
Nepean, Ontario, Canada K2E 7M4
Tel: (800) GANDALF or (613) 723-6500
Fax: (613) 228-9510

GTE
Tel: (800) 888-8799 or (214) 718-5608

Hayes ISDN Technologies
501 Second St., Ste. 300
San Francisco, CA 94107
Tel: (415) 974-5544
Fax: (415) 543-5810

Hermstedt GmbH
Kaefertaler Strasse 164
D-68167 Mannheim, Germany
Tel: +49 (621) 3 38 16-0
Fax: +49 (621) 3 38 16-12

IBM
Networking Systems Division
3039 Cornwallis Rd.
Research Triangle Park, NC 27709
Tel: (800) 426-2255 or (919) 543-7421
Fax: (919) 543-5417

INS (Inter Networking Systems)
P.O. Box 101312
D-44543 Castrop-Rauxel, Germany
Tel: +49 2305 356505
Fax: +49 2305 24511
E-mail: info@ins.de

Intel Corp.
5200 N.E. Elam Young Parkway
Hillsboro, OR 97124-6497
FaxBack: (800) 525-3019
Tel: (800) 538-3373
+44-1793-431155, in Europe
(503) 264-7354, worldwide
Intel BBS: (503) 264-7999 (modem settings 8-N-1, up to 14.4 Kbps)
Tech. support: (503) 629-7000

Internet Engineering Task Force (IETF)
c/o Corporation for National Research Initiatives
1895 Preston White Dr., Ste. 100
Reston, VA 22091
Tel: (703) 620-8990
Web: http://www.ietf.org

ISDN Systems Corporation
8320 Old Courthouse Rd., Ste. 200
Vienna, VA 22182
Tel: (703) 883-0933

ISDN*Tek
P.O. Box 3000
San Gregorio, CA 94074
Tel: (415) 712-3000
Fax: (415) 712-3003
Web: http://www.isdntek.com

Livingston Enterprises, Inc.
4464 Willow Rd.
Pleasanton, CA 94588
Tel: (800) 458-9966 or (510) 426-0770
Fax: (510) 426-8951

Lucent Microelectronics (formerly AT&T Microelectronics)
943 Holmdel Rd.
Holmdel, NJ 07733
Tel: (908) 946-1151
Fax: (908) 946-9146
Web: http://www.research.att.com

MCI
Tel: (214) 701-6745 or (800) MCI-ISDN

MERGE Technologies Group, Inc.
211 Gateway Rd. West, Ste. 201
Napa, CA 94558
Tel (800) 824-7763
Fax: (707) 252-6687

Microsoft
One Microsoft Way
Redmond, WA 98052-6399
Tel: (800) 426-9400 or (206) 882-8080
Fax: (206) 93-MSFAX
Web: http://www.microsoft.com

MITEL Corporation
360 Legget Dr.
Kanata, Ontario, Canada K2K 1X3
Tel: (613) 592-2122 (ask for Paul Mannone or Peter Merriman)

Motorola ISG
Technical Support Center
Huntsville, AL 35805
Tel: (205) 726-0798 or (800) 221-4380
Web: http://www.mot.com

Motorola UDS
5000 Bradford Dr.
Huntsville, AL 35805
Tel: (205) 430-8000

Ms Telematica
via S. Marcellina 8
20125 Milan, Italy
Tel: +39-2-66102315
Fax: +39-2-66102708
E-mail: mstelema@icil64.cilea.it

NCSA Mosaic
Web: http://www.ncsa.uiuc.edu/SDG/SDGIntro.html

netCS Informationstechnik GmbH
Feuerbachstr. 47-49
12163 Berlin 41, Germany
Tel: +49.30/856 999-0
Fax: +49.30/855 52 18
E-mail: sales@netcs.com or support@netcs.com

NetManage, Inc.
10725 N. De Anza Blvd.
Cupertino, CA 95014
Tel: (408) 973-7171
Fax: (408) 257-6405
Web: http://www.netmanage.com

Netscape
501 E. Middlefield Rd.
Mountain View, CA 94043
Tel: (800) NETSITE or (415) 254-1900
Fax: (415) 528-4124
Web: http://home.netscape.com

Network Express, Inc.
4251 Plymouth Rd.
Ann Arbor, MI 48105
Tel: (313) 761-5005
Fax: (313) 995-1114
E-mail: info@nei.com

Nevada Bell
Tel: Small business (702) 333-4811
Large business (702) 688-7100

North American ISDN Users Forum (NIUF)
Tel: (301) 975-2937

Northern Telecom
2221 Lakeside Blvd.
Richardson, TX 75082-4399
Tel: (800) NORTHERN or (972) 684-1000
Fax: (972) 684-3907
Web: http://www.nortel.com

Novell
1555 N. Technology Way
Orem, UT 84057-2399
Tel: (800) 453-1267 or (801) 222-6000
Fax: (800) NOVLFAX
Web: http://www.novell.com

Nynex
ISDN Sales Hotline: (800) 438-4736
New England states: (617) 743-2466

OnNet
Web: http://www.onnet-ec.com/

Pacific Bell
ISDN Service Center: (800) 472-4736
24 Hr. Automated: (800) 995-0346

Paxdata Networks Limited
Communications House
Frogmore Rd.
Hemel Hempstead HERTS HP3 9RW, UK
Tel: 0442 236336
Fax: 0442 236343
Marketing: Jim Fitzpatrick (jim@paxdata.demon.co.uk)
Technical: Giles Heron (giles@paxdata.demon.co.uk)

Proteon, Inc.
9 Technology Dr.
Westborough, MA 01581
Tel: (800) 545-7464 or (508) 898-2800
Fax: (508) 366-8901
Web: http://www.proteon.com

Rochester
ISDN Information: (716) 777-1234

Shiva
Edinborough Corporate Center
Shiva Park
Stanwell St.
Edinburgh EH6 5NG, Scotland
Web: http://www.shiva.com

Siemens Components, Inc.
Integrated Circuit Division
2191 Laurelwood Rd.
Santa Clara, CA 95054-1514
Tel: (408) 980-4500

Silicon Graphics, Inc.
2011 N. Shoreline Blvd.
Mountain View, CA 94043-1389
Tel: (800) 800-7441 or (415) 960-1980
Fax: (415) 961-0595
Web: http://www.sgi.com

Southwestern Bell
Austin, TX
Tel: (800)-SWB-ISDN
Dallas, TX: (214) 268-1403
North Houston, TX: (713) 537-3930
South Houston, TX: (713) 567-4300
San Antonio, TX: (210) 351-8050
ISDN availability other locations: (800) 992-ISDN

Spider Systems Limited
Spider House
Peach St.
Wokingham, England RG11 1XH
Tel: 0734 771055
Fax: 0734 771214

Spry
3535 128th Ave., SE
Bellevue, WA 98006
Tel: (800) SPRY-NET or (206) 957-8000
Fax: (206) 957-6000
Web: http://www.sprynet.com
E-mail: mailto:service@sprynet.com

Stentor (Canada)
ISDN "Facts by Fax": (800) 578-ISDN
Steve Finlay: (604) 654-7504
Glen Duxbury: (403) 945-8130

Sun Microsystems
2550 Garcia Ave.
Mountain View, CA 94043-1100
Tel: (800) 821-4643, (800) 821-4642, or (CA) (415) 960-1300
Fax: (415) 969-9131
Web: http://www.sun.com

SunLink
650 Champ Ave.
P.O. Box 170
Sunbury, PA 17801
Tel: (717) 286-5764
Fax: (717) 988-1890
Web: http://www.onnet-ec.com/

Telebit
One Executive Dr.
Chelmsford, MA 01824
Tel: (800) 989-8888 or (508) 441-2181
Fax: (508) 441-9060
Web: http://www.telebit.com

Telenetworks
625 Second St., Ste. 100
Petaluma, CA 94952
Tel: (707) 778-8737
Fax: (707) 778-7476
E-mail: info@tn.com

Teleos
2 Meridian Rd.
Eatontown, NJ 07724
Tel: (908) 389-5700
Fax: (908) 544-9890
Web: http://www.teleoscom.com

Tele-Path Industries, Inc. (TPI)
221 South Yorkshire St.
Salem, VA 24153
Tel: (540) 375-0500
Fax: (540) 375-0505
Web: http://www.ttc.com

Telesoft International, Inc.
4029 Capital of Texas Hwy., South Ste. 220
Austin, TX 78704
Tel: (512) 373-4224
Fax: (512) 447-1024

Telrad Telecommunications, Inc.
135 Crossways Park Dr.
Woodbury, NY 11797
Tel: (516) 921-8300 or (800) 645-1350

Trillium
11812 San Vicente, Ste. 500
Los Angeles, CA 90049
Tel: (310) 479-0500
Fax: (310) 575-0172
E-mail: marketing@trillium.com

Trumpet Software International
21660 East Copley Dr., Ste. 340
Diamond Bar, CA 91765
Tel: (909) 861-4400
Fax: (909) 861-0215
Web: http://www.trumpet.com/

U S West
Ron Miller: (303) 965-7153
Ron Woldeit: (206) 447-4029
Denver, CO: (800) 246-5226

US Robotics
Sales: (800) 342-5877
Fax: (847) 676-7320
E-mail: sales@usr.com
Support: (847) 982-5151
Fax: (847) 676-7314
E-mail: support@usr.com
Web: http://www.usr.com/

US Sprint
Rick Simonson: (913) 624-4162

WebSurfer
Web: http://www.netmanage.com/netmanage/apps/
    websurfer.html

Wiltel
Justin Remington: (918) 588-5069

WinTapestry
Web: http://www.frontiertech.com/

WinWeb
Web: http://galaxy.einet.net/EINet/clients.html

Zydacron, Inc.
670 Commercial St.
Manchester, NH 03101
Tel: (603) 647-1000
Fax: (603) 647-9470

ZyXEL Communications, Inc.
4920 East La Palma Ave.
Anaheim, CA 92807
Tel: (800) 255-4101
Fax: (714) 693-8811
Web: http://www.zyxel.com

C

ISDN Bibliography and Online Resources

Our goal in providing this appendix is not to tell you how to use an online information service or the Internet in general, or CompuServe or the World Wide Web in particular. Nor do we want to provide the be-all and end-all of ISDN resources. Rather, we just want to tell you what information is available on CompuServe and the Internet, what it's made up of, and why you might find it interesting. We also want to point you at the books and materials about ISDN that we've found most useful in the course of researching and writing this book.

This appendix focuses first on what's up on CompuServe and the Internet, how best to interact with it, and what kinds of things you can and cannot find up there. It tells you how to be effective when you work with CompuServe or the Internet, from the standpoint of knowing what to look for, which kinds of questions you can ask,

387

and the answers you're likely to get. It also helps you to understand just what kind of help you can expect to get from the online community and what to do if you can't get the help you need. Then, at the conclusion of this appendix, we include an ISDN section at the head of the Bibliographies and Resources section.

By now, you've probably noticed that we've mentioned only CompuServe and the Internet as sources of online information. "What about the others?" you might ask. Yes, we know there's also America Online, Prodigy, GEnie, and a bunch of other lesser contenders in this field. But none of them have staked a presence in the area of technical information and support on line as CompuServe has, nor do any of them have the breadth and reach of the Internet.

That's why we focus the bulk of our discussion in this appendix to these two information sources, even though there are more to choose from. In the next-to-last section, titled Other Online Resources, we'll try to give you some ideas about other places worth looking, but this will be a set of cursory suggestions, rather than an in-depth investigation.

What Does "Online" Really Mean?

In the context of our discussion, "online" means that you have to log in to somebody else's network (frequently using a modem) to access their information collection rather than your own network. Although this may sound inconvenient—and it sometimes is—the benefits invariably outweigh any inconvenience, costs, and effort that might be involved.

For the record, these benefits include:

- Free access to technical support operations for questions and answers via forums (CompuServe) or newsgroups and mailing lists (the Internet). Even if you never ask a question yourself, reading other people's questions (and the answers that go with them) can be enormously informative.

- Access to online sources for software patches and fixes for a broad range of products. Rather than waiting for the vendor to send you a disk, or paying long-distance charges to access their private bulletin board, you can get the latest versions of software (or the tools to turn your software into the latest version) with a local phone call and a (sometimes lengthy) download.
- Access to shareware and freeware that can extend your network's capabilities or increase your personal productivity. Much of the software this book's authors use for things like screen shots, graphics, file compression, and more originated on the Internet or CompuServe. A little prospecting can work wonders in this area!
- The biggest benefit by far is the opportunity to meet and interact with your peers and colleagues in the networking profession and to learn from other people's experiences and mistakes. You'll also have the occasional chance to learn from the wisdom of real experts, including the developers of the software or hardware you're using, or world-renowned gurus from a variety of fields.

All in all, there's a lot to be gained from going on line to look for information on just about any subject, but especially for technical and computer-related subjects. Since that's where networking fits pretty neatly, these resources are excellent (some would argue, indispensable) sources for information on the whole gamut of networking topics, products, technologies, and issues.

Now that we've gotten you all excited about the possibilities inherent in online information access, let's talk about the costs. Whether you join up with CompuServe, get onto the Internet, or, like this book's authors, do both; you can't join up without incurring some costs.

For CompuServe, this involves a series of account options, with associated monthly fees and additional charges for online time (usually above a certain number of "free" monthly hours). A light user shouldn't have to spend more than $10 to $15 a month for the service, but if you make regular downloads or spend significant amounts of time on line, it's easy to spend $50 to $100 a month, or more.

For the Internet, you'll have to arrange for a connection with an Internet service provider (ISP), and select one of the many options available for an Internet connection. For individuals or small businesses, we recommend using ISDN, or at least a V.34 modem, with a PPP connection. Prices vary from location to location, but you should expect to pay between $80 and $150 a month for ISDN service with this kind of connection, or about half that with a dial-up POTS connection. This usually entitles you to 10 to 20 hours per month of "free" online time, after which an hourly fee will be charged for additional hours.

There are lots of other Internet account options available from most ISPs, which can vary from dial on demand to dedicated accounts or according to the bandwidth of the connection involved (modem, ISDN, T1, T3, etc.). If you're interested in attaching your network to the Internet or need more bandwidth than an ISDN connection can provide, talk to your local ISPs or to national ISPs that offer service in your area. If you shop carefully for the best combination of price and service, you should be able to find something you can live with!

As with any other service, whether it's CompuServe, the Internet, or both, you'll want to do your best to learn how to use these information conduits effectively, to get the best bang for your bucks. Please consult the bibliographies at the end of this appendix for a list of resources that can help you learn what it takes to get the best use of either or both of these services.

The CompuServe Information Service

The CompuServe Information Service (CIS) is an electronic information service that offers a selection of thousands of topics for your perusal.

CompuServe, a for-a-fee service, requires an individual account (called a membership number) with an accompanying password to be accessed. There are many ways to obtain trial access at no charge, but if you want to play on CompuServe, sooner or later you have to pay for the privilege. CompuServe charges a monthly membership fee, in addition to a fee for connection time. Some of the services available on CompuServe have additional charges as well. Be warned! It's easy to spend time—and money—on CompuServe.

Forums for Conversation and Investigation

When you access CompuServe, it's necessary to select an area of interest to focus your exploration of the information treasures available. On CompuServe, information is organized into forums. A forum is an area dedicated to a particular subject or a collection of related subjects, and each forum contains one or more of the following:

- Message board: Features electronic conversations organized by specific subjects into sections related to particular topics (ISDN or the name of an ISDN vendor is probably what you'd look for as the focus for a section or forum on ISDN). A given sequence of messages, chained together by a common subject or by replies to an original message, is called a thread. It's important to notice that threads may read like conversations but that messages in a thread can be separated from one another by hours or days. Following threads is a favorite pastime for those who spend time on CompuServe.
- Conference room: An electronic analog to the real thing, it brings individuals together to exchange ideas and information in real time. It's much like a conference telephone call except that, rather than talk to each other, the participants communicate by typing on their keyboards. Conference rooms are not for the faint of heart, and they can be frustrating for those with limited touch-typing skills.
- File library: A collection of files organized by subject that can be downloaded for further perusal and use. Examples of file types found in CompuServe libraries include

archived collections of interesting threads, documents of all kinds, and a variety of software ranging from patches and fixes for programs to entire programs.

In all, many, many worlds of information are available on CompuServe, any or all of which can by themselves be a completely absorbing source of information, gossip, software, and activity. With all its elements taken together, CompuServe is a perfect example of what might be called an "electronic information warehouse."

Getting a CompuServe Membership

You can obtain an account over the telephone or by writing to CompuServe and requesting a membership. For telephone inquiries, ask for Representative 200. Here are the numbers to use:

- Within the United States (except Ohio), including Alaska, Hawaii, Puerto Rico, and the American Virgin Islands, call toll free at 800-848-8199.
- Outside the United States, in Canada, and in Ohio, call 614-457-8650.

Telephone hours are from 8 A.M. to 10 P.M. Eastern time Monday through Friday and from noon to 5 P.M. on Saturday. Written inquiries for a CompuServe account should be directed to:

CompuServe, Inc.
Attn: Customer Service
P.O. Box 20212
5000 Arlington Centre Boulevard
Columbus, OH 43220

Accessing CompuServe

To get access to CompuServe, you must equip your computer with a modem and attach that modem to a telephone line. You also need some kind of communications program, to let your computer "talk" to CompuServe by using the modem and to help you find your way around its online universe. Finally, you have to obtain a telephone number for CompuServe—most of them are local numbers, especially in the United States—that's appropriate for the type and speed of modem you're using. At this point, CompuServe isn't available via ISDN outside the Columbus, Ohio, area (CompuServe's hometown), but keep your eyes peeled, because that kind of access is surely just a matter of time.

At present, though, connection-time charges are based on how fast your modem is (faster modems cost more), but the higher charges are typically offset by even faster transfer speeds. If your CompuServe bill is $30 a month or higher, most high-speed modems will pay for themselves in six months or less based on the reductions in fees you realize by using one.

After you are connected to CompuServe, you enter your membership number and your password. First-time users should follow the instructions provided by your CompuServe representative or in the *CompuServe Starter Kit* that's available from CompuServe (for an additional fee).

After you're logged in, getting directly to a named CompuServe forum is easy, as long as you know the name of the forum you're after. When you simply type **GO <NAME>** from the CompuServe prompt, you are presented with a menu of additional choices for that forum. To get started with your information mining efforts, use the **FIND** command with ISDN, a vendor's name, or a product name that you're after. This will normally produce a list of forums that you can visit, to further explore potential sources of information.

The Many Forums of CompuServe

There are plenty of vendors and networking communities represented on CompuServe. You'll find a rich selection of Novell forums (GO NetWire) and Microsoft-related forums and libraries, for everything from vanilla Windows to Windows for Workgroups, Windows 95, and Windows NT Server (use GO MICROSOFT to get to the root of the Microsoft forums; don't skip the Microsoft

Knowledge Base at GO MSKB, either). You'll also find plenty of IBM-related forums (GO IBM) or OS/2-related information (GO OS/2). Don't forget to use the FIND command to locate other vendors and products, either.

The Internet

The Internet, as a wag might put it, is a "whole 'nother story." There are more riches to be found on the Internet than you could shake a stick at. This won't stop us from pointing you at a few good stops along the way, but it will effectively prevent us from covering all the possible bases. Rather than trying to tell you where all the goodies are, we're going to explain how to search for the information you seek.

Our primary approach to the Internet requires that you have access to the World Wide Web (WWW), usually known as the Web. The Web is a worldwide collection of hypertext information servers that is made easy to navigate through the use of hypertext links, which let you jump effortlessly from document to document (or within a document) simply by activating a link on a document you're examining (for most users, this requires no more effort than clicking on a word or graphic on your display). Secondarily, access to electronic mail and/or USENET newsgroups will be quite helpful as well.

Searching for Satisfaction

In much the same way that the FIND command on CompuServe lets you ask for information by company or product name, the Web sports a number of database front ends, called "search engines," that will let you enter a keyword (or several, in fact) for search. These programs will return a collection of hypertext links to sites that match your keywords to various locations on the Web, ready for you to double-click on them and investigate further.

The name used to attach to Web resources is called a URL (an acronym for uniform resource locator, a way to designate sites and information accessible through the Web). Here are the URLs for a handful of popular, and useful, Web search engines. If you simply point your Web browser at one of these, you'll be able to get pointers to the information you're looking for.

Sometimes, using the right tools can make using the World Wide Web for research much simpler. A class of software tools called *search engines* can examine huge amounts of information to help you locate Web sites of potential interest. Here's how most of them work:

- Somewhere in the background, laboring in patient anonymity, you'll find automated Web-traversing programs, often called *robots* or *spiders*, that do nothing but follow link after link around the Web ad infinitum. Each time they get to a new Web document, they peruse and catalog its contents, storing the information up for transmission to a database elsewhere on the Web.
- At regular intervals, these automated information gatherers will transmit their recent acquisitions to their parent database, where the information is sifted, categorized, and stored.
- When you run a search engine, you're actually searching the database that's been compiled and managed through the initial efforts of the robots and spiders, but which is handled by a fully functional database management system that communicates with a customized program for your search form.
- Using the keywords or search terms you provide to the form, the database locates "hits" (exact matches) and also "near hits" (matches with less than the full set of terms supplied, or based on educated guesses about what you're *really* trying to locate).
- The hits are returned to the background search program by the database, where they are transformed into a Web document to return the results of the search for your perusal.

If you're lucky, all this activity will produce references to some materials that you can actually use!

The Search Engines of (Our) Choice

We'd like to share some pointers to our favorite search engines with you, which you'll find in Table D.1. This is not an exhaustive catalog of such tools, but all of them will produce interesting results if you use "CGI" or "CGI scripts" as search input.

Table C.1 These Web search engines can make looking for ISDN-related materials much less taxing.

Search Engine Name and Information	URL
EINet Galaxy, MCI spinoff EINet's engine	http://www.einet.net
Lycos, Carnegie-Mellon engine	http://lycos.cs.cmu.edu
W3 Org Virtual Library, W3 Org outsourced project	http://www.stars.com
Wandex, MIT spinoff's engine	http://www.netgen.com/cgi/wandex
WebCrawler, University of Washington engine	http://webcrawler.cs.washington.edu/WebCrawler/WebQuery.html
World Wide Web Worm (WWWW), University of Colorado engine	http://www.cs.colorado.edu:80/home/mcbryan/WWWW.html
Yahoo	http://www.yahoo.com

When you're using these search tools, the most important thing to remember is that the more specific you can make your search request, the more directly related the results will be to what you're looking for. Thus, if you're looking for information about ISDN terminal adapters, you might try using "ISDN TA" or "TA" as your search term instead of simply using "ISDN." Although you may get plenty of nothing when using search terms that are too specific, that's better than looking through a plenitude of irrelevant materials when nothing is all that's in there!

The Web has to be experienced to be believed. Since the authors' initial exposure to it about two years ago, it's completely changed the way we approach research of any kind. We hope you'll find it to be useful, but we must warn you, it's also completely addicting!

Other Ways to Get Internet Satisfaction

When it comes to classifying the kinds of information you'll en-counter on the Internet in any search for networking information, specifications, and examples, here's what you're most likely to find:

Focused Newsgroups

Focused newsgroups are basically congregations of interested indi-viduals, who congregate around a specific topic on USENET, BIT-NET, or one of the other regular message exchange areas on the Internet.

Where networking is concerned, this involves a handful of prima-rily USENET newsgroups with varying levels of interest in (and coverage of) networking- or vendor-specific or related topics, like NetWare, LAN Server, or Windows NT, networking protocols or products, related technologies like Ethernet, Token-Ring, or FDDI, and other related areas.

To begin with, you'll want to obtain a list of the newsgroups that your Internet service provider (ISP) carries. Normally, you will al-ready have access to this list through whatever news reader you're using, but you can usually get a plain-text version of this list just by asking for it.

Then, take this plain-text file and open it with your favorite editor or word processor that contains a search command. By entering the name of the company, technology, or product that you're interested in, you can see if there are any newsgroups devoted to its coverage (a recent check on our part discovered several hits for the term "isdn" including *comp.dcom.isdn*, *de.comm.isdn*, *fido.ger.isdn*, and *relog.isdn*). Of these, two are aimed at German audiences (*de.comm.isdn* and *fido.ger.idsn*), we use *comp.dcom.isdn* as a terrific source of information, and we know nothing about the relog.isdn list, since we found it empty.

In fact, the only way to tell if a newsgroup can do you any good is to drop in for a while and read its traffic. You should be able to tell, in a day or two, if the topics and coverage are interesting and informative.

If they are, you should consider subscribing to the newsgroup, or at least dropping in from time to time to read the traffic. Remember, too, that these newsgroups are a great source of technical information and that they often have vendor technical support employees assigned to read them, ready to answer technical questions on your behalf.

Focused Mailing Lists

Focused mailing lists originate from targeted mail servers that collect message traffic from active correspondents and then broadcast the accumulated traffic to anyone who signs up for the mailing list.

Entering and leaving a mailing list takes a little more effort than subscribing to or leaving a USENET newsgroup, but otherwise these two categories provide the same kind of information: daily message traffic—sometimes quite voluminous—focused on networking or related topics.

Locating mailing lists can sometimes be tricky. Although you often learn about them only by reading message traffic on newsgroups, you can sometimes find them mentioned in search engine output or by asking a users' group or a technical support person focused on a particular topic or area. Even so, they can be incredibly useful.

Information Collections from "Interested Parties"

Sometimes individuals with special interests in a particular area, such as networking, will collect information about their area of concern and publish it in a variety of forms that can range from Web pages to file archives available on private or public servers.

Although such collections can often be eclectic and idiosyncratic, the best of them can offer outstanding "jumping-off points" for investigating any particular topic. This is as true for networking as it is for other topics.

As with mailing lists, finding these gems can be a matter of hit or miss. By watching the message traffic on newsgroups or mailing lists, you'll figure out who the gurus or forward-looking individuals are. By looking in their messages for pointers to Web pages or other resources (which you'll often find in the .sig, or signature, files at the end of their messages), you can sometimes get pointers to great sources of information.

In the same vein, if you see that particular individuals are consistent and reliable sources of good information on a particular topic, send them an e-mail message and request that they share their list of recommended online resources with you. You may not always get a response (some of these people are very busy), but it never hurts to ask, and the occasional answer can provide a real treasure trove of information pointers!

The best source of ISDN information on the Internet, bar none, may be found at the following WWW URL: http://www.alumni.caltech.edu/~dank/isdn/. This is Dan Kegel's ISDN Web page, and it's got pointers to everything worth knowing about ISDN on the Internet (no kidding!). If you can get there, you can get all the online information about ISDN that you'll ever need.

Information from Special Interest Groups

Special interest groups cover a multitude of approaches to their topics: They can be trade or industry organizations, research or standards groups, or even companies involved in particular activities.

Often, the groups with vested interests in a technology will provide information on that technology, along with pointers to other sources as well. This is as true for networking as it is for other topics, but because these groups are nonpareils of Web and Internet presence, they are often among the best places to start looking.

It's often been said that "It's not *what* you know, it's *who* you know that counts." When it comes to locating Internet resources, this may sometimes seem more like "*where* you know," but the principle remains pretty much the same. Thus, for particular topics, you shouldn't point your search engine only at company, product, or technology names; try pointing it at the names of such groups as well. Here, again, these can be incredible sources of useful information.

Dan Kegel's page includes a section entitled "ISDN User Groups"; look here for information about local and national groups, most of which have their own mailing lists, file archives, and Web servers that you can explore for good ISDN information (and contacts for consultants, equipment dealers, etc.).

Other Online Resources

Many companies that are too small, too poor, or otherwise disinclined to participate on CompuServe or the Internet will maintain their own private bulletin board systems (BBSs), which you can dial up and investigate. These are always free, but they're also almost always long-distance calls, so what you save in connect time costs to a service provider you'll probably end up paying to your long-distance company instead.

Nevertheless, when other avenues fail to turn up what you're looking for, it's a good idea to call the vendor and ask if they offer a BBS. This kind of setup often gives the opportunity to communicate with technical support via e-mail, instead of enduring "eternal hold" while waiting to speak to a real human being, and can often provide direct access to software patches, fixes, upgrades, frequently asked questions (FAQs), and other kinds of useful documentation.

In the same vein, many companies offer FAXback services that can ship paper-based documentation, order forms, and other goodies to your fax machine. This has the advantage of costing you only as much long-distance time as it takes you to request the information you're after; after that, the transmission costs are usually borne by the vendor.

Digging for information is an endeavor in which persistence usually pays off. If you're bound and determined to get the facts, figures, or help you need, you'll eventually be able to get it. Just be sure to leave no resource uninvestigated, no possible avenue untraveled, and no stone unturned!

Noncomputerized Resources Worth Investigating

Even though they may not be as dynamic and interactive as online resources, don't overlook the information you can glean from more conventional paper-based publications. (We know you've got to be somewhat open-minded in this regard, because you're reading this book!) Nevertheless, we'll do our best to acquaint you with some books, magazines, and publishers to check out in your quest for the latest and greatest networking information. You should find this information in the bibliographies at the end of this appendix and on Dan Kegel's page (check the listings under the title "ISDN Periodicals and Magazines" for some useful resources).

Summary

In this appendix, we've tried to point you at the best and brightest of online (and other) information resources. Over the years, we've learned that both CompuServe and the Internet are essential to our research, but you will probably be able to get by with only one or the other. Whatever your choice of online information, however, we're sure you'll become dependent on it in no time (if you aren't already). It's definitely one of those things that, as soon as it becomes familiar, you wonder how you ever managed without it! In the bibliographies that follow, we try to provide some tools to bring you up to speed quickly enough to make the investment pay off right away.

Bibliographies and Resources

ISDN

Angell, David: *ISDN For Dummies*, 2nd Edition: Copyright 1996, IDG Books Worldwide, Indianapolis, IN. The best introductory book on ISDN available, this book covers everything a small office or home user will need to know on the subject.

Bryce, James Y.: *Using ISDN*, 2nd Edition: Copyright 1995, Que Corporation, Indianapolis, IN. One of the best and most comprehensive of the general overview books on ISDN, this book is good for general references and PC specifics.

Hopkins, Gerald L.: *The ISDN Literacy Book*: Copyright 1994, Addison-Wesley Publishing Company, Reading, MA. A great comprehensive introduction to ISDN for managers and technicians alike.

Motorola University Press: *The Basics Book of ISDN*: Copyright 1992, Motorola (published by Addison-Wesley Publishing Company, Reading, MA). A short and useful introduction to ISDN terms and technology.

Stallings, William: *ISDN An Introduction*: Copyright 1989, Macmillan Publishing Company, a division of Macmillan, New York, NY. Stallings has a prodigious understanding of ISDN. An exhaustive examination of ISDN from the high levels to the nitty-gritty technical details.

General

Aboba, Bernard: *The Online User's Encyclopedia*: Copyright 1993, Addison-Wesley Publishing Company, Reading, MA. A general book that covers online topics from A to Z, this tome defies description but is incredibly useful.

CompuServe

Wagner, Richard: *Inside CompuServe*, 3rd Edition: Copyright 1996, New Riders Publishing, Indianapolis, IN. A useful overview of how CompuServe behaves, what kinds of access software are worth considering, and what sorts of resources it contains.

Wang, Wallace: *CompuServe for Dummies*, 2nd Edition: Copyright 1995, IDG Books Worldwide, Indianapolis, IN. One of the best all-around resources on CompuServe available, this book covers software, organization, and effective "surfing" techniques.

Wiggins, Robert and Ed Tittel: *The Trail Guide to CompuServe*: Copyright 1994, Addison Wesley Publishing Company, Reading, MA. A quick overview of the CompuServe Information Manager (CIM) software for Windows and Macintosh and a quick, but useful, guide to resources on line. Includes a chapter on network-related forums and topics.

Internet

December, John and Neil Randall: *The World Wide Web Unleashed*, 2nd Edition: Copyright 1996, SAMS Publishing, Indianapolis, IN. The best of the general WWW reference books, this one covers all the topics, including one of the most comprehensive guides to online resources we've ever seen anywhere.

Dern, Daniel: *The Internet Guide for New Users*, 2nd Edition: Copyright 1996, McGraw-Hill, New York, NY. One of the best all-around Internet books, this one covers a little bit of everything, including programs to use and places to look for information.

Krol, Ed: *The Whole Internet User's Guide*, 2nd Edition: Copyright 1995, O'Reilly & Associates, Sebastopol, CA. Another of the best Internet books around, this was the earliest and is still a personal favorite.

Levine, John R. and Carol Baroudi: *The Internet for Dummies*, 3rd Edition: Copyright 1996, IDG Books Worldwide, Indianapolis, IN. An excellent overview of the Internet's many protocols, programs, and capabilities.

Tittel, Ed and Margaret Robbins: *Internet Access Essentials*: Copyright 1994, AP Professional, Boston, MA. The fourth of the three best all-around Internet books, this one was cowritten by one of this book's authors, which means he thinks it's pretty darned good indeed!

D

Glossary

- **23B + D.** The primary rate interface (PRI) in ISDN. A circuit with a wide range of frequencies that is divided into twenty-three 64 Kbps "bearer" channels for carrying voice, data, video, or other information simultaneously and one D "delta" 16 Kbps channel for telephony data. See also PRI (primary rate interface).

- **2B + D.** The basic rate interface (BRI) in ISDN. A single ISDN circuit divided into two 64 Kbps digital B channels for voice or data and one 16 Kbps D channel for low-speed data and signaling. Either or both of the 64 Kbps channels may be used for voice or data. In ISDN, 2B + D is carried on one or two pairs of wires (depending on the interface). See also BRI.

- **5ESS.** A digital central office switching system made by AT&T.

- **Analog.** Most current residential telephone lines are analog. Technically, it is an electrical circuit that is represented by means of continuous, variable physical quantities (such as voltages and frequencies), as opposed to discrete representations (like the 0/1, off/on representation of digital circuits).

- **B channel.** A "bearer" channel is a fundamental component of ISDN interfaces. It carries 64 Kbps in either direction, is circuit switched, and can carry either voice or data. See also BRI (basic rate interface) and ISDN.

- **BONDing.** Bandwidth ON Demand (sometimes written BONDING) is the automatic combining of both B channels into a 128 Kbps channel for faster data transfer.

- **BRI (basic rate interface).** One of the two types of interfaces in ISDN. BRI consists of two bearer or B channels and one data or D channel. Each B channel is 64 Kbps "clear" of digital bandwidth, which means that the full 64 Kbps is available to your application. The B channel carries the traffic. Any network control signaling is done external to the B channel. The D channel is a 16 Kbps packet-switching circuit. The network control signals are transmitted over this circuit. End user applications can also use the D channel for low-speed data-only transmissions. One BRI standard is the U interface, which uses two wires. Another BRI standard is the S/T interface, which uses four wires.

- **CCS (comon channel signaling).** An integral part of ISDN known as signaling system 7, CCS is a method for sending call-related information between switching systems by means of a dedicated signaling channel. This signaling channel is separate from the bearer or B channels. CCS allows services such as call forwarding and call waiting to be provided anywhere in the network. Other acronyms for common channel signaling are CCSS, CCSS7, and SS7.

- **Centrex.** Centrex is a type of business telephone service. It is like having a private branch exchange (PBX) located in your local central office. Centrex is basically single-line telephone service delivered to individual desks (the same as you get at your house) with additional features.

- **CO (central office).** The central office is a facility that serves local telephone subscribers. In the CO, subscribers' lines are joined to switching equipment that allows them to connect to each other for both local and long-distance calls.

- **CPE (customer-provided equipment, customer premise equipment).** Telephone equipment key systems, PBXs, NT1s, answering machines, and so on that resides on the customer's premises.

- **D channel.** In an ISDN interface, the data or D channel is used to carry control signals and customer call data in a packet-switched mode. In the BRI (basic rate interface) the D channel operates at 16 Kbps, part of which will handle setup, teardown, and other characteristics of the call. Also, 9600 bps will be free for a separate conversation by the user. In the PRI (primary rate interface), the D channel runs at 64 Kbps. The D channel is sometimes referred to as the delta channel. See also BRI, PRI, and ISDN.

- **DMS100.** A digital central office switching system made by Northern Telecom.

- **EKTS (electronic key telephone service).** This is a service that provides PBX-like capabilities using ISDN add-on features. It ties these add-on features to keys on your ISDN telephone, allowing you to have a hold button or a forward button, for example.

- **FPS (frames per second).** This term is most often used when talking about the speed of video capture and playback. It refers to the number of frames per second of video images displayed on the screen. The higher the frame rate, the more fluid the motion appears. The highest, or best, quality frame rate available is 30 fps. Lower frame rates (below 10) still appear as motion but are noticeably "jerky," and zero fps corresponds to a still frame (no motion).

- **Gbps (Gigabits per second).** A measure of bandwidth or throughput, based on 2^{30} (1,073,741,824) bits per second (slightly over a billion).

- **IEC.** See IXC (inter exchange carrier).

- **ISDN (Integrated Services Digital Network).** ISDN is the telephone network using all-digital rather than analog signals. It is a type of telephone service in which voice, data, and video information is digitized and transmitted at high speed over a single, public switched network. With ISDN, existing switches and wires (in most cases) are upgraded so that the basic "call" is a 64 Kbps end-to-end channel. ISDN comes in two basic flavors: basic rate interface (or BRI) and primary rate interface (or PRI). See also BRI (basic rate interface) and PRI (primary rate interface).

• **ISP (Internet service provider).** An organization that provides access to the Internet, typically for a fee (determined by the bandwidth and availability of the connection provided).

• **IXC (inter exchange carrier).** Also referred to as IEC. Any common carrier authorized by the Federal Communications Commission (FCC) to carry customer transmissions between local access and transport areas (LATAs). AT&T, MCI, and Sprint are examples of inter exchange carriers.

• **Kbps (Kilobits per second).** A measure of bandwidth or throughput, based on 2^{10} (1024) bits per second as a measure.

• **LATA (local access and transport area).** A geographic territory used primarily by local telephone companies to determine charges for intrastate calls. As a result of the Bell divestiture, switched calls that both begin and end at points within the LATA (intra-LATA) are generally the sole responsibility of the local telephone company, whereas calls that cross outside the LATA (inter-LATA) are passed on to an inter exchange carrier (IXC).

• **LEC (local exchange carrier).** The local phone companies—either a Regional Bell Operating Company (RBOC) or an independent phone company (e.g., GTE)—that provide local transmission services. See also RBOC.

• **Local loop.** The physical wires that run from the subscriber's telephone equipment to the switching system in the telephone company's central office.

• **Loop qual (local loop qualification).** This is the process of checking the local loop distance—the distance between the customer's telephone equipment and the central office switch. If this distance exceeds 18,000 feet, additional equipment, such as repeaters, is added to the line to boost or enhance the signal. See also Repeater.

- **Mbps (Megabits per second).** A unit of bandwidth or through-put based on 2^{20} (1,048,576) bits per second (a little over a million).

- **MUX (multiplexer).** An electronic device for combining multiple data or voice signals into one signal group for transmission over a high-speed trunk.

- **NI-1 (National ISDN-1).** National ISDN-1 is a specification for a "standard" ISDN phone line. The goal is for National ISDN-1 to become a set of standards to which every manufacturer can conform. For example, ISDN phones that conform to the National ISDN-1 standard will work, regardless of the central office the customer is connected to. Future standards, denoted as NI-2 and NI-3, are currently being developed.

- **NT1 (network termination type 1).** The NT1 is the classic ISDN "black box." The NT1 is a customer premise device that converts the two-wire line (or U interface) coming from your telephone company to a four-wire line (or S/T interface). The NT-1 connects between the ISDN phone line and the terminal adapter (such as the ISDN board in an Intel ProShare Video System). It supports network maintenance functions such as loop testing. Up to eight terminal devices may be addressed by an NT-1.

- **NT2 (ISDN, network termination type 2).** An intelligent customer premise device, such as a digital PBX, that can perform switching and concentration. See also NT1.

- **Packet switching.** Sending data in packets through a network to some remote location. The data to be sent is subdivided into individual packets of data, each having a unique identification (ID) and each carrying its destination address. The packets can go by different routes and may arrive in an order different from that in which they were sent. The packet ID lets the data be reassembled in proper sequence.

- **PBX.** See Private branch exchange.

- **POP (point of presence).** A long-distance carrier's office in your local community. A POP is the place where your long-distance carrier, or IXC, terminates your long-distance lines just before those lines are connected to your local phone company's lines or to your own direct hookup. Each IXC can have multiple POPs within one LATA. All long-distance phone connections go through the POPs.

- **POTS (plain old telephone service).** The basic analog telephone service: standard single-line telephones, telephone lines, and access to the public switched network.

- **PRI (primary rate interface).** The primary rate interface (that which is delivered to the customer's premises) provides 23B + D or 30B + D running at 1.544 megabits per second and 2.048 megabits per second, respectively.

- **Private branch exchange (PBX).** A PBX is a private telephone switch. It is connected to groups of lines from one or more central offices and to all of the telephones at the location served by the PBX.

- **RBOC (Regional Bell Operating Company).** One of seven regional telephone companies created by the AT&T divestiture: Nynex, Bell Atlantic, Bell South, Southwestern Bell, US West, Pacific Telesis, and Ameritech.

- **Repeater.** Equipment that is inserted at some point along the transmission line to amplify the signal. Repeaters are often used to "boost" a signal traveling over long distances, as in the case of lines that fail the local loop qualification test. See also Loop qual and Local loop.

- **Restricted service line.** An ISDN trunk capable of operating at 56 Kbps. Restricted service line is common in the United States and Japan.

- **Service order number.** See SON.

- **SPID (service profile identifier).** The SPID number is issued by the telephone company and is used to identify your ISDN line to the central office switch. The Intel ProShare Video installation software prompts you for your SPID number, so it is important that you have this number on hand.

- **S/T interface.** A four-wire ISDN circuit. The more common ISDN circuit is the U interface.

- **SLC (subscriber-loop carrier).** Computerized substation of phone company for ISDN outside the 3.4 mile range of the central office switch; used instead of a repeater.

- **SON (service order number).** The number used by the local exchange carrier (LEC) to track your ISDN order.

- **SVN (subscriber verification number).** The number used by the inter exchange carrier (IXC) to track your ISDN order.

- **T-1 (also sometimes written T1).** A 1.544 megabit per second transmission method.

- **TE (ISDN terminal equipment).** The equipment that is attached to the end of the ISDN line, an Intel ProShare Video System 200, for example.

- **TE1 (ISDN terminal equipment type 1).** ISDN terminal equipment designed to interface directly to the S/T interface.

- **TE2 (ISDN terminal equipment type 2).** Any equipment that has the ability to interface to the S/T interface for control/communications purposes via an ISDN terminal adapter.

- **Trunk.** A communication channel between switching devices or central offices.

- **U interface.** A two-wire ISDN circuit: essentially today's standard one-pair telephone company local loop made of twisted wire. The U interface is the most common ISDN interface.

- **Unrestricted service line.** An ISDN trunk capable of operating at 64 Kbps. Unrestricted service line is standard in Europe; some are available in the United States.

Index

A

413

About AP PROFESSIONAL

AP PROFESSIONAL, an imprint of Academic Press, a division of Harcourt Brace & Company, was founded in 1993 to provide high quality, innovative products for the computer community. For over 50 years, Academic Press has been a world leader in documenting scientific and technical research.

AP PROFESSIONAL continues this tradition by providing its readers with exemplary publications that bring new topics to light and offer fresh views on prominent topics. Often, today's computer books are underdeveloped clones, published in haste and promoted in series. Readers tend to be neglected by the lack of commitment from other publishers to produce quality products. It is our business to provide you with clearly written, educational publications that contain valuable information you will find truly useful. AP PROFESSIONAL has grown quickly and has established a reputation for fine products because of this commitment to excellence.

Through our strong reputation at Academic Press, and one of the most experienced editorial boards in computer publishing, AP PROFESSIONAL has also contracted many of the best writers in the computer community. Each book undergoes three stages of editing (technical, developmental, and copyediting) before going through the traditional book publishing production process. These extensive measures ensure clear, informative, and accurate publications.

It is our hope that you will be pleased with your decision to purchase this book, and that it will exceed your expectations. We are committed to making the AP PROFESSIONAL logo a sign of excellence for all computer users and hope that you will come to rely on the quality of our publications.

Enjoy!

Jeffrey M. Pepper
Vice President, Editorial Director

Related Titles from AP PROFESSIONAL

TWAY, *Multimedia In Action!*

VACCA, *JavaScript Development*

VACCA, *VRML: Bringing Virtual Reality to the Internet*

VAUGHAN-NICHOLS, *Intranets*

WATKINS/MARENKA, *The Internet Edge in Business*

WAYNER, *Disappearing Cryptography*

WAYNER, *Java and JavaScript Programming*

WENIG, *Wireless LANs*

WIKLUND, *Usability in Practice*

Ordering Information

 AP PROFESSIONAL
An imprint of ACADEMIC PRESS
A division of HARCOURT BRACE & COMPANY

ORDERS (USA and Canada): 1-800-3131-APP or APP@acad.com
AP Professional Orders: 6277 Sea Harbor Dr., Orlando, FL 32821-9816

Europe/Middle East/Africa: 0-11-44 (0) 181-300-3322
Orders: AP Professional 24-28 Oval Rd., London NW1 7DX

Japan/Korea: 03-3234-3911-5
Orders: Harcourt Brace Japan, Inc., Ichibancho Central Building 22-1, Ichibancho Chiyoda-Ku, Tokyo 102

Australia: 02-517-8999
Orders: Harcourt Brace & Co., Australia, Locked Bag 16, Marrickville, NSW 2204 Australia

Other International: (407) 345-3800
AP Professional Orders: 6277 Sea Harbor Dr., Orlando, FL 32821-9816

Editorial: 1300 Boylston St., Chestnut Hill, MA 02167 (617) 232-0500

Web: http://www.apnet.com/approfessional